5 . 50

An Anthology of Black Arts & Culture

STORMS

OF THE

HEART

An Anthology of Black Arts & Culture

STORMS OF THE HEART

Edited by **KWESI OWUSU**

First published in 1988 by Camden Press Ltd
43 Camden Passage, London N1 8EB,
England

Set in 11/12 Garamond Med.
by Photosetting and Secretarial
Services, Yeovil
and printed and bound by
A. Wheaton & Co. Limited, Exeter, Devon

Designed by Ruhi Hamid

This book has been published with
subsidy from the Arts Council of Great
Britain

British Library CIP Data
Storms of the heart: an anthology of
Black arts and culture.
1. Black arts
I. Owusu, Kwesi
700' .8996

ISBN 0-948491-35-3

Art Editor Frances Borzello

Cover illustration based on a
photograph by Mirella Ricciardi

To Alfred Fagon, actor, poet, buried anonymously by the London Metropolitan police.

And in memory of Naa Shormeh Nortey, heartfelt messages of the world you left for our ancestors ... aoow, yaa ba.

C O N T E N T S

In de beginnin
wuz de word
And de word wuz ours
to change de worl
as we like
In we own image an likeness

Jacob Ross

Prelims

I N T R O D U C T I O N

Black arts refers to the creative expressions of the African and Asian communities in Britain, both continental and diasporan; expressions highly informed by what Franz Fanon would have called 'combat breathing', a living, interminable challenge to imperialism in the metropolis. The state of consciousness which informs them articulates the dialectics of race, sex and class within the context of the exploitative and endemic racism of capitalist social relations.

Over the last four decades or so, Black arts in Britain have made significant advances, perhaps more so than in any other period in their history. They occupy strategic positions and territories on the contemporary cultural landscape, enjoying 'visible' profiles in a broad range of old and new art forms, in the media and in the cultural industries. These profiles have been achieved in spite of fragile infrastructures, gross public underfunding and the disorganic effects of state culture.

The backdrop to these advances has been the socio-cultural and political impact of post-war emigration from the Caribbean, Asia and Africa; the resurgence of Third World cultural movements in the wake of independence; and the development of an anti-racist movement. Post-war immigration is particularly significant, for it gave Black arts and culture a broader social milieu of practice and engagement. By breaking the isolation of the artists already resident here and popularising a complex range of discourses, it radically changed the context for their appreciation and consumption. Immigration reinforced the popular traditions of Black arts and culture and helped pose alternatives to the elitist appropriation of Black artists and movements. Nineteenth century Black writers like Equino and Gronnisaw, for example, were used to embellish predominantly white middle class movements like slave abolition.

A cultural celebration like the Notting Hill Carnival, with its decidedly Black character and community organisation, as well as its dynamic fusion of apparently disparate aesthetic, social and political elements, does not just exalt new cultural ways of seeing and celebrating life. With the systematic suppression, particularly since the Industrial Revolution, of British mass festivals and popular recreations, it symbolises a crucial affirmation of the right to mass, popular organisation and creative expression. Its significance lies at the very heart of British culture and history.

Post-war immigration has brought together two pertinent histories/herstories of Black arts: the long strand of artistic and creative endeavour embedded in British culture which goes back to the days of Roman occupation and the Black emperor Septimus Severus (208-211), and the indigenous cultures of Africa, Asia and the Caribbean. This merger and potent synthesis provides contemporary Black arts with relevance and dynamism. The contradictions and legacies of Britain's past are crystallised in the works of Black artists and cultural practitioners. They colour the ideological canvas before the artist makes a brush stroke and fill the air before the musician blows a note. They provide Black artists with the raw material for social and political resolution.

The resurgence of Third World cultural movements has made an immense contribution to the ever-increasing confidence of the Black arts movement in its search for and affirmation of 'we own aesthetics'. A common point of departure for many Black artists is the defiance of formal artistic boundaries, specialisation and the fragmentation of social experience. There is a conscious articulation of diverse and disparate elements of creativity, often organised in new and exciting spaces. Many Black artists work in various media simultaneously, forging creative links, collaborations and alliances. This state of consciousness, a reflection of African and Asian attitudes to creativity, is called orature. Pitika Ntuli reminds us that it is 'more than the fusion of art forms... It is the conception and reality of a total view of life. It is a capsule of feeling, thinking, imagination, taste and hearing... It is a weapon against the encroaching atomisation of life. it is the beginning come full circle on a higher plane.'

An interesting dimension of orature is that it gives to Black arts an internationalist character as artists and cultural workers defy formal definitions of the geo-political to connect with creative centres of inspiration in Africa, Asia and the Caribbean. Black arts are therefore in a constant state of tension with the ideologies of appropriation such as 'ethnic arts', 'minority arts', and 'Black British arts', which attempt to ghettoise them within the British nation-state.

The search for aesthetics has been complemented by attempts to rescue Black art forms and cultural practices from the ideologies and histories of Eurocentrism. There is a general recognition that the domination of Black cultures and the development of modern European art movements are two sides of the same coin. All the contributors in this anthology take this problematic seriously.

The enormity of the task is not so much daunting as revealing of the pervasiveness of the problem. The process of historical excavation and reclamation can be positive as well as painful. Black appropriation is central to even such progressive and libertarian European movements as Cubism and Surrealism. If there is a subtle joke in Picasso's 'discovery' of African artefacts in a friend's shop in Paris, it is not the impossibility of quantifying the aesthetic impact on him with such a flimsy anecdote but the casualness with which the story is passed on. The Eurocentric attitude of trivialising to deny the profound is like slicing the canvas of history to use as a blindfold.

Not many people doubt Surrealism's commitment to new ways of percéption and cultural practice. Few of the movement's historians, however, have explored the extent of the impact of African, Asian and Middle Eastern cultures on it and even more significantly, its commitment to a new and equal relationship with them. Yet the surrealist André Breton said: 'Surrealism consents to be a homage (to the orient), as the eye hovers over the pearl.' The debt still waits to be recognised, not least in the contributions of 'negritude' intellectuals like Aimé Cesaire, Franz Fanon, Birago Diop, Léopold Senghor, Lamine Senghor and others. Almost subconsciously, Jean Paul Sartre tries to exorcise the ghost of appropriation from the mansion of Surrealism when he describes Cesaire as having chosen to 're-enter into himself backwards', an acute allusion to Surrealism's definition of itself in 1925 as 'the cry of the mind turning back on itself'.

This anthology speaks directly to the concerns and interests of Black artists in Britain today. It features the voices of Black artists ourselves as we talk, argue, explore and celebrate creativity in a complex array of media and approaches. For me, the appropriation of such a space is important and exciting because we are used to a dominant media which talks about us, to us and on us. Experts are in plentiful supply in the media, doubling as journalists, researchers, consultants and officers and advisers of funding bodies. In this book, the contributors themselves define their priorities and creative intentions, establishing the basis of dialogue and discussion through their own work and experience. The emphases may vary, the strategies may reflect diverse priorities and concerns, but together the articles reflect the dynamism of the Black arts movement and its impact on British society.

The anthology is also a contribution to the enormous task of Black arts documentation. In the hectic schedules of our daily work, meeting deadlines or working non-stop to keep body and soul together, we have little time to document. Sometimes the only evidence of a past exhibition is a catalogue; live perfomances literally evaporate into the historical wind; and our many useful conversations and debates go un-recorded. One result is the syndrome of the historical gap, the impression of always seeming to be starting anew.

It is important for us to engage in collective documentation, situating our work and interventions on broader contemplative terrains which support our many multi-media/cross media interventions and collaborations. Consequently the book avoids 'art form' compartmentalization and adopts a thematic format which explores common grounds of creative concern and intention. Brief introductions at the beginning of each of the three sections contextualise the articles.

Last but not least, I believe that the ideas represented in the book are crucial for the Britain of the eighties and nineties. This may seem a paradox, since it is becoming increasingly unfashionable, not to mention difficult, to discuss ideas or to get to the heart of the matter. Ideas now come packaged like detergent, orange juice or pop stars. Image and style are in and presentation, tool of advertising agencies and media hacks, pays scant attention to content. In the dominant cultural industries, events provide a façade for the stifling silence of underlying ideas, concepts and problematics seldom discussed. Famous personalities die, rows and scandals erupt and subside, and time rolls on. It is crucial to turn the tide of post-modernist complacency and pessimism, crucial to seize the time. We have to start talking, signifying the beautiful moments of our lives to mobilize a new future.

E N C O U N T E R S

CLAIMING SPACES FROM THE WHIRLWIND

Emancipate yourself from mental slavery; none but ourselves can free our minds.
Bob Marley

This section focuses on the Black presence in Europe's cultural landscape and the struggles to claim aesthetic, discursive and political spaces from dominant institutions and ideologies. The interventions of Black artists are, for the most part, explorations across the frontiers of definition, representation, creative production and experience, and social power. In 'Emergence 2', Pratibha Parmar alludes to the importance of such explorations when she states that 'the kinds of space we have, don't have, or are denied access to, can empower us or render us powerless'.

Creativity is as significant for the process it nurtures as for its products. Process is not a mere means to an end, but an engagement with life itself. It is the live show of aesthetic and political resolution. In the encounters with dominant institutions and ideologies, territories are won and lost in a constant positioning and re-positioning, signposts are set up or struck down, and new languages are born defying the silence.

The aims and objectives of Black artists and movements are many and the means of achieving them multi-dimensional and com-

plex, reflecting a rich array of concerns, commitments and demands. Black arts and culture in Britain have grown in a historical landscape that has largely remained hostile, trivialising their potential and intentions whilst embellishing itself with their beauty and dynamism. Consequently the work of many contemporary Black artists has focused on turning back the tide of appropriation, snatching victories from the whirlwind, creating authentic profiles, always surviving, dreaming and celebrating.

The opening piece, Ben Okri's 'Meditations on Othello', is a critical excursion into the distorted world of Black representation in western culture. He questions the historical treatment of the Black tragic hero and highlights the moral contradictions involved in the representation of a less than authentic voice. Okri's historical perspective on theatre broadens out into a social critique of contemporary significance which sets the tone for the rest of the section. David Dabydeen continues the historical investigation with an account of depictions of Blacks in seventeenth and eighteenth century English art. Nadir Tharani examines how Eurocentrism relates to South Asian arts and Rasheed Araeen details a contemporary experience, relevant for its confirmation of the historical trajectories.

Tam Joseph, Keith Piper and Donald Rodney are visual artists whose work explores new ways of seeing and articulating the demands of the Black experience. In a striving for social relevance and engagement, Tam Joseph has collaborated with Gavin Jantjes on the mural *The Dream, The Rumour and the Poet's Song*, a refreshing antidote to inner city grey and drab on Brixton's front line. Piper and Rodney's statement on theory and practice, a forthright demand that both come together, is addressed to both the art establishment and the Black arts movement: 'The claim of Gilbert and George that "we want our art to speak across the barriers of knowledge directly to people about their life and not about the knowledge of art" is hollow rhetoric.' They also state that 'many of our one-time comrades in struggle have found themselves coaxed into the claws of the capitalist art market through the private gallery system'. At the *From Two Worlds* exhibition at the Whitechapel Art Gallery in 1986, I watched people's elated responses to Piper's startling art, to the bold paintings and the broadcasts of revolutionary speeches and poems emerging from sculptured heads.

Pratibha Parmar's 'Emergence 2' provides a context for the articles on specific interventions within particular spaces. It shows how memories of migration, displacement and reclamation inform the work of two 'proud creative spirits', the artists Chila Burman and Sutapa Biswas. 'The Politics of Space' is Shaheen Haque's elaboration of similar themes from her personal experience as a Black women architect.

Double Edge is a young Black theatre company based in London which for two years was locked in battle with one of England's most powerful institutions, the Church of England, after it took charge of a disused church hall to get a home for its activities. The problem of homelessness undermines the progress of Black arts in a fundamental way. Adeola Solanke's article charts the progress of the intervention to claim concrete space and highlights the collisions and collusions of legal and political forces.

The experience of J. D. Douglas in organising the Paul Robeson exhibition deals with the area of Black media representation and historical reclamation. Paul Robeson is one of the most significant voices of this century, but, tarred with the brush of cold war politics, he is barely mentioned in the dominant media of the US, his own country. Here in Britain most people remember him only for his rendition of 'Ol' Man River' or as 'honorary Welshman', due to his involvement with Welsh miners and influence on Welsh male choirs. His significance as an artist with an extraordinary perception of the dialectics of race and class who fought to uphold his personal and artistic integrity, generally remains unexplored. Douglas sets out to correct these anomalies and to claim a space for reliving memorable Black experience and achievement to inform present day practices.

Jide Odusina's article broadens out the discussion on media representation by examining the subject of arts coverage in the Black-controlled media and programmes devoted to Black publics.

The dominant media consistently censors Black creativity and attempts to control its impact. 'Ceddo: The People's Account and IBA Censorship' tells of the problems of getting a film screened which 'presents a view from within the Black communities of the consequences in the domain of public order of the persistently lawless — not yet to say racist — policing we experience.'

'Is African Music Being Colonised?' reports on the controversy involving African artists in London and white promoters of African music which confirms the historical trajectories of a racism fashioned in liberal benevolence and patronage. In 'Walking Away With the Music', the only Black kora player in Britain, young Tunde Jegede and his mother, Galina Chester, make a statement on the commercialisation and promotion of African music and musicians in Britain.

The articles have been chosen to give a sense of not only the debates and controversies but also the dynamic pace of events and the conflicts of interests and priorities.

BEN OKRI

LEAPING OUT OF SHAKESPEARE'S TERROR

FIVE MEDITATIONS ON OTHELLO

ONE

I have not been able to stop thinking about *Othello* since I saw a production of the play at London's Barbican. It was the first time I had seen it performed on stage. I was practically the only Black person in the audience. The seats beside me were occupied by three white girls. They noisily crackled their packets of sweets and giggled a lot. I wanted to tell them to be quiet. But I suspected that if I spoke faces would turn towards me. After a while I couldn't bear it any longer. When I spoke, what I feared happened. Faces turned, eyes lit up in recognition. My skin glowed. I felt myself illuminated, unable to hide.

I used to agree with C. L. R. James that *Othello* is not a play about race. The Royal Shakespeare Company thought so as well. They had Ben Kingsley play Othello in the tradition of the Arab moor that Edmund Kean made popular, the only type Coleridge could accept. Ben Kingsley played the part lyrically and it was obvious that he had been doing some unsuccessful weight-lifting to give the character the stature it deserves, but there were times when his colour made nonsense of the part. With the peculiar stage lighting in some scenes it was often difficult to see the difference between his complexion and that of the other actors and actresses. The chromatic tension of the play was thereby rendered harmless. In addition to this, they imposed on the play a vaguely homosexual theme and a psychiatric condition called the Othello syndrome which is a form of psychotic jealousy. None of these helped to make the play credible. These two elements form one long line of evading some of the terrors that are at the heart of the play.

When people don't really want to face something they often become pretentious. The whole business of Othello as an Arab was popularised by Coleridge and Charles Lamb. They did not want to face the full implications of Othello's blackness. They did not want him in their dreams. They also did not want to confront the powerful sexual element in the play. If you take away Othello's colour then you don't really have the depths of the tragedy. A 'tawny Othello' is much more comfortable to take. If it did not begin as a play about race, then its history has made it one.

The emotional explosiveness of *Othello* depends utterly on seeing it acted on stage. Othello's colour is not real on the page. It

1

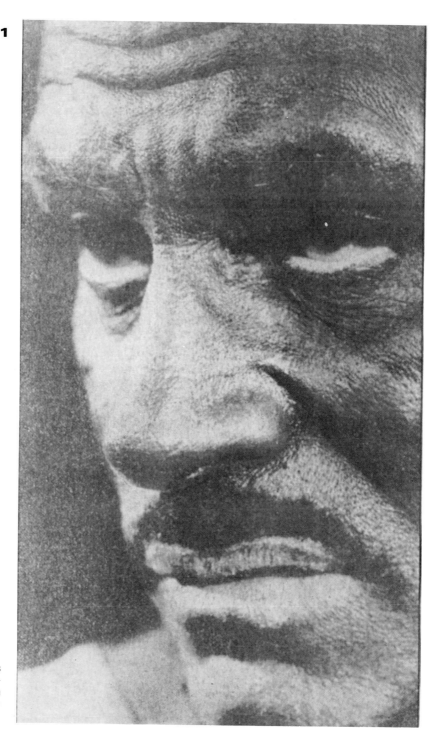

Sir Lawrence Olivier as Othello in the 1964 National Theatre production at the Old Vic. Photo by Angus McBean.

1

can be avoided. Coleridge himself confessed to the 'beautiful compromise' he makes in reading the play. But when he saw it on stage he was revolted by the 'wedded caresses' of Othello and Desdemona. To reduce the colour is to diminish the force of the sex. Working together they can be quite unbearable.

Shakespeare chose his tragic figure well, and then stacked the cards against him. I find it strange that Othello is the only Black man in the universe of the play. He is isolated by colour. He cannot hide on the stage. And his position in society makes his isolation deeper. It is a terrifying position to be in. Honourable, trusting, and surrounded by people who could see him as their worst nightmare. The loneliness of colour made worse by the solitude of power. To whom could he turn? Who could he trust? Trapped in a code of honour which, in a victim, is nothing more than a code of weakness, it is safer for him to trust those who seemed trustworthy. To begin to doubt would bring on insanity for he would have to doubt everyone. And then his mortal terror would begin. He would find himself in the labyrinths of that nightmare of history from which there is no escape. That is perhaps why towards the end of the play his dementia thunders as if in the monstrous echo chamber of his skin.

Sian Thomas as Desdemona, Joseph Marcell as Othello in the Lyric Theatre, Hammersmith, production of 1984. Photo by Ray Abbott.

2

TWO

Every age presents Othello in relation to how they perceive the 'other'. What else can explain the hostility of critics towards Black actors playing the role? It took thirty-two years for English critics to accept Ira Aldridge in the nineteenth century. He was successful with his Othello everywhere else. When critics saw Paul Robeson play the part in 1943 they said it was like seeing the play for the first time and that Iago became 'a credible villain' when a Black man acted Othello. And yet Othello continues to be white underneath.

Our perception of the other gives the measure of our humanity, our courage, and our imagination. Iago represents those who cannot accept the other. He cannot accept himself. He makes colour the victim of his failings. The imagery of Black as unnatural comes from him: he smears it through the play. It is an extraordinary idea: Shakespeare presents this character who is Black, and therefore clearly alien, and then shows that he is not so alien after all, and paints his humanity right down to his jealous soul. And on the other hand we have Iago, who is white, familiar, but who is actually the real alien to humanity and love. It's almost as if Shakespeare were saying: 'It is not those who look different who are the real strangers. For the dangerous ones to succeed in their evil they will be of your familiar colour, and speak with your voice. Don't look for them in startling differences. Look for them within, where they are harder to find.' Iago is a schemer who functions, unrecognised, in the pack, in crowds.

Iago is a lonely and bitter man. He is the man who utterly refuses to transcend himself. He does not accept reality and he refuses to face history. And yet he is, in his twisted way, an intelligent man. He has not found the vocation in which to utilise his considerable imaginative gifts. He is the supreme test for those who would not see clearly. He thinks more intensely than anyone else in the play. In fact he has the mind of a playwright, manipulating people round his plots. When the plot gets out of hand, when the characters don't behave as expected, like a 'bad' playwright he kills them off. Iago is the scourge for those whose thinking is muddled. He depends on their faulty vision to pervert reality.

One of the great themes of the play, for me, is the war between appearance and reality. Appearance strives to be but reality is. Appearance can command the gaze, distort things, but reality is the eternal present. It is what things are in all secret phases. It is what appearance strives to become. Reality is the future of all secrets.

Othello is caught in the nightmare that history has made real. And there is something frightening about a majestic man who believes what they say about him. He believes too much in appearances. Here is a man of royal birth, who was taken a slave, and rose to become a general. Whatever bitterness or bewilderment he might have had has been taken from him. In its place he has been fed bubbles of power. He fed them to himself. In this sense Iago is the most wickedly perceptive person in the play: so clearly does he see the shallowness of Othello's rise, how much he must have paid, how much rage he must have repressed. And because Othello couldn't really release his rage, as it would hinder his rise, he couldn't therefore transform his anger into something higher. He couldn't transcend his jealousy when it swooped into his soul like a green bird of prey. All Iago had to do was get that repressed rage to turn on itself and to open up in Othello the element of self-destruction.

Othello can't really be an honest man. He couldn't have risen that high and in such fearful isolation if he were. Unlike Iago, he accepts too much. He even wholly accepts the blind logic of the world in which he has sacrificed his history for ambition. That is why he had to be so trusting. Trapped in ambition, marked by his colour, refusing to confront his predicament, he is the authentic self-betrayer. He is the white man's myth of the Black man. But he is also a negative myth for Black people in the west. Signposts along roads that can lead to hell also have their own peculiar value.

THREE

It must be admitted that there is something unbelievably simple about Othello. He comfortably personifies jealousy, and his particular manifestation of it is taken as a quality of his otherness. But there he is, a man of royal birth, taken as a slave, and he has no bitterness. He doesn't possess an ounce of anger, or even a sense of injustice. It is difficult to believe that he got that far as a warrior, climbed so high in office, and yet possessed no cunning and no ability to penetrate appearances. Othello is too simple to be true. The most irritating thing of all is his nobility, which, in his predicament, is nothing more than naivety. When a Black man in the west is portrayed as noble it usually means that he is neutralised. When white people speak so highly of a Black man's nobility they are usually referring to his impotence. It is Othello's neutrality and social impotence that really frightens me.

James Baldwin has said that people will face in your life only what they would face in theirs. But to this must be first added the condition that people accept your humanity as being essentially equal to theirs. I find it odd that Shakespeare should concede nobility to Othello, but not rage. It is possible that Shakespeare, as a white man, could not fully concede Othello an equal status of humanity. It seems that the only way white people can see Black people, and begin to accept them, without really having to face them, is by lessening their internal realities. Their external difference, their skin colour, is romanticised, taken as exotic. And their souls are filled with blankness. This is why white people can know what Black people suffer daily all over the globe and not be really bruised in their humanity; because they assume that Black people are used to their pain, that they feel things differently, and that suffering is their unchanging condition. When you reduce the reality of the other there is the dubious benefit of not having to face the fullness of their being, their contradictions, their agonies.

Those who hate Black people and those who romanticise them mean the same thing when one speaks of the colour as ugly and the other speaks of it as charming. Both of them deny Black as being its own unique condition and existing as itself. The weirdest thing about Othello is that his colour is empty history. It is the accepted thing to comment on Othello's jealousy, but few critics seem to realise that his colour, his otherness, must imply a specific history in white society. It seems that in the castle of Othello's skin Shakespeare poured whiteness. It is possible that Othello actually is a blackened white man.

But he certainly is a lost man. It is striking that his author cheats him of a satisfying period of sex with Desdemona. Instead of sex, Othello is allowed coitus interruptus. Instead of anger, he is given an almost idiotic naivety. He has no real friends in the universe of the play. In spite of his apparel of power and glory, he is a naked man, a deluded man. And why does he have to be trapped in that unending cycle of murder and suicide? Could it be murder because you can't deny someone's humanity and not expect them to be violent? Or that in an abnormal situation only an abnormal kind of speech becomes possible? And suicide because the abnormal reality is overwhelming, and no human solution seems possible? Or because it too can be a twisted affirmation of freedom? But it is also a fantasy, a wishing away of reality: it solves the problem of race. In the play it is amazing that Othello's suicide is seen as an extension of his nobility. When in fact it is the inescapable logic of his impotence. The whole machinery of the play is set into motion by the presence of this lone Black man. By the end he kills himself. Iago who is responsible for so many deaths is dragged away, unrepentant, to some vague punishment. The universe of the play becomes homogeneous, diminished. There are always alternatives. Othello's survival would have been fascinating. We always need the other.

FOUR

Two centuries of Othello committing murder and suicide on the stage has produced no significant change in attitude towards Black people. I doubt that *Othello* as a play really disturbs as many people as it should. Society has become too smothered by complacency. Add to this the fact that Othello as a lone Black man on the stage is not threatening. White audiences must merely look upon his phenomenon. It is a basic truth of literature that if you can't enter the centre of a work, then it can't really shake you up. How can white people imagine themselves in Othello's predicament? History does not support it. Othello is a character with only one road leading out of him, but none lead into him. It is quite certain that the Black person's response to Othello is more secret, and much more anguished, than can be imagined. It is often unbearably lonely to know that you can empathise with them, but they rarely would empathise with you. As a Black man it hurts to watch Othello.

Which brings me to another element. If Othello is quite harmless, then Iago is the real enemy. And yet I can't wholly blame Othello for trusting him. Of all the people in the play, with the natural exception of Desdemona, Iago is the only one who expresses what he feels for Othello. He is lying, but nonetheless he expresses. It means a lot to the isolated to have someone declare their affection. Even the victim wants to be loved. But any Black man who has gone out with a white woman knows that there are a lot of Iagos around. If the woman is considered 'desirable' then the situation is more insidious. The question the new Iagos ask themselves is: why him and not me? Then they might put it down to the myth of the Black man's rampant sexuality — a myth invented by white people in the first place. It is crucial to Iago's obsession that Othello is successful. If Othello were a failure and hadn't won Desdemona's love he would not begin to exist in Iago's hell. It is also crucial that Iago is a failed human being. He is full of self-loathing. The real jealousy at work in the play is Iago's. When he speaks of jealousy as a green-eyed monster Iago knows what he is talking about. He's been there. He's stuck there. He has lived with jealousy for long. The fascinating and at the same time repellent thing about Iago is his refusal to confront his failure. The angle of his humanity is very thin. He is the man of short cuts. And so he becomes a specialist in the art of projecting his bitterness. And to crown all this, he has to mask his resentment, his self-obsession. And so he mingles with the crowds of humanity.

Iago today would not be a member of a fanatical racist group: they would be too ignorant, too unintelligent, for him. He is not that much of a failure. He would attend the right marches, say the right things, and he would be unmistakably vocal in his objection to 'racism'. He would be invisible because he is — almost — like everyone else. He lives in the closed universe between cynicism and hell. He is the perfect hypocrite in the sense that you would never think of applying the word to him. And he is an almost flawless actor and a superb ironist. Most of what Iago says has the sinister truth of an ice pick. It is the fact that he speaks from his own condition which gives his utterances their weird and elusive honesty. His smile should send shudders of terror through us. But it warms us a little, because we despise him and feel bad about it, because he too is human, and more seriously because we don't really know him. But he knows us. He has insinuated himself into our lives. And he loathes us, loathes everything. And in our midst he spins his web of hate. Iago is a more authentic creation than Othello. Wherever human beings fail to transcend aspects of themselves there lies the conditions for the birth of an Iago. He is the universal negative man, foil for heroes. There isn't one of us who hasn't glimpsed that curiously satisfying vengeance of drawing the hated world into the depths of our own hell. It is Iago's complete and secretive dedication which makes him so unique.

Othello, today, would not be a radical. He is too ambitious to let anger get in the way. He has come from nothing and has fought his way up in a new world. He wouldn't want to face the truth about himself because it would destroy him. He wouldn't want to face the falsity of his yearnings. To face his predicament would mean accepting the fact that he has become a willing victim of the dream that enslaved him in the first place. He is merely rising up the ladder imposed on him, not building his own.

And then there is Desdemona, innocent and sweet and passive. She and Othello are an unfortunate pair. Neither of them has any cunning. She is too young to perceive Othello's danger. She takes too much for granted and believes too much in the simplicity of everything and everyone.They are mutually deluded. What did she see in him? She saw his nobility, rather than his vulnerability, his strength, rather than the weakness of his position. She is just the type who likes romances and is seduced by exoticism. Today she might be an ardent lover of a glamorised Africa. She would be just the kind of girl who believes that love makes everything right, and that the world would want for her what she wants for herself. She would not have particularly heard of slavery. She would be shocked to hear that Black people are treated badly because of their colour, that they have their homes burnt down, and are beaten up and mercilessly discriminated against. She would be shocked because she 'has been protected from reality', to borrow a line from Harriet Sergeant. The source of their delusion is ignorance. She is the redemption, and the victim, and the vengeance of her history.

FIVE

Desdemona fell in love with Othello because of his stories. He had lived a heroic life. Her father thought he had used sorcery on her. There is no greater sorcery than poetry, than the imagination of the story-teller. Desdemona is a bit of a rebel and her humanity is large. But humanity without scepticism, without knowledge, is dangerous. In real terms she would not find happiness in her choice unless she became a little wise along the way, and the costliest price is always paid for wisdom: the tearing down of as many illusions and lies as the human frame can bear. She would have to love Othello without illusions. It would be a hard kind of love, a rigorous love, that demands constant vigilance. She would have to alter the way she sees her history, and that would alter almost everything else. She would have to be strong and capable of living with a kind of loneliness. There would be many compensations but she would have to manage the tremendous difficulty of being both romantic and wise. And this is the crux of Desdemona's situation. Romantics reduce Black people to a fantasy. And then they love the illusion they themselves have created. Romantics do not face Black people as they are, each in their own particular individualities. Between Desdemona and Othello is a doomed alliance, for he too doesn't face her reality. He never questions the true basis of her love, and consequently doesn't understand her illusions, her lack of cunning and fear. Neither of them knew their predicament and so they didn't stand a chance. And love alone is never enough. That is how victims who remain unaware, blind to their predicament, are always betrayed. They are betrayed as much by those who don't care about them as by those who love them.

I think that the play is less about jealousy than is commonly maintained. I think it is more about accepting the other, about opening the doors of consciousness to more of reality. Or having to become less human. Rejecting is easy: all it takes is to be confused and to be ignorant. But to face the complexity of others, their history, the bands of their raw humanity — that takes courage, and is rare.

Whose heart is not pierced when at the end of the play Othello asks Lodovico that in his letters telling of the tragedy he should 'speak of me as I am: nothing extenuate, nor set down in malice. Then you must speak of one that loved not wisely, but too well.'? These are the crucial lines of the play. Speak of me as I am. Don't beautify me. Don't simplify me. Don't make me less. Don't make me more either. I am not even sure if Shakespeare faced up to that injunction, which is probably the most challenging to a writer. But he put the injunction there. And because he did he spoke from the depths of Othello's life. That failure to love wisely applies to every main figure in the play, to Desdemona, to her father, to Iago, and, really, to all of us. Here Othello is speaking at the threshold of death. An incomplete creation, a man who throws no shadows, a man who has no secret life, he is about to pass into our dreams. It doesn't really matter that Shakespeare didn't, and quite possibly couldn't, get Othello fully in focus, nor looked at him closely enough. What matters is that because of Shakespeare's genius Othello haunts the English stage. He won't go away. He is unable to hide on stage but he is always there, a reminder of his unexplained presence in the white consciousness, and a symbol of the fact that Black people and white are bound on the terrible bed of history. Doomed to his relentless cycle, he will not vanish from our dreams. And yet I dream of ways of liberating him from bondage.

The Ghanaian writer, Kojo Laing, insists that you can choose your sins. You can also choose your nightmares. Somewhere between their marriage and his murder Othello must wake up to the necessity of his vigilance. Leaping out of Shakespeare's terror, he could stand luminous and transcendent. Franz Fanon might have been thinking of the long nightmare at the end of Othello's sleep when he wrote in the closing sentences of *Black Masks, White Skins*: 'O my body, make of me a man who always questions'.

When victims stop seeing themselves as victims and discover the powers of transformations, forces are born on this planet. The possibilities of a new history depends on it. What is done with these possibilities depends on how wisely we love. And ultimately we are bound in fate with whoever the other may be. We are bound in the fact that we have to deal with one another. There's no way round it. Rilke seemed to me to be saying something of this when he wrote: 'That's what fate means:/ to be facing each other/ and nothing but each other/ and to be doing it forever.'

The way we see the other is connected to the way we see ourselves. The other is ourselves as the stranger.

DAVID
DABYDEEN

BLACKS IN

EIGHTEENTH CENTURY ART AND SOCIETY

On 5 April 1723, the *Daily Journal* reported on the influx of Black people in the country and on fears of London being 'swamped' by these immigrants:

> 'Tis said there is a great number of Blacks come daily into this City, so that 'tis thought in a short Time, if they be not suppress'd, the City will swarm with them.

Such anxiety typified white responses to Black people living in their midst over a period of four centuries. By the end of the sixteenth century it had become fashionable for aristocratic families in England to own a Black houseboy, and hundreds of Africans were consequently imported into the country.[1] Their increase was a source of grievance to Queen Elizabeth I who in July 1598 dispatched an open letter to the Lord Mayor and Aldermen of London, and to the Mayors and Sheriffs of other towns, ordering their immediate deportation. The Royal letter spoke of the 'diverse blackamoors brought into this realme, of which kinde of people there are allready here too manie'. The attempt at deportation failed — the owners of Blacks naturally refused to surrender their prized property — and in 1601 Queen Elizabeth (who, curiously, employed Black slaves in her own Court) issued another proclamation commanding their banishment in which she expressed her 'discontent' at the 'great number of negars and Blackamoors which (as she is informed) are crept into this realm'. For the first time in English history, Blacks were used as scapegoats for social evils: Queen Elizabeth blamed them for consuming food in a time of shortages, food which should go to English people who are 'greatly annoyed' as a result; in addition, the Blacks were 'infidels, having no understanding of Christ or his Gospel'. In spite of the threat to prosecute owners who refused to comply with the new order, Blacks remained in the kingdom and, as Peter Fryer states, 'from that day to this, there has been a continuous black presence in Britain'.[2]

In the eighteenth century their numbers were substantial enough to elicit comment from foreign travellers and natives alike. One German visitor in 1710 was moved to remark that 'there are, in fact, such a quantity of Moors of both sexes in England that I have not seen before'; at the other end of the century, in 1788, Philip Thicknesse observed that 'London abounds with an incredible number of these black men... in every country town, nay

3

4

in almost every village are to be seen a little race of mulattoes, mischievous as monkies and infinitely more dangerous'.[3] The multiplicity of such statements suggest that the Englishman, wherever he went, could not avoid seeing real Blacks on the city streets. Certainly, whenever he looked up, the chances were that he would be faced with the painted image of a Black. The city was littered with signboards and tradesigns which imposed themselves upon the consciousness, visually and audibly: if in the Middle Ages it was the religious peal of churchbells which dominated the senses, by the eighteenth century it was the commercial creaking of signboards which claimed the Englishman's ear. He no longer looked to the church steeple's weathercock, but to the signboard, for his favourite topic of conversation:

> But when the swinging Signs your Ears offend With creaking Noise, then rainy Floods impend (John Gay, *Trivia*, Bk 1, 11. 157-8)

As Ambrose Heal[4] reminds us, the 'Blackamoor's Head' (with variations like 'Black Boy and Horse', 'Black Boy and Sugar Loaf' and 'Black Boy and Tobacco Roll') was one of the commonest motifs on such signboards. A city like London then, if not actually 'swamped' (to borrow the infamous term from our present Prime Minister) by flesh-and-blood alien Blacks, was 'swamped' by

6

images of blacks. London in the eighteenth century was *visually* black in this respect.

Not surprisingly, Black people figure in hundreds of seventeenth and eighteenth century English paintings and prints. Judging from their widespread presence in English art it can be said that they had become very much a part of white society. They are to be found in the most unexpected places, participating in the society as if they had *always* been there: in *A View of Cheapside*, 1761, we discover, unexpectedly, among the crowd of white Londoners, a Black horn-player in the company of white musicians. He appears to be totally integrated into the society, he behaves naturally and unselfconsciously, and is observed by the artist likewise. Seventeenth and eighteenth century art testifies to the variety of their occupations, Blacks being depicted as footmen, coachmen, pageboys, soldiers, sailors, musicians, actresses, prostitutes, beggars, prisoners, pimps, highway robbers, streetsellers, and other similar roles. They were not by any means passive or subservient in their roles: in *The Rabbits*, 1792, the Black rabbitseller has a ready and withering answer to the Lady's objections to his goods. 'O la, how it smells — sure it's not fresh,' the lady protests, to which he replies, 'Be gar Misse, dat no fair —If Blacke Man take you by Leg so — you smell too.' Such a display of wit and quick thinking by the Black is not uncommon in eighteenth century prints, suggesting that Blacks were noted for their brilliant comic repartee. On a serious level such boldness was no doubt a strategy for survival in the alien world of the white. Blacks in white society have, historically, had to live by their wits, in every sense. By answering back, by retaliating, they provoked respect from whites (if only out of fear) and preserved self-esteem among themselves. Of course the more common and historic method of retaliation would have been a blend of physical and verbal force: Francis, a large eighteenth century Black, walking down the Strand, minding his own business, was confronted by a jeering white who asked him, 'Well, blackie, what news from the devil?'. Francis, without much fuss, let loose a punch which flattened him to the ground, and walked away saying, 'He send you dat — how you like it?'.[5] Francis' response anticipates the barbed and witty curses, and the broken pavement stones, hurled simultaneously at police in retaliation against their bullying, in the Brixton rebellion of 1981.

English art shows the experience of the Black at both ends of society, English painting depicting his situation among the upper classes, and the English print his contact with the lower orders. What emerges from English painting is a sense of the solitude of Blacks in the alien environment of the aristocratic household. The group portrait or conversation piece, such as Hogarth's *Wollaston Family*, tends to show the Black as a mute background figure going about his duties unnoticed and unacknowledged. Here he is barely more than a blob of black paint, a shadowy figure with no personality or expression, for the Wollastons have commissioned the artist to include the Black in the picture only as a token of their affluence and colonial business interests, not as an individual in his own right: among the sitters are a daughter of a Bank of England Director, a Portugal merchant and Director of the Royal Exchange Assurance, and a future South Sea Company Director and Governor of Virginia. In Wheatley's *Family Group (fig. 7)*, the Black is at the edge of the picture and slightly to the back, spatially divided from the white aristocratic family to whom he is a servant but to whom he does not really belong, except in the economic sense. They are all standing or sitting or bubbling with activity, whereas he kneels silently, not participating in their happiness. Even the dog is more part of the family's affections than the Black, the dog being a central not a peripheral detail. In fact Blacks and dogs shared the same status in the aristocratic household. The *London Advertiser* of 1756 carried a notice by Matthew Dyer informing the public that he made 'silver padlocks for Blacks or Dogs; collars, etc.' *The Tatler* of 1710 carried a spoof letter by a

Black boy complaining that his lady's 'parrot who came over with me from our country is as much esteemed by her as I am. Besides this, the shock dog has a collar that cost as much as mine.'[6] English ladies posed for their portraits either with their pet lamb, their pet lapdog or their pet Black (*figures 4-6*). Sometimes both dog and Black are present in the same picture, both gazing respectfully at their owner, as in Dandridge's *Young Girl with Dog and Negro Attendant* (Yale Centre for British Art).

Such a configuration of white master/mistress, dog, and Black servant, is frequent in English painting. In John Riley's *Charles Seymore, 6th Duke of Somerset*, Black servant boy and black dog adopt the same attitude of admiration for their Master. The Black and the dog are mirror images of each other. Similarly, in David Morier's *Henry, 10th Earl of Pembroke*, the Earl is being admired simultaneously by Black groom and dog; the Black groom, standing behind the Earl, admires him from one angle, whilst the dog, sitting at his feet, admires him from another. A hierarchy of power relationships is being revealed: the superior white (superior in social and human terms) is surrounded by inferior creatures, the Black and the dog, who share more or less the same status.

Comparisons between the physiognomy of Blacks and animals are also made in English art, an extreme and comic example being Rowlandson's *Broad Grins*. More subtle is John Wootton's *The Racehorse Lamprey* in which the head of the Black groom and that of the dark horse are wedged together at the edge of the painting. Apart from the identification effected through colour, the two 'creatures' adopt the same perspective in looking out at us. European artists were liable to make the same juxtaposition between African and animal: in Aelbert Cuyp's *Starting for the Chase* the Black groom and the black horse are paired off not only by colour but, as in the Wootton painting, by parallels in profile and perspective. Indeed the closer one looks at the face of the Black groom the more one sees a resemblance to the horse's face, and vice-versa.

Such comparison between African and animal, however unintentional or unconscious in the artist's mind, is nevertheless a reflection upon the dominant white ideology which equated the two. Richard Eden in the mid-sixteenth century described Africans as 'a people of beastly lyvynge'. Such an English response was to prevail over the next two centuries at least —in 1774 Edward Long elaborates upon Eden's observation, stating that the African's 'faculties of smell are truly bestial, not less their commerce with the other sexes; in these acts they are libidinous and shameless as monkeys, or baboons. The equally hot temperament of their women has given probability to the charge of their admitting these animals frequently to their embrace.'[7] Indeed, the moral justification of the slave trade rested largely on the refusal to classify the Black as a human being. Hence Lord Chesterfield could argue that Africans were 'the most ignorant and unpolished people in the world, little better than lions, tigers, leopards, and other wild beasts, which that country produces in great numbers'. It was thus morally acceptable 'to buy a great many of them to sell again to advantage in the West Indies'.[8] Lord Grosvenor could argue in Parliament that the slave trade was 'an unamiable trade' but could add, with no recognition of the callousness of his comparison, that 'so also were many others: the trade of a butcher was an unamiable trade, but it was a very necessary one, not withstanding'.[9] The processing of Blacks and of mutton was obviously identical: it is this stark and sordid ideology which lurks beneath the 'polite' images of Blacks, dogs, horses and other animals in the paintings of Wootton *et al.*

What emerges from such paintings is a sense of the loneliness and humiliation of Blacks in white aristocratic company. The Black existed merely to reflect upon the superiority of the white. In van Dyck's *Henrietta of Lorraine (figure 3)*, the Black is a mere aesthetic foil. The lady's tallness comes out in relation to his smallness, and his dark skin throws into relief the whiteness of her skin. (In real life Blacks were greatly prized for the intensity of their colour, as the 'For Sale' advertisements in English newspapers indicate. The *Williamson's Liverpool Advertiser* of 20 April 1756 carries this advertisement: 'Wanted immediately a Black Boy. He must be of a deep black complexion...' The Black boy offered for sale in 1771 at a public auction at Lichfield is described as 'friendly, officious, sound, healthy, fond of labour, and for colour, an excellent fine black.')[10] His blood-coloured clothing contrasts with her dignified, sombre dress: he is 'natural' in the pejorative sense of the word whereas she is 'civilised'. Mental qualities are thus being revealed. Her social and human superiority is further emphasized in his backward position as well as in his upward gaze of adoration which she ignores: the Black is the external spectator internalized, for we too, the spectators, are meant to adopt this servile perspective in beholding her image. Finally the *aesthetic* image of Madonna and Child mirror the *political,* imperial notion of Mother Country and Child Colony: a political statement, however unintentional, is being transmitted via art. The same kind of analysis can be made of several other paintings which place the Black servant and white owner in an identical relationship of dominance and inferiority — works like Peter Lely's *Elizabeth Countess of Dysart* and Joseph Wright's *Two Girls and Negro Servant.*

7

Other colonized people, like Indians, receive the same treatment: in Peter Lely's *Charlotte Fitzroy* (*figure 8*) the Indian boy (like the African in Dandridge's painting) kneels in homage at the foot of the white female, offering a tray of fruit; in John Mortimer's *Portrait of a Young Man with Servant*, the Indian servant, standing behind his Master, looks up to him admiringly. These images serve to remind us that Indians and Africans shared the same lowly status in seventeenth and eighteenth century England. They were both sold publicly through newspaper advertisements: in 1709, the *Tatler* advertises 'a Black Indian Boy, 12 Years of Age, fit to wait on a Gentleman, to be disposed of at Denis's Coffee-house in Finch-Lane near the Royal Exchange'.

Newspaper advertisements of this period for African children are too numerous to mention. Like the African, the Indian slave-servant in England frequently ran away from his owner — in 1737 an advertisement appears for a runaway 'East-India Tawny Black',

8

8 Charlotte Fitzroy, by Peter Lely, York City Art Gallery.

and in 1743, for a 'Runaway Bengal Boy'.[11] The frequency of such 'hue-and cry' advertisements indicates the harshness of the Black experience in seventeenth and eighteenth century England. Although apparently well-clothed and well-fed (relative to the condition of the white English poor), Blacks took to the streets whenever the opportunity to escape arose, partly out of the loneliness and alienation of existence in white aristocratic society, partly out of the physical punishments they suffered. The newspaper advertisements often reveal their battered condition: John White, a 15 year old Black who ran away from his master in 1686 is described as having 'upon his throat a great Scar'; in the same year we read of Tom Black who bore 'a scar in his Head lately broken'; two years later comes news of another runaway with 'a scar on his Temple, a great many Scars on his Neck'.[12] In van Dyck's *Henrietta of Lorraine* the white lady rests her hand lightly on the Black boy's shoulders, but we are not to be deceived by the polite images of art.

What the van Dyck painting and others of its kind finally reveal is an even deeper corruption in English (and European) treatment of Blacks, which is the corruption of commercialism, for what we are seeing is a degenerate version of the religious iconography of Madonna and Magi. In paintings of the *Adoration of the Magi,* one of the Kings paying homage to Madonna and Child was normally a Black man or Black youth.[13] In Medieval and Renaissance religious art the Black Magus is a dignified, regal figure, splendidly apparelled and bearing rich gifts. He stands proudly and upright *before* or *beside* Mary. In some paintings he dominates the scene, his energy and upright stance contrasting sharply with the elderly, feeble and kneeling white Magi. He is of equal human status with his fellow whites, and he confronts Mary, the white woman, on a basis of equality. By the era of the slave trade this image has been debased, with the Black reduced to feeble impotence. The image of the Black Magus attending the Madonna in an attitude of human equality is debased into the image of the Black slave-servant attending the secular White Mistress in an attitude of inferiority and humiliation. He has become a diminutive creature, either standing behind his Mistress or kneeling at her feet, his impotence in art being an accurate reflection upon his real physical and psychological emasculation in English and colonial societies. The pregnancy of the secular Madonna to whom he presents his gift (Elizabeth, the Countess of Dysart, in the Lely painting, was pregnant at the time; the Black boy's bowl of flowers reflects upon her fertility) further complicates the allusion to the iconography of the *Adoration of the Magi.*

If English paintings on the whole yield a sense of the lowly status and loneliness of the Black among the aristocracy, then English prints reveal the other aspect of his experience of white society: his active participation in the subculture of the lower classes, his full and equal sharing in their experience of violence and vulgarity. In Cooper's *Sailors Fleet Wedding Entertainment* for instance, the Black, more towards the centre of the picture, is a happy, lusty figure; he grabs merrily at an old prostitute who, alas, responds to his sexual heat by setting fire to his turban, their activity adding to the comic disorder. His setback here is only temporary for other prints show lower-class white women only too eager to receive the attention of the Black. In William Humphrey's 1772 print, *High Life Below Stairs*, the Black butler fondles the white maid who responds warmly to his affections, their surreptitious frolics taking place in the privacy of the servants' quarters. Other prints of Black and white prostitutes touting their talents together or of Black and white soldiers participating jointly in riot and disorder indicate the extent to which the common people forged alliances for reasons of survival.

Although these prints tend to caricature Black people, emphasising sexuality or violent tendencies, we can nevertheless perceive through the haze of myth this historical truth — that Blacks were assimilated into lower-class white society to a considerable degree, finding pleasure, companionship and a degree of protection among the ranks of the common people. When in 1768 Sir John Fielding, the magistrate, complained that the English 'mob' protected runaway Blacks, making it impossible to recapture them,[14] we can well believe him, given the evidence of class-cooperation revealed in popular prints. What the Blacks gave to the English society in return, apart from two centuries of cheap or free labour, cannot be readily described: the records, visual or scribal, were compiled by whites who neglected to adopt a Black perspective on English society. A little evidence has filtered through: we know for instance that by 1787 white Londoners were dancing to Black dance music — the 'Black hops' was the latest craze.[15] That this scrap about Black music should have survived the centuries signifies the stereotypic association of Blacks with 'rhythm': more 'serious' and 'respectable' contributions to the cultural, intellectual and scientific life of English society were unrecorded and so remain beyond the recall of historians.

With regard to the images of art, a series of other questions are raised for the historian to consider: why, for instance, are the images of Blacks in English art mostly of males? Was this because the Black population in England, who were brought over to work, were overwhelmingly male, or was the white male artist nervous or guilty about depicting Black women? Why were white women, from the evidence of portrait painting, and from social records, so fond of possessing litt!e Black boys — what psychological and sexual politics and neuroses were at play in the English boudoir or bedroom?

NOTES

1. For the early history of Blacks in Britain, see J. Walvin, *Black and White: The Negro and English Society 1555-1945*, London 1973; J. Walvin, *The Black Presence. A Documentary History of the Negro in England, 1555-1860*, London 1971; F. Shyllon, *Black People in Britain 1555-1833*, Oxford Univ. Press 1977; F. Shyllon, *Black Slaves in Britain*, Oxford Univ. Press 1974; P. Edwards and J. Walvin, *Black Personalities in the Era of the Slave Trade* London 1983; P. Fryer, *Staying Power: The History of Black People in Britain*, London and Sydney 1984.
2. Fryer, op. cit., p. 12.
3. P. Thickness, *A Year's Journey through France and Part of Spain*, 2nd edition, London 1788, II, pp. 102 f.
4. Sir Ambrose Heal, 'London Shop-Signs', in *Notes and Queries*, CLXXVI, 1939; see also the Heal Collection of Tradecards in the British Museum's Dept. of Prints and Drawings.
5. Fryer, op. cit., p. 88. For another example of Black wit in an English print, see Henry Heath's *Fresh Fish*, 1828, in the Yale Centre for British Art Collection of Prints.
6. Walvin, *Black and White*, p. 60; Shyllon, *Black People in Britain*, p. 29.
7. Walvin, *Black and White*, pp. 6, 163.
8. *The Letters of the Earl of Chesterfield to his Son*, ed. C. Strachey, 3rd ed., London 1932, P. 116.
9. *Report of the Debate on a Motion for the Abolition of the Slave Trade*, London 1791, p. 47.
10. Shyllon, *Black People in Britain*, pp. 13, 15.
11. Fryer, op. cit., p. 78.
12. Fryer, ibid., p. 23.
13. The Black Magi figure has been analysed in depth most recently by P.H. Kaplan in his doctoral dissertation, *Ruler, Saint and Servant: Blacks in European Art to 1520*, Boston University 1983.
14. Fryer, op. cit., p. 71.
15. Fryer, ibid., p. 81.

Hogarth's Blacks by David Dabydeen, from which this chapter is taken, was first published by Dangaroo Press in 1985. This version has fewer pictures than the original.

OBSERVERS ARE WORRIED

TAM JOSEPH

9

Two Faces of the Law,
1985, acrylic on canvas,
9 Tam Joseph.

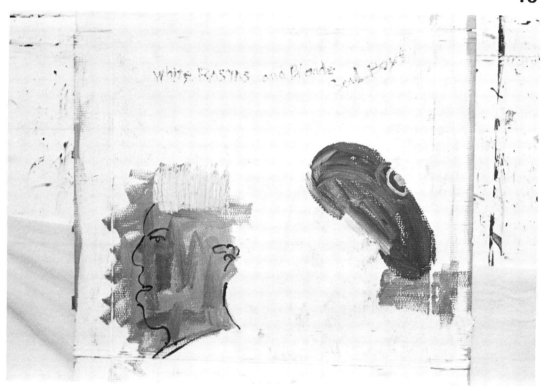

White Rastas and Blond
Soul Boys, by Tam Jo-
10 seph.

11

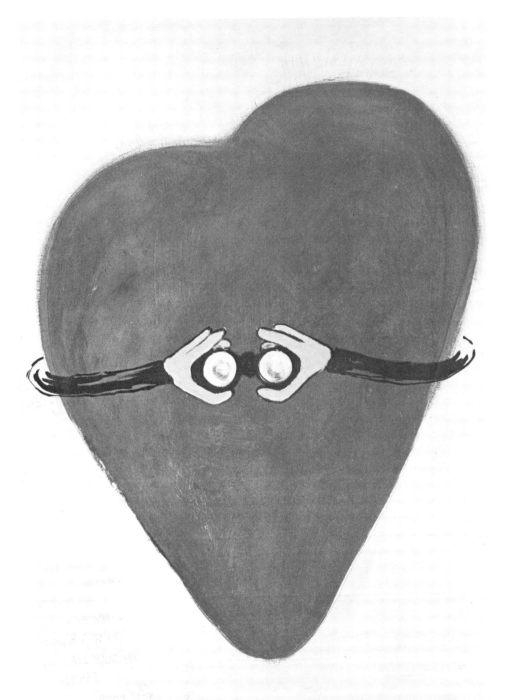

Seek and Ye Shall Find,
1985, acrylic on canvas,
11 Tam Joseph.

12

The Struggle, 1986, stai-
ned sycamore and rope,
12 Tam Joseph.

13

Good at Sports   likes music   Needs surveillance

UK School Report, 1983, acrylic on canvas, Tam
13 Joseph.

14

Has Anyone Seen Tony Birbeck?, 1983, acrylic
14 on canvas, Tam Joseph.

Monkey Dey Chop, Tam
5 Joseph.

15

16

Spirit of the Carnival,
1983, acrylic on paper,
6 Tam Joseph.

17

17 De Man Call Tam, Tam Joseph.

18 The Crime Rate is Rising, 1985, acrylic on canvas, Tam Joseph.

18

HEADS UNDER THE SANDS

OF SOUTH ASIAN ARTS

NADIR THARANI

WESTERN APPROPRIATION

ONE

In 1915 Ananda K. Coomaraswamy, the Indian art historian and cr[...] commented in the *Athenaeum* magazine that to say 'the East is East and the West is West is simply to hide one's head in the sand'. In Britain today this polarisation still persists. And despite all efforts, it is our heads that have been hidden in the sands, a fate shared by South Asian art forms.

In spite of the size of the South Asian community, we are strangely absent from the TV screens or the colour supplements. Heera, the Bhangra rock band, have earned three gold and platinum discs for the fastest selling records in this country. But they have yet to feature in popular music programmes. Even though Bhangra music has been around for over a decade, most magazines have ignored it. L. Shankar, who has recorded with saxophonist Jan Gabarek on the German ECM jazz label, can be heard on German radio. His concerts and those of the vocalist Ramamani of the Karnataka College of Percussion sell out on the continent. Subramanian, another South Asian violinist, records in Denmark, sells compact discs in France and the USA, composes for and plays with jazz musicians Herbie Hancock and Stephan Grappelli but has yet to feature in any contemporary music festival in Britain. South Asian dance forms feature in the 'folk' section of the listings of the weekly magazines, in contrast to 'classical' European dance, a classification that is inaccurate with regard to the historical origins and development of South Asian performing arts. The litany is endless.

The space denied within the dominant discourse, both mainstream and alternative, is similarly restricted on the streets where South Asians are subjected to an extremely high number of physical attacks. Unemployment within the Pakistani and Bangladeshi communities is also very high. Such statistics bear no correspondence to the media representation of South Asians as cooks, shopkeepers and businessmen. The diverse practices that constitute South Asian arts also tend to be simplified into an idealised whole.

One of the reasons advanced for this state of affairs is the Eurocentric nature of the cultural discourse in Britain, coupled with ignorance of the long and diverse history of South Asian cultural forms. But a cursory glance at the media reveals that this discourse is not monolithic. It is possible, after all, to watch *Club Mix* on Channel Four or listen to reggae music on Radio One. It would seem that the reasons for such exclusions are much more complex than the analyses which posit such simplistic dichotomies as mainstream versus minority. The elements that constitute the cultural discourse interact within a constantly changing terrain that not only admits historical determinations but also responds to contemporary social pressures and tendencies.

The representations of South Asian arts, their production and dissemination, (or their absence), are not only subject to the same ordering pressures as other art forms but also to their specific relationship with Europe. These representations condition and are conditioned by the depiction of South Asians and their history. To describe this history constitutes a separate project, but an outline can be traced here. One of the main organising features is the opposition referred to by Coomaraswamy and elaborated in Edward Said's *Orientalism*. The discourse locates the East as despotic, stagnant and stranded in history.

TWO

A stone's throw out on either hand
From that well-ordered road we tread,
And all the world is wild and strange..
For we have reached the oldest land
Wherein the Powers of Darkness range
Rudyard Kipling

The presentation of the East as *strange*, a perception linked to the fear of the unknown, was expressed as long ago as the thirteenth century at a time when Europe was locked in medieval superstition. The alleged immobility or the so-called static character of South Asian art (and society) was suggested by Sonnerat in the eighteenth century and by Hegel. The German philosopher was largely responsible for stressing the spiritual and subjective aspects of South Asian arts, a view that was elaborated by Coomaraswamy at the beginning of this century. The Romantic movement with its longing for distant and exotic landscapes created images of India and Indian art that persist to this day. The 'unattractive' aspects of South Asian arts were attributed to the despotic nature of the society. Even the climate was indicted. The hot climate had not only resulted in stagnation, but had prevented the 'perfection' of various art forms. Western acceptance of these concepts was part of the process of the definition of Europe's own culture, vision and reality by situating South Asia as part of the 'other'. This process was stimulated by the rise in the eighteenth century of ideologies that we now term Modernism. Modernism's various aspects, often at variance with each other but always sharing similar positions in the overall schema, posited themselves as part of the grand order of Reason, as a liberating ideology that sought the global and unilinear development of society. It was an endeavour that required a fervent belief in Science, for Science was supposed to make Progress possible and enable Reason to triumph. Underpinning and motivating this programme was the unparalleled growth in Europe's material wealth and power which fuelled its imperial and colonial ambitions. The ideologies of the Enlightenment were an integral feature of the process that would return South Asia to the folds of history, to the path of Progress, a manoeuvre that required Europe's guidance and physical presence.

The interaction of these ideologies with the South Asian art forms and cultures varied from region to region and from one historical conjuncture to the other. Forms and cultures were subverted, subordinated, or even bolstered, depending on their nature and historical circumstances. This interaction led in some cases to an ossification of many traditional art forms.

More importantly, especially with the perception of South Asian arts in Europe, the major characteristic of this collision was to pose a false dichotomy between tradition and modernity by equating the former with backwardness and stagnation. That which was old, that which had come to pass, was no longer relevant. It is a view that is still assiduously projected and propagated; it stands guard over each discussion of South Asian arts, delineating and restricting every encounter.

20

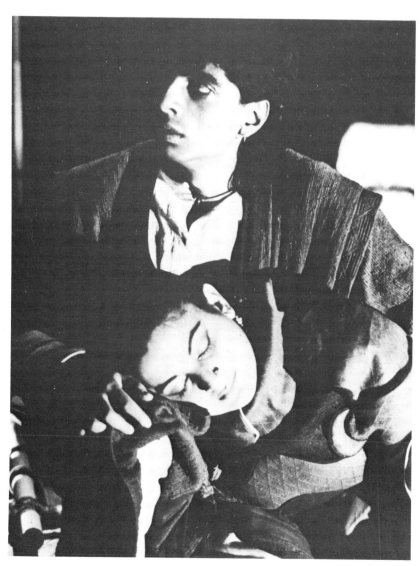

Yogesh Bhatt and Sudha Bhuchar in The Broken Thigh, Tara Arts Theatre
20 Company, 1986.

THREE

**Do not be mournful over your fate —
Lift from the heart cares of tomorrow,
Do not be tearful over the age gone by;
Do not ask for tales of the time of sorrow;
All lamentations are finished — ask no more.
Faiz Ahmed Faiz**

Faced with this antagonistic environment, South Asian artists and critics in Britain have often responded by retreating to a position that upholds South Asian art forms as immutable. It is a viewpoint that manifests itself in a variety of forms that reflect the diverse aspirations and composition of the South Asian community. Some critics, citing the long history of these art forms, demand complete immersion in this culture as a prerequisite for its appreciation. Others, ignoring the problematic of the 'real', lament the impossibility of translating literature even though this has not inhibited the appreciation of the writings of Homer, Garcia Marquez, or Milan Kundera. Divisions between 'folk' and 'classical' are perpetuated without an examination of their historical interdependence or their class origins. A cultivated connoisseurship excludes the popularisation of these art forms, an act that would seek to engage the social realities of Britain, and consequently provoke an interest in the second generation who form a third of the South Asian population.

This retrenchment, this regrouping against a hostile culture, is a form of regression comparable to the use of religion as a bastion against the same threat. During the last decade this trend has been effected and supported by the art establishment's creation of a special domain that subsumes South Asian arts under categories such as *minority* or *ethnic*. This marginalisation together with the protectionist penchant for tradition perpetuates the historical judgements on South Asian arts and confirms its representation as strange and exotic, its location as the other. It reinforces the opposition between tradition and contemporaneity bestowed by Modernism. This allows the dominant culture to continue to appropriate and install these forms within its own divergent terrain, subjecting them to the wand of Reason after activating them with the motor of Progress.

This appropriation allowed Owen Jones in 1853, in *A Catalogue of Ornamental Art*, to declare that 'the principles (of Indian decorative patterns) belong to us...'; principles which, according to William Morris, inspired 'those who first had to do with the movement of which the foundation of our art schools was a part' and who 'called the attention of our pattern designers to the beautiful works of the East'. Such assertions permit Jean Paul Gaultier to dress his models in the South Indian *lungi* (similar to the sarong) on the cover of *Harpers and Queen* and 'stun' Paris; or allow designer Laurent Goldstein to present the male garb of Pakistan in *The Observer*, 22 March 87, and to describe it as being inspired by Mozart's *Requiem*. South Asian music may have inspired and been utilised by La Monte Young, Philip Glass, G. Holst, Messiaen, John Cage and Stockhausen amongst others, but has yet to be featured on the airwaves as part of normal programming. Appropriation allows the *shalway khamiz*, one of the dress forms of South Asia, to be paraded down the aisles of Paris fashion shows to rapturous applause. Yet when worn by Asian women at an antenatal clinic in England, it provokes 'the voice of the midwife' to 'automatically rise, as if the women wouldn't understand' even though 'sometimes the woman was a lawyer or teacher speaking perfect English'.[3]

21

FOUR

The transmutation inherent in appropriation raises a problem which underlies most discourses on 'minority' arts, the question of what constitutes South Asian arts in this country. Is it the use of South Asian aesthetic motifs or is it the origins of the artists which defines South Asian arts in Britain? Are we to classify art forms on the basis of 'ethnicity', a reduction also advocated in the nineteenth century?

A majority of South Asian artists here still use South Asian art forms, partly due to the pressures of the dominant discourse which sees 'ethnicity' as a classificatory category for all aspects of life. It is a question which requires further debate although that is not the main intention of this article.

What I have attempted here is to suggest that the discourses of Modernism, traditionalism, 'minority' arts, and the transformations of appropriation, usually posited in opposition to each other, are in fact facets of the same amorphous discourse whose operations result in the exclusion or misrepresentation of South Asian art forms.

The struggle against these divergent facets is indissolubly linked to the re-examination of the history of Modernism and its various modes of operations within South Asia and demands a more than passing acquaintance with South Asian history. It requires a knowledge and awareness of the various levels of cultural practices and the study of texts such as *Vishnudhar-mottara*, a major work on Indian painting. This would throw light on the manner of operation of the dominant culture, its ubiquitous tendency to appropriate, and its habit of exorcising our languages. It would also check the regression into traditionalism. The latter tendency is far removed from Kadri Gopalnath's experimental playing of raga vasantha on the saxophone or the use of the dramatic structures of Gujirati folk theatre by film director Ketan Metha in his *Bhavni Bhavai*.

The struggle for space cannot be simplified into a quantitative demand nor should it be restricted to the use of South Asian forms. What is really urgent is to challenge the dominant representations of South Asia and South Asian art forms by using any combination of forms. If the choice is South Asian art forms, then these should be rooted in the social realities here. They should, if necessary, also marshall and subordinate elements from other cultures within their overall framework. This will result in a development of these forms which would be both pertinent and vital. It is a challenge that is inextricably linked to other struggles against the state, to our heads emerging from the sands.

NOTES

1. Analysis by the official Labour Force survey reported in the *Guardian,* 8 January 1987.
2. See 'Strange Delights', *Artrage,* no. 16 on how this is reinforced by contemporary reviewers and writers.
3. 'The baby they just call Patel', *Guardian*, 3 December 1986.

EMERGENCE 2

PRATIBHA PARMAR

**Personal fragmentation has a collective beginning in the vast landscapes of barren mountains and tumultuous seas.
The diasporan dance continues its wide movements, abrupt dislocation, violent moments.
Yet there remains the flame of inspiration to live out joyful visions.**

It is in that moment of emergence where we assert our identity, our desires, and reclaim our histories that we move from being an object to a subject. It is this movement from object to subject through a creative engagement with the themes of roots, herstory, and representation in writing and visual arts by Asian women, that I wish to explore.

We use images, sounds and visual metaphors to highlight our realities of disorder, alienation, contradictions as well as the optimistic concern with the celebrations of difference. Differences of history, of gender, race, sexuality and nationality have created the territory of the 'other'.

Central to our creative endeavours are our conscious and unconscious memories of migration and displacement. Indian people have been scattered all over the globe for centuries: colonisation and slavery took our ancestors in ships as indentured labourers to work on sugar plantations in the Caribbean, as railway workers in Africa and on rubber plantations in South East Asia.

Of necessity we have had to move between cultures and languages of domination, and in doing so have developed unique responses to questions of identity. In becoming distant from our pasts and struggling against the insecurity of our present, we have searched for a vocabulary to intervene into certain spaces.

Spaces can be real and imagined, spaces can tell stories and unfold histories. Spaces can be interrupted, appropriated and transformed through artistic and literary practices.

The appropriation and use of space are political acts. The kinds of spaces we have, don't have, or are denied access to, can empower us or render us powerless.

This is an exploration into how some individual Asian women, often defined as 'the other', marginal, or invisible, women born in and through the diaspora, have interrupted and/or reappropriated a number of different cultural territories. Our experiences of exclusion from the centres of culture and power have sharpened our awareness for the need to come in from the margins. They have alerted us to the unjust and alienating structures that work to exclude us and our experiences.

These interruptions are also about not accepting such closures
but changing the structures and forging new languages, different
modes of uttering and invoking responses.

> Moving from silence into speech is for the oppressed,
> the colonized, the exploited, and those who stand
> and struggle side by side, a gesture of defiance that
> heals, that makes new life, and new growth possible.
> It is that act of speech, of 'talking back' that is no
> mere gesture of empty words, that is the expression
> of moving from object to subject, that is the liberated
> voice.[2]

Writing has been one of the most popular and accessible means of
making that journey from object to subject for Black women all
over the world. Storytelling, the oral tradition which forms the
basis for much of the passing down of history and legends, myths
and poetry, has been an integral part of many of our communities
and cultures. It constitutes the memory banks of tradition and a
means of passing down of culture from one generation to the next.
Stories began to be written down as migration, displacement and
enforced movement became a common occurrence for racial and
cultural communities all over the world. Writing became a way to
voice the search for selfhood and signal the historical contexts of
our lives.

> She stood under the glimmer of yesterday's sunset as
> the ancestral
> voices
> of her mothers beckoned for remembrance.
> Resonances of half forgotten memories
> embedded in recesses centuries old
> fluttered like autumn leaves as she struggled to find a
> way into her past.
> Unlocking the herstory of her people's pain,
> she discovers a pain so deep
> its serrated edge leaves an iconography of despair.
> Having drowned for so long in the other's history,
> she leaps out to write her own
> filling the silent absences of their history.
> I shall subvert their fables and write ourselves into a
> history of lived
> moments.

Since Alice Walker won the Pulitzer prize, sections of the

publishing industry in Britain have finally acknowledged Black women's writings. While their motivations may be purely financial, we are at least seeing more Black women's books on the bookshelves. In reclaiming the written word, Black women have become signifiers of a political and historical moment by taking control over representations of themselves and interpreting their own lives. As a political gesture, these writings are a direct intervention into literary traditions which have for too long stereotyped and marginalised such voices: a challenge to the politics of domination that would render us voiceless.

Poetry, novels, short stories, autobiographical narratives, political and discursive writings, have been the predominant forms of writing for women. Black women are writing today fired by many needs. Some feel an urgency to fill out absences in history, while others are concerned with creating images of ourselves which are authentic and textured, devoid of racial or sexual stereotypes. Still others write to create imaginary landscapes where Black women are heroines and in control of their own destinies. Whether we write to reclaim, affirm or celebrate ourselves and our subjectivities, Black women's writings continue to grow and intensify.

Though writing cannot always be a substitute for action, words are nevertheless powerful weapons in the struggle against imprisonment, exclusion and invisibility. Neglect, absences and distortions about Black and Third World people are common features in much European writing. As a Black woman who is a product of the Asian diaspora, words offer me a means of channelling my diverse emotional and intellectual energies into a creative form. I write for many reasons. I want to change ideas and ideologies that only serve the interests of the dominant majority. I wish to document histories and herstories that far too often fall victim to a deliberate amnesia. I want to reflect our realities and help create spaces where it is possible to offer an ever-changing imagery of ourselves.

It has been a long and painful journey to accept and proclaim my identity as a writer. This reluctance to name myself was partly because of the tyranny of fiction and poetry as the only legitimate form of writing in certain circles, when for years I wrote only non-fiction. But this hegemony of fiction was not the only obstacle: the lack of images of Asian women as articulate, literate and confident individuals fought against the predominance of the pervasive mythical image of the writer as white male. To exorcise the ghost of this image, and reclaim the women from my cultural traditions, still continues.

My personal herstory of displacement is not unique. Migrants all over the world are part of the modern world system and carry with them a legacy of loss and fragmentation.

> Reflecting ourselves in each other's eyes, we will move forward and
> create our own worlds,
> speaking in tongues which will resonate our unspoken dreams.
> As the sun descended in the north she awoke in the south,
> the early morning rays travelled through time and space helping to
> unravel her sense of self.
> Rising, rising, rising from yesterday's silence to tomorrow's dreams.
> In that transient moment she traversed that space between the
> consciousness of victim to that of the survivor.

The power of transformation inherent in the word is present, too, in the symbols and images that Black women as painters and artists explore on canvases. It has never been a given that Asian women as artists and as visionaries exist as proud creative spirits; yet in recent years, through the diverse but vocal Black art forums, the mainstream art world has witnessed a number of Asian women emerging as strong artistic voices challenging definitions of Asian women as the other, invisible and marginalised.

Chila Kumari Burman and Sutapa Biswas are part of this new generation of artists whose works provide a textured and visual interpretation of aspects of the Asian experience. Their works have challenged the notion that art and artistic activity is the preserve of a small elite as well as providing a direct intervention into artistic discourses which presume a particular gender, class and race position of 'the artist'.

Chila Kumari Burman was born in Liverpool and studied at the Slade. Her photographs, paintings, prints and etchings record her development as an artist rooted in a history and a culture quite different from the one she encounters in the art world. Her works are essays into several themes: the female body, the unity of women internationally, environmental concerns, policing in the Black communities and representations of Asian women. They are a metaphor for the different realities which exist side by side yet are sharply divided and hostile to each other, offering a non-verbal insight into the complex relationship between politics and art. Her images are a direct testimony to a particular world, a reality not transferred onto canvas as mere documentary evidence but as an imaginative offering of her individual interpretation and experience.

From the beginning of her artistic career, Chila Burman has been concerned with how public spaces are occupied by graffiti: 'My work is concerned with scratches, marks on walls and surfaces, as I feel that the study of these is as valid as the study of high art. It is not so much the literary message in graffiti which I want to explore, because nothing could compare with the personal spontaneity of the individual graffitist, but rather I have concentrated on the vitality of line, variety, richness of colour, texture, pattern, together with the crudeness, violence and delicacy of marks. Using silkscreen, lithography, etching, drawing, mixed media and painting, I have tried to achieve a combination of freedom, abstraction, political and personal feelings, with myself as the medium through which unconscious and conscious emotions and impulses are integrated. The relations of colour, pattern, form and texture become the subject for my own personal interpretations and associations.'

There is drama in many of Chila's prints. *If you and I don't awaken and see what this man is doing to us then it will be too late. They may have the gas ovens built and going before you realise that they're already hot: Malcolm X (fig. 22)* shows through the use of acid the slow disintegration of a policeman's helmet and face as his truncheon falls sharply onto a Black youth during the 1981 uprisings. In this image, a Black artist bears witness to the terror of the state, but also confronts that power by burning up the policeman with acid.

If you and I don't awaken and see what this man is doing to us then it will be too late. They may have the gas ovens built and going before you realise that they're already hot: Malcolm X, photo-aquatint, etching and silkscreen, 30 x 24", 1984, **22** Chila Kumari Burman.

Blue Oppression Wired, gouache and oil pastel, 30 x 24", 1980, Chila **23** Kumari Burman.

22

23

A series of Chila's prints entitled *Blue Oppression Wired, (fig. 23)* illuminates the notion of barred and confined spaces in the urban environment which are slowly straining and stretching under the weight of resistance.

> Not for her the incantation of survival, 'to be or not to be' which belongs to those who have the luxury of such choices. The passion to uncover and be the chronicler of her stories is her daily
> motif.
> Having drowned for long in the other's history, she leaps out to write
> her own.
> Construct/deconstruct the myriad meanings of her being.
> Charting the journeys, voicing the silences,
> she searches to reassemble this herstory,
> to reconstruct the complex algebra of her lives.

Sutapa Biswas was born in India and has grown up with her family in Southall. Her work is strongly influenced by ancient Hindu mythologies and iconography as well as by the everyday experiences around her. Her work is a journey which has taken her into her cultural and historical past as a way of recreating her present and inventing her future.

Sutapa's paintings and drawings are history paintings which depict 'happenings and experiences which dissipate into the background. The setting could be the domestic scene or an hour of conversation'; they are inspired by a need to inform and challenge the viewer. She shows images of Asian women which are wry, humorous and powerful. Humour and satire are strong elements in Sutapa's work and pull one into a world where women are fierce in their righteous anger. For instance, in her painting, *Housewives with Steak Knives, (fig. 24)* the traditional image of Kali, a goddess of war, wielding the weapons of resistance in her many arms symbolises the defiance of Asian women universally. Intimate and sensual, fiery and heroic, the women in Sutapa's drawings are rounded wholes, exuding a liveliness and poetic resonance.

The Pied Piper of Hamelin, inspired by a visit to India, demands an involvement from the viewer. The vibrancy of the colours and the interplay of the different dimensions creates a frieze effect, engaging us in complex dialogue about the dominance of western tourism against the economic poverty of the rickshaw wallah and the richness of Indian art and architecture.

24 Housewives with Steak Knives, Sutapa Biswas.

As she sat searching for herself in the mirror
she zeroed in on that one point which reflected the
continuum of her
many beings.
She had tasted the bile of hateful contraries,
images that this hostile landscape had conjured up for
her.
Having drowned for so long in the other's history,
she leaps out to write
her own.

It is not only in the subject matter that Sutapa challenges the
aesthetic of the individual artist motivated by the ethos of an
'artist' and oblivious to the surrounding material and political
influences. The images in her works provide a narrative of
particular experiences: images of Asian women in our totality,
women not on the margin, silent or-mute.

The materials an artist uses are often symbolic signifiers of
economic, cultural and gender positions. One of the striking
features of Sutapa's works is her use of pastels. There is nothing
soft or feminine in her choice of pastels as a medium for many of
her drawings. The sheer size of her pictures and the intensity of

colour signal assertively in mainstream visual spaces, challenging expectations of 'high art'.

The cultural impact made by women such as Chila Burman and Sutapa Biswas is crucial, reverberating under the umbrella of Black arts in Britain, and equally importantly, intervening in mainstream artistic practice and theory.

As writers and artists we are creating a textual whole which constitutes a collage of our plural identities, shifting the boundaries of cultural meanings and processes. Through its reference to various traditions, our work demands that it not be marginalised or ghettoised. We have employed a number of sites for cultural struggle and redefinition and involved ourselves in an active process of self-identification. Our work reasserts difference and reconstructs our subjectivity against the assimilation and invisibility of our 'otherness'. Our words and images of anger, passion, and compassion as well as of humour and wit, challenge the definition of us as the silent, acquiescing 'other'.

> In continuing the tradition of her mothers, she pioneers new ways of
> seeing.
> Weaving patterns of survival and creation with silken threads she
> confronts the harshness of the dark grey concrete canvas.
> Building fires which reflect her desires,
> she speaks, moves, colours, writes and sings with many voices but the
> rhythm remains the same.
> Women, exchanging silent words of understanding, nurturing,
> circling,
> sharing.
> Creative spirals, sweeping, sweeping, sweeping into an arc of
> lightness, movement and change.
> Rising, rising, rising from yesterday's silence to tomorrow's dreams.

NOTES

1. Emergency 1 was originally written as a prose poem and a narrative for a video on Black women artists and poets. The film was made by Pratibha Parmar and is distributed by Circles.
2. Bell Hooks, 'Talking Back', in *Discourse: Journal for Theoretical studies in Media and Culture*, no. 8 1986-87, edited by Trinh T Minh-ha. This issue titled, 'She, The Inappropriate/d Other', contains many interesting articles.

THE POLITICS OF SPACE

OF A BLACK WOMAN ARCHITECT

SHAHEEN
HAQUE

THE EXPERIENCE

By shaping the space in which one moves and has experiences, architecture is the very landscape of human life. Unlike other forms of art, architecture is not just aimed at an audience; it is also inhabited and used by people. It is thus potentially a social art of the highest order.
Nunzia Rondanini.

If you had asked me sixteen years ago, 'What is architecture?' I would have been hard pressed to reply. However, since then I have trained and spent the last seven years of my life as one. Traditionally, architecture is seen as the art of design and construction of buildings. It is about the spatial relationships that buildings and parts of buildings have with each other. It is therefore about the physical form a building takes and the space it leaves around it.

As a Black woman architect I believe that architecture is also informed by the politics of space. It is essentially about the power structures that fund the white male middle class architects who make up the body of the profession in Britain. They create the physical environment in which we live and reinforce through their designs their problematic definition of women, Black people and the working class. White middle class architects reinforce through the built form their stereotypes of how Black and working class people live. Inevitably the buildings they produce reflect a limited response to the arts and to the social life of the people they design for and, by doing so, limit the life choices of the Black and working class.

On the left, environment issues have been taken up as legitimate areas of political concern but architecture is still not generally seen as a political issue. Whilst there has been widespread criticism of post war modernist architecture in the inner city, epitomised by the high rise council block, it took the Black uprisings of the 1980s to precipitate official action. Haringey Council has for example now embarked on a rehabilitation project on Broadwater Farm to 'better the facilities on the estate'.

STARTING A CAREER IN ARCHITECTURE

My parents lived in the East End of London where I was born. Their experiences of racism and the poverty of the physical environment made them move out of the area. Because we came from a financially poor background my parents placed a huge emphasis on education. When I was young, my mother borrowed a book called *Careers for Girls* from a neighbour and made me choose a career. I started the book at A and never got any further than architecture. I was hooked. My interest in drawing and painting could be encompassed by architecture. After a lot of explaining and persuading, my parents agreed on my choice. This was the easy part as I later realised. The most difficult part came once I got through my A-levels and started at a school of architecture. The seven years I was there were literally spent in confusion and isolation.

I was unprepared for being not only the one Asian woman but also the only Black woman on the course. Coming from a working class background also made it difficult for me to participate fully in the discussions and debates about art and architecture. The lectures particularly reinforced the dominance of western art and architecture and portrayed them as the most important influence on architectural design. Other significant forms such as Islamic and African architecture were relegated and merely seen as precursors for the more important western traditions.

Whole academic terms were, for example, spent studying Renaissance architecture whereas a two-hour morning lecture was deemed sufficient to cover Egyptian and Islamic architecture. African and Asian architecture were completely negated in the curriculum. When I reached the third year I decided to deal with this negation by doing a dissertation on the influence of sufism in Islamic architecture. Working on this dissertation gave me a sense of the wealth of an alternative knowledge and history of architecture which up until then had been denied me. However, my personal tutor openly stated that he could give me no help on the subject not only because he knew nothing about it but also because he was not interested.

Another example of Eurocentric bias and arrogance was when two Nigerian male students submitted work for the formal crit procedure using models from their particular experience of housing in Nigeria. The tutors refused to acknowledge this experience and pressurised them to re-submit the work using European models. This attitude forced one of them to drop out of the course. The other persevered but like me faced a catalogue of indifference and arrogance. During his last year he explored the possibility of developing a health centre in Nigeria for his comprehensive design study. From the onset, he was actively discouraged and told to base his model on European architecture and buildings here. Thus he was denied any meaningful support even though he had made it clear that he had no intention of practising architecture in Europe.

I survived the racist architectural education and graduated. But I found the experience of working in private practices very similar to my college days. To begin with, my fellow graduates had relatively little problem in securing work. I applied for numerous jobs but didn't get very far. When I eventually got a job I was paid £1,000 less than my white male colleagues. This is a common experience for most women, particularly Black women. Working in a private practice was a difficult and contradictory experience. As I became increasingly aware of myself as a Black woman in a white, male-dominated profession, I decided to find alternative employment. I joined a local authority committed to equal representation of its workforce and to the importance of consultation with the community in the design process. The authority was also committed to co-operative and multi-disciplinary working.

After three years however I realise that whilst the political sentiments may be very noble, the day-to-day realities are fraught with race, sex and class contradictions. Some of the comments one hears daily range from 'Black people can't speak properly', through 'they are incapable of doing the job they are employed to do', to 'they only got the job because they are Black'. Sexism is also rampant in the architectural industry. Male architects and quantity surveyors specify various products and materials using trade literature full of images of scantily-clad women selling manufacturers' products ranging from roofing materials to rubber pipes. Not surprisingly these men are unable to deal with women architects as equals in a professional capacity.

The pressure to be doubly competent in my work is great. I have to prove with every job and contract that I am better than my male colleagues. Recently, a staunchly conservative quantity surveyor stated that there were only two people in the architectural team of fourteen who worked to deadlines and cost limits. He had to admit that both of them were women. One of them was Black.

INTERVENTIONS

Despite the problems in the profession, I feel it is important to talk about the interventions we have been trying to make in order to contribute to a new and relevant discourse of architecture. Presently there are a number of feminist groups that come together to discuss and explore ideas around feminist design. But these groups are made up of predominantly white and middle class women and have so far failed to provide a space for Black women's interventions. This has meant that as Black women we have had to find our own ways and terms of formulating a discourse that reflects our needs.

It is important for Black women to develop a political confidence since it is only through this that I feel it is possible for us to have the power to effect changes in our space. We also have to inform the process of change with our own particular experiences. I bring to it my own background, a reality of living with my parents and brother in a single bedroom flat with no bathroom. This box negated our very basic material and cultural needs.

British architecture has in the main concentrated on western models and informed them with particular class ideologies to develop housing designs which cater for the needs of the white nuclear family. A major flaw in the dominant discourse is its failure to take on board the needs of the different Black communities living in the inner cities. Black people are not seen as permanent citizens and here to stay. An acceptance of the permanency of the Black presence would have a radical effect on the way architects and white society in general view the Black community. Architecture would need to move away from its Eurocentric basis and embrace a wider cultural concept of design and housing needs. This would also have implications for other communities such as the gay and disabled. By catering for the needs of the extended family, for example, design would take on board new sets of space requirements which conform to the needs of larger groups of people living together.

I have begun to discuss some of these issues and possibilities in a working party, but to achieve real progress we need to break down our profession's exclusionism and link up with workers in the housing departments, tenant groups and the community. I also feel that to ensure that the housing needs of the Black communities are met, it is essential for Black architects to work with their own communities to establish a design principle.

For example, I recently came into contact with a white woman who had visited and studied housing design in India. Her reason for not being allowed into the kitchen of an Indian family was, she thought, because Indian people believed that the kitchen was a dirty place! She obviously had no understanding of the subtleties of Indian culture. There are a range of possible reasons why she was denied access to the kitchen, from the fact that she was a guest, to the ritualisation of the art of cooking which in Hindu religion requires the non-admittance of 'strangers' to the purified haven of the kitchen.

Currently I am working on an arts education project which involves designing facilities such as a performance space, cinema, recording studio and community offices into three existing buildings. The design brief was to link up the spaces in the buildings with walkways. The walkways had been designed by white male architects in a very traditional way. After studying models from India, I have been able to persuade the design team to use these models in the design, convincing them of their viability and appropriateness. The use of non-European architectural styles and models is important because we are designing for a multi-racial community. It is a sure way of establishing from the outset that the building is for the whole community. This is particularly crucial because buildings which currently house arts facilities are usually associated with the middle classes and patronised by them. The architecture therefore re-inforces this identity and association.

We intend to involve the local communities in the detailed design of the building through a series of public consultation meetings. These consultations will have to address the tendency of architects to see themselves as professionals who know better than their 'clients', and will raise the issue of language as used by architects. Architects currently present their drawings and ideas in a drawn form and language which mystifies the whole design process. Plans and drawings are couched in a language which requires familiarity and the skill to interpret. This is a problem which distances the architect from the community and makes it difficult for people to intervene in the organisation of the very spaces they inhabit and experience throughout their lives. The miserable failure of inner city architecture as a result of modernism has led us to involve the community in the design process.

It is interesting to note the response of the architectural profession as a whole to the recent debates around community architecture. While previously only a small number of architects with a social conscience have sought to involve the communities they are designing and building for, the idea is now gaining popularity and being seen by an increasing number of architects (still relatively small) as the way forward. The architectural press and the professional body as a whole is fiercely resisting the idea and pushing the works of modernists such as Le Corbusier as a valid approach to design. In order to make architecture respond to the needs of the community, it is essential that architects radically rethink the ways by which we design buildings and organise spaces. This inevitably means the breaking down of the profession's elitism, reassessing architectural education and crucially involving our communities in the whole architectural process.

CREATIVE SPACE

THE CHURCH OF ENGLAND

DOUBLE EDGE VERSUS

There is a tendency for commentaries on Black arts to focus on problems. Problems relating to the lack of funding, of fair critical feedback from the media, of adequate training facilities, all of which crucially affect the work of artists. This article is about a solution to a particularly pressing problem, one which undermines the stability of the sector in a fundamental way: the problem of homelessness.

ADEOLA SOLANKE

25

St. Michael's Parish Hall,
25 Greenland Street.

The difficulty in finding a base with adequate facilities and security of tenure is a devil that sooner or later rears its ugly head for all but the most fortunate groups. Without a solid base from which to operate, it is difficult to pursue programmes thoroughly and consolidate progress. But to find one is a Herculean task in today's property market. London is in the throes of a housing crisis of enormous proportions. Those who are fortunate enough to find suitable accommodation confront the problem of rapidly rising rents, which can mean that premises are unaffordable even when found. When members of Double Edge Theatre Company found themselves faced with the prospect of life on the streets in December 1985, they decided something drastic had to be done. 'Empty buildings and homeless people go together,' quips the squatters' graffiti. The company took heed. It took charge of a large, disused church hall near London's Camden Town — and found itself in a real-life drama involving the local council, the police and one of the country's most entrenched and powerful institutions, the Church of England.

What brought this young theatre group and this bastion of the state into a confrontation which spanned eighteen months and involved three (unsuccessful) eviction events? The answer lies a stone's throw from Camden Town tube station in the innocuous shape of St. Michael's parish hall on Greenland Street. It is an unlikely site from which to launch a challenge to the establishment, but its location near a bustling high street establishes the property as ideal for a Black arts centre in an area lacking in satisfactory recreational provision for its Black population. The empty, run-down building, an ugly duckling to passers-by, looked like a beautiful swan to Double Edge members Michael Donovan, Helen Clarke and Derrick Blackwood, who saw the chance to avert their immediate crisis and to pursue their dream of creating a permanent Black arts centre.

Double Edge Theatre Company was formed in 1984 by two young Black theatre arts students, Derrick Blackwood and Clarence Smith, who met and worked together at Rose Bruford Performing Arts School, a channel for the creative energies of several Black actors. The aim of the company is to provide theatre which addresses and reflects the concerns and aspirations of young Black people in Britain. The first production was *Johnny was a Good Man*, a study of heroin addiction and youth's waste in a society in which Black youngsters are beset with the difficulties of dealing with a racist culture at the same time as they are wrestling with the general upheavals of adolescence. Camden Council included it in its drug education campaign. The artistic policy of the company deviated from the dominant tradition of liberal multi-racial theatre in presenting an all-Black cast dealing with a theme inspired by the Black experience, and incorporating issues of class conflict and racial values.

The company followed this with *The Remnant*, an allegorical look at African history which examined the choices and pitfalls before Black people today in the light of historical experience.

Why does a group like Double Edge exist? Helen speaks passionately about what motivates them: 'When we're planning our programme the starting point has to be thinking about ourselves, our history, our culture. Why are we here? What is the significance of being Black? How did we come here? We have been told since we were young at school that history is white. We've been told about figures like Henry VIII, and Christopher Columbus and Sir Francis Drake, and they are supposed to be the stuff of history. We don't figure in it. But when you look into the matter we see Black people have been around since the year dot. White man's history is warped. Their version of history suggests that we as Black people should be eternally grateful to them for what they've done for and to us. The question is, what have they done? What haven't we done for ourselves? We're trying to tackle these questions.'

Such efforts are often launched from inauspicious places. The group's first home was in the front rooms of members. From these it progressed to a small space, 'a little tiny box' says Derrick, in Kentish Town Afro-Caribbean Community Centre. The circumstances they met there will sound familiar to many Black groups: inadequate space (five by twelve feet for three people), inadequate facilites and limited access to those that were offered. 'The group was sharing the hall with so many other users it was impossible for us to rehearse properly. The Centre wasn't really housing a theatre company; we were like an odd appendage floating about the place,' Michael remembers. That was in October 1985.

The situation was critical and the options were few. Derrick Blackwood remembers approaching the Roundhouse, the first national Black arts centre, set up with initial funding from the Greater London Council and also located in Camden. 'Remi Kapo, the co-ordinator, gave me a million reasons why he couldn't help us. But to me Camden Council had put enough money into the project to justify the inclusion of a Camden-based Black arts group.'

Camden Council, approached directly, made two suggestions: one, offering Double Edge the use of a portacabin; the other, offering financial support and other kinds of necessary backing if the group succeeded in securing premises for itself. 'We were told by Camden Council that any group finding itself in a position to house itself could approach the council for the funding of the property, either by way of rent, licenses, leases or, in certain cases, by purchasing the property,' Michael Donovan recalls.

As it happened, it did not take long for the company to locate a suitable space. Derrick, who was born and bred in Camden, already knew of St. Michael's and knew it had been empty for years. Enquiries revealed that the building was the property of the Church, under the management of the Reverend Alan Page, Archdeacon of Hampstead and the immediate ecclesiastical power in the parish. Double Edge had to decide quickly. 'Initially, we simply wanted to use the space, but we weren't sure on what basis. The dream was to have our own base ultimately, but our accommodation crisis brought the long-term goal to the forefront. Around Christmas we saw a light on in the building, so we knew we had to act. We hoped that the Church, being a caring institution, would understand our plight. It was either that or see our company collapse. It was an emergency. It meant that negotiations had to follow afterwards.'

And so it happened that one chilly morning around New Year 1986, a disused church property was resurrected into a living force. As Double Edge moved into the space, it also moved into a new stage of its development, one which was to prove as problematic as positive. 'As soon as we entered, we knew we were home: a stage, a bar area, a large hall, good lighting, all asking to be transformed into a thriving arts centre.' Making the dream come true was to depend on four key factors: the Church had to be persuaded to sell, the Council lobbied to fulfil its promises, police opposition to a Black arts centre overcome and a separate company, independent of Double Edge, had to be created to champion the cause.

The relationship with the police kicked off to a memorable start on the second night of the squat when a squadron of local officers arrived. 'There were only two of us there,' one of the group remembers, 'and many of them. The only thing that saved us was the fact that they underestimated us. We knew the law on squatters' rights; but they were the law. We tried to explain our plans and the officer in charge came out with the quote of the decade: "We don't make treaties with Argies!". The tone of that comment suggests the character of the police's attitude to us.' At that stage it appears that the police did not want to risk a confrontation and so left. 'That was the beginning of the real battle for St. Michael's. If they had known what we were about they would have forced us out. They underestimated our capabilities. We learned how to negotiate with the system and how to use official structures and mechanisms, like those of the Church and Council. They thought we were jokers. They were wrong.'

The formation of a company to take charge of the task of securing the building was imperative. The development of Camden United Theatre happened gradually as local groups and interested individuals rallied round Double Edge and worked voluntarily to get the scheme off the ground. The aim was to establish an arts centre which would pull resources into one area for the benefit of as many groups as possible. Rehearsal and performance space would be provided at cheap rates as part of the drive to make Black theatre economically viable and less dependent on the whims of funding agencies. 'As administrator, I longed to get Double Edge as self-sufficient as possible. Funding is so unstable. Every year there are cuts and it's only the fittest that survive. One thing we didn't want was to deprive other local groups of resources by bidding for the building in a unilateral manner. Other groups wanted the space too, and so Camden United Theatre, an amalgam of all the different interests involved, came about,' says Helen. Although Double Edge initiated CUT, it could not run it: 'It was too big a job and would have undermined our work as a theatre company, which is to provide Black theatre. CUT was created to manage Camden United Theatre for Double Edge and the other users of the space. It has its own workforce and work programme and the prospects of CUT members are linked to the success of the initiative. We want to give young unknowns the chance to show what they can do. Our emphasis is with the small, the local, the growing. You don't have to have been funded for years to gain access to this space.'

The job before CUT was daunting. Helen, who had been away on a GLC-run arts administration course, returned in July 1986 to find an excellent practice ground to test all the course had taught her. Of all the skills she had picked up, she found none so useful as the ones to do with negotiation. 'The arts admin course taught me diplomacy. I learned how to talk to people to get what I wanted. How to enter a situation and achieve an objective. How to manage an office and its resources effectively. It was a crash course in human relationships. I went to work in various organisations, well-funded and poorly-funded. On placements I observed how people coped without much money and what others achieved with a lot of money. I worked with the National Theatre where they had six administrators to do the job Michael and I were doing at Double Edge. So I learned how to do the work of five extra people by getting to the root of tasks and cutting out unnecessary work. I also worked with people who showed me that lack of resources is not an excuse for shoddy work.'

To realise its object of purchasing the building and converting it into an arts centre, it was necessary to persuade the church to sell the building, since Camden Council would not give financial help without proof of willingness to sell. Father Page's first eviction order in January 1986 had been pursued as far as the High Court until members of Double Edge persuaded him to give them a hearing. A second eviction order in July 1986 acted as a spur to CUT to establish itself as a viable concern. 'To them we seemed like a load of pests, only interested in getting free premises. What they hadn't been shown was our professional attitude and serious purpose. We realised we had to give them an account of why we were there and why we felt we should stay there.'

26 Double Edge Theatre Company poster.

26

The outcome was a report called *Camden United Now.* 'The report justified our presence there. We spoke about why we felt a Black arts centre was needed in that particular place. We indicated how each nook and cranny of the building was to be used. We provided a financial analysis of what we expected our income and expenditure to be for the first year of the theatre's life, and a breakdown of how our programming activities would help in the running of its economy. Terry Morris, a volunteer with CUT, did a lot of the ground-work for this and the effect was astonishing.'

The report was sent to funding bodies, councillors, Double Edge's bank manager and the Church. Straight away it improved the relationship with Father Page who was persuaded to reconsider his eviction bid. CUT's battle was also assisted by the Church's internal circumstances. One event in particular gave them unexpected ammunition and scope. In January 1986, around the time of the squat, the Church had issued a report called *Faith in the City*, which looked at the role of the Church in the inner city. The report was presented by the Archbishop of Canterbury's Commission on Urban Priority Areas (UPA), set up to examine 'the strengths and weaknesses of the Church's life and mission in the inner city'. In the words of the commission: 'If our report has a distinctive stance, it arises from our determination to investigate the urban situation by bringing to bear upon it those basic Christian principles of justice and compassion.' (Introduction p.xiv.) The report recognised that people in the UPAs were on the whole made powerless by their poverty: 'They are trapped in housing and in environments over which they have little control. They lack the means and opportunity — which so many of us take for granted — of making choices in their lives.'

The report identified property as a crucial issue in its examination of its relationship with Black people, many of whom are relegated to living in UPAs. The Church is a major property owner in Britain. The 1986 Report and Accounts of the Church Commissioners (the body which manages the 'historic' resources of the Church), shows that it owns £44.8 million worth of commercial, agricultural and residential property in the UK and some commercial property in the USA. Property income rose by 4% in the last financial year, and total income was £150.8 million. The capital value of the property portfolio rose to £1003 million at December 31 1986, and of the total property portfolio commercial properties totalled £564 million. The commissioners are engaged in a policy of selling Church property to release funds for more profitable forms of investment, and the Big Bang has created plenty of opportunities to pursue this policy as competition for space in the City and West End grows. The Church Commissioners' Report and Accounts showed that proceeds from sales frequently went into retail developments, although the commissioners also purchased a lucrative freehold in the City to be redeveloped to be let as office space. Rent from shops yielded the most money within the commercial property section.

The use of redundant buildings represents a political and ethical hot potato for the Church. What is its position when a property is sought by both high-paying private concerns and poor community groups? Does the property automatically go to the highest bidder? Not necessarily, according to the Church Commissioners. The section headed 'The Sale of Redundant Buildings ' (pp. 152-3) states: 'Where a redundant building is not required by another Christian denomination, and is not a candidate for preservation by some other means... the Church Commissioners have to make choices about the sale of the site... In some places, the commercial site value may exceed the price that can be afforded if the site is to be used for community purposes... The Commissioners are then faced with a difficult decision: to realise the full value of the site, in order to make more money available to further the work and mission of the Church throughout the diocese and beyond, or to accept a lower price in order to allow the needs of the local community to be met... The Church of England alone has the discretion... to sell to other than the highest bidder.'

Having secured the Church's approval for its presence in the building with the *Camden United Now* report, CUT's next task was to persuade the Church to exercise its discretion in the sale of St. Michael's. CUT's stand presented the country with a test case about the Church's sincerity and willingness to take non-financial matters into account. The Commission had urged diocesan authorities to avoid giving the 'impression... of a rich and uncaring institution' (p. 153). One of the four Black members of the *Faith in the City* commission was Reverend Barry Thawley, vicar of St. Matthews Church in Brixton, a well-known venue for Black cultural events. Reverend Thawley is the chair of the Association of Black Clergy, a group which pressures the Church to acknowledge the strength it derives from its Black flock by catering for the needs of Black people in its internal and external operations. Barry Thawley and another Black clergyman, Theo Samuels, vice-chair of the Association and chair of the London Diocesan Race Relations Group, were key figures in the fight to implement the Commission's recommendation that a standing committee on Black concerns be introduced as a permanent feature of the Church's decision-making structure, an aim achieved in December 1986. By linking up with these progressive forces within the Church, CUT was able to direct its energies more effectively: 'We decided the best approach was to get the Church lobbying the Church,' says Derrick.

Advice and support from Camden Council was equally valuable. Jeff Morris from the Race Relations Unit and Junior Douglas, a Black officer in the Arts and Recreation department, were just two of the people who came to CUT's assistance. Brian Barford, head of the Grants Unit, gave advice which helped the group formulate a strategy for Council support. A grant of £25,000 from the Race Relations Unit helped purchase necessary equipment and set in motion a programme of activities. Greater London Arts contributed a grant of £1,000 for a jazz season.

The Council made a major intervention in July 1986 when Father Page, without any warning, imposed another eviction order. A deputation from the Council lent its weight to the efforts of Thawley and Samuels on behalf of CUT and the matter permeated far enough up the London Diocesan hierarchy for the Bishop of Edmonton to step in. Father Page was adamant that the group had to go, but CUT made it clear that it was prepared to fight to defend what it had achieved. The Church was reluctant for the situation to end in a showdown and so, after discussions, it was agreed that the group could continue to use the premises on condition that it allowed access to the Church's chartered surveyors to show prospective customers round the premises. CUT decided to make a bid if St. Michael's was put on the market and began talking to Camden Council about capital funding for its purchase. 'We found out about the Area Committee, which is the central body controlling all the departments within the Council and the source of funds. If you're awarded a grant from the Area Committee, you stand an excellent chance of getting funding from other committees. We also looked up the civil rights team who helped us establish our rights as squatters within the building. The Church wouldn't take rent from us because that would give us tenant status. A worker from the team was assigned to us and clarified our relationship with the police and other involved parties.'

While this was going on, CUT began a series of events. A performing arts festival in July 1986 showcased the talents of over forty acts. This was followed by a jazz season, CUT in the Jazz, which included the Courtney Pine Quartet and IDJ dance group. In the autumn, Staunch Poets and Players premiered their play *The Balmyard*, which has since toured England and the Caribbean; Double Edge staged its third production *Song of Songs*; and a drama group from Azania, The Azanian National Theatre, performed *Burning Embers*, which had been a success at the Edinburgh Festival earlier that year. Letters of support came from all quarters. Greater London Arts praised the work of Double Edge as 'a valuable resource for the community in North London... the loss of which would be a blow to the cultural life of the area.' The Camden Committee for Community Relations wrote: 'In the fields of drama, education and community development in Camden, the activities of Double Edge are exemplary.' In addition, the group now had legal assistance from Tony McKenzie, a college friend of Michael's who worked with a South London law centre.

Things were moving well and CUT applied for an entertainments licence. Only one body objected to the application: the Metropolitan Police. 'In recent months there have been events

27

27 Double Edge actor in performance.

at these premises which have attracted large numbers of people,' went one objection, which assumed that any gathering of Black people must mean trouble and therefore necessitate a police presence. The letter referred to 'mobs' and 'throngs' in true gutter-press fashion, and anticipated 'serious public order problems thus placing a severe strain on police resources.' The police also alleged that an incident involving a dispute at a local minicab office was attributable to CUT.

Members were baffled by these allegations and pointed out that at no time had the police questioned them on such matters, nor had any member been arrested for any crime. They were angry that the police had made allegations which undermined their reputation without giving them the right to reply. Ironically it was

28 Double Edge actresses in performance.

this underhand behaviour by the police which delivered the group its trump card. Not only did the police make these comments to the Council, they took them to Father Page and so precipitated a third eviction attempt in March 1987. This turned the tide.

On March 5, CUT workers arrived at their workplace to find the doors barred and policemen guarding the premises. The Civil Rights Unit was called and a worker attended as an observer. After a few hours, CUT members regained access to the building. Their first task was to find out what had provoked Father Page.

Perhaps there is a divine providence which protects helpless groups against bullying institutions. The commotion outside the building attracted the attention of a solicitor, Trevor Asserson, employed by the law firm on the same block. His intervention and legal expertise steered the course of events and perhaps went some way to make the Church regret its strong-arm tactics. Having re-established CUT's status in the building, Asserson arranged a meeting to discuss Father Page's sudden action. To get the Church to agree to a meeting, CUT had to organise a picket outside Lambeth Palace, the Archbishop of Canterbury's London residence. This meeting was a breakthrough, bringing together Father Page, Father Philip Dyson, Dean of the parish, and Archdeacon Derek Hayward, an important figure in church financial affairs as the Controller of the London Church Fund. It became clear at this meeting that the allegations against CUT were unfounded, leaving the Church in the wrong and compelled to make concessions.

At this time of writing (autumn 1987) it has been agreed that the building will be initially offered for sale to CUT and not placed on the open market, and that any variance in the price arrived at by the CUT and Church surveyors will be resolved by arbitration. The Church itself, through its Urban Fund, may even be able to help. CUT is arranging for charitable status, as this will affect the price at which the Church can sell it the building, and has also gained permission to embark on a rebuilding programme to fulfil the conditions of an entertainments licence.

A mixture of political acumen, bravado, street wiseness had combined to bring about the current state of affairs. Was it worth it? They all say yes. 'Many lessons have been learned,' comments Derrick. 'When the time comes to act you get your hard core and you move and mobilise more support on the way. In meetings there's always the rhetoric and posturing but we needed more people when our backs were against the wall. There'll always be an intelligentsia intellectualising revolution, but what we've done proves that it's the ragamuffin that pulls you through. We know the meaning of that in our bones. In the end, it's non-respect for the system that enables you to fight the system.'

J.D.
DOUGLAS

PAUL ROBESON

ORGANISING THE EXHIBITION

The visitor's book of the exhibition *Paul Robeson — Citizen of the World*, shown at Swiss Cottage Library, London, from March 21 to April 25 1987, was filled with comments reflecting varying degrees of admiration and just the occasional negative statement.

Two statements that stood out were from people who knew little about Paul Robeson before they walked into the exhibition space. The first said, 'I've never heard of him before, but from what I see and read, I am impressed that there is a man (Black) that everyone can be proud of. I don't have the right words to express my admiration!' The second said, 'Found this exhibition most informative and interesting. Went from almost lack of knowledge to a great source of information.'

Most people respond warmly to the personality of Paul Robeson, even when they have barely heard of him or know little of his impressive life and works. He has an extraordinary presence and his artistic achievement elicits immediate respect and admiration. That relatively few people are aware of his achievements and the full impact of his career and struggles is outrageous.

The exhibition aimed to make a contribution to redressing the balance by reclaiming his memory and keeping it alive. The issues raised and the difficulties encountered in the process are pertinent to Black historical documentation and the problematic task of reminding the present of our past achievements.

Paul Robeson was born on 9 April 1898 in Princeton, New Jersey. He attended Rutgers University and then Columbia University Law school where he earned a law degree. From 1914 to 1919 Robeson was known primarily as an athlete. During these five years he thrilled the sports world with his immense talents as a football, baseball and basketball player.

In the early twenties he gained critical acclaim for his starring role in two of Eugene O'Neill's plays, *Emperor Jones* and *All God's Chillun*. He then moved on to the concert stage and thrilled audiences with his repertoire of negro spirituals. As his fame as a singer spread, he travelled first to Europe and then to Asia and beyond. In 1928 he appeared in the London production of the stage musical *Showboat*. Two years later, in 1930, he played the role of Shakespeare's tragic hero, Othello, with Peggy Ashcroft as Desdemona, at the Savoy Theatre in London. Of his performance, the *Morning Post* wrote, 'There has been no Othello on our stage,

29 Paul Robeson, National Film Archive, London.

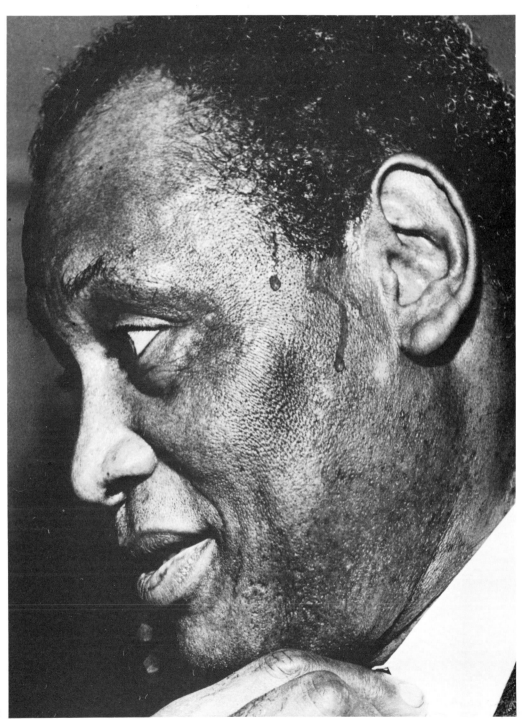

certainly for forty years, to compare with his dignity, simplicity and true passion.' He repeated the role thirteen years later in New York and the production became the longest-running Shakespearian play on Broadway. He made eleven films including *Emperor Jones*, *Showboat*, *King Solomon's Mines*, *Jericho* and *Proud Valley*. It must be said, however, that Robeson is most commonly known for his rich baritone voice and his rendition of *Ol' Man River*.

As a boy growing up in New Jersey, Paul Robeson had a deep sympathy for the social underdog. As he grew in stature as an artist, so did his strong feelings towards socialism. One of his most famous statements reflects this growing commitment when he said, 'The artist must elect to fight for freedom or for slavery. I have made my choice. I have no alternative.'

In 1938 Paul Robeson was asked by a *Daily Mirror* reporter what he would give up for an ideal. His answer was 'my career'. Twelve years after that bold statement, Robeson found himself in that exact position. He had spoken relentlessly against the injustices he saw in America and the authorities did not like it. In 1950, his passport was revoked and he was not allowed to travel outside the United States. Concert halls were barred to him, his records were removed from shops and his every move monitored by the FBI. The US authorities even tried to make Robeson a non-person by removing all his achievements wherever they were recorded or documented. In 1958, after a long legal battle, he regained his passport and was once more able to travel. In 1959, Paul Robeson played Othello for the final time at Stratford-on-Avon. He undertook a world concert tour and returned to America in the early sixties. Shortly afterwards he retired from public life. He died in 1976. C. L. R. James said about Robeson: 'To have spent half an hour in his company or to have ten minutes alone with him was something that you remembered for days. If I had to sum up his personality in one word, or rather two, I would say a combination of immense power and great gentleness.'

The history of the Paul Robeson exhibition, *Citizen of the World*, is not as straightforward as might be imagined. Being in the right place at the right time was as important a factor as my determination to see it happen. Throughout my endeavours, I met some kind and lovely people. I also, on occasion, crossed paths with individuals I wished I had not met.

My interest in Paul Robeson goes back to the early 1980s when I was working as the Ethnic Minorities Co-ordinator for the Cardiff Broadcasting Corporation. Part of my job was to ensure that the radio station, owned jointly by private concerns and the community, had a reasonable amount of programmes of ethnic

30 Leaflets from the Paul Robeson exhibition.

THE GLC PRESENT
PAUL ROBESON: A FILM TRIBUTE

5TH MAY, 1985
QUEEN ELIZABETH HALL, SOUTH BANK, BELVEDERE ROAD SE1

3.00 *The Proud Valley* (1940)
£2.00 (£1.00 for school children
students, senior citizens, unemployed) (PG)

4.30 *Lecture on Paul Robeson* A
lecture will be given by John
Akomfrah, from the Black Audio
Film Collective, on Paul Robeson
Film and Politics, in the Queen
Elizabeth Hall. (Admission free, no
pre-booking)

7.00 *Jericho* (1937) and *Song of
Freedom* (1936) These films are
made available by kind permission of Raymond Rohauer.
£2.00 (£1.30 for school
children students, senior
citizens unemployed) (U)

Tickets available from Queen
Elizabeth Hall, South Bank,
Belvedere Road SE1 928 3191
(Credit Card Hotline 928
8800) or by post from Box
Office, Royal Festival
Hall, London SE1 8XX.

STOLL PICTURE THEATRE
Kingsway
PAUL ROBESON
THE SONG OF

Paul
ROBESON
EXHIBITION

GLC present an exhibition on the life
and works of Paul Robeson (1898-76)

24 April—16 May
At the Royal Festival Hall
10am—10pm admission free

A film tribute will be held at the
Queen Elizabeth Hall on 5 May

LONDON AGAINST RACISM
GLC

Paul
ROBESON
MEMORIAL CONCERT

Presented by the GLC
May at 7pm
the Queen Elizabeth Hall

ring (in alphabetical order)
Dawn • Dame Peggy Ashcroft
on Morlais (Welsh Choir)
las • Martha Edwards
elch • Willard White
• Joe Marcell

.50—£8.00
ffice 01-928 3191
8 8800 10am—8pm

Paul Robeson – Citizen of the World
An Exhibition by J.D. Douglas
21 March—25 April 1987

minority interest, though no one could tell me what this meant!

As I was more or less left to my own devices, I concentrated making programmes that were either about Black people or Black issues. In 1983, I was researching a play on the 1919 Cardiff riots. I spent most of my lunch hours in Cardiff Central Library. One day as I entered, I saw the face of a Black man on a medium-sized poster. What attracted me was not so much the face, but the position of the poster. Someone had placed it on a board that was almost at ground level. My curiosity aroused, I walked up. By the time I was standing next to it, the poster did not even rise above my knee. Behind the board was a door that led into a small room from which issued the voice of Paul Robeson singing *Mama's Little Curly Headed Boy*. I recognised the voice as that of the man who sang *Ol' Man River*, but at that time, I did not know any other Robeson songs. As I entered the room, I saw a small collection of books in a glass case, some album sleeves and some magazine and newspaper cuttings crudely placed on the wall. There was however some special magic in that room, a quality that was invisible yet all round me. I felt unable to walk away until I had satisfied some inner need, a need I did not know existed until I came into that library. Within a few minutes, I decided to make a radio programme about the collection of items on Robeson. The programme was well received and subsequently repeated.

By 1984, I had left CBC and was working for the London Borough of Wandsworth as the ethnic arts officer. I felt that the collection of items would form an interesting display in the Lavender Hill library exhibition hall, supplemented by the little mementoes of Robeson I had begun collecting since leaving Cardiff. My first task was to locate the collection I had seen at Cardiff Centre Library. After several telephone calls over three months, I found out that the items had belonged to a Mr. Ken Goodlands from Bristol, undoubtedly one of Robeson's biggest fans. When he died, Mrs Martha Edwards from Ponty-Clean in Mid-Glamorgan was given the responsibility of looking after the collection. She had been instrumental in the Cardiff display.

I negotiated with Martha Edwards and received the go-ahead to stage the exhibition at Lavender Hill library in June 1984. Around the same time, I spoke to many individuals who had either known or worked with Robeson. One such special meeting was with the late Marie Seton, who in 1958 had written the definitive biography of Robeson. She not only gave me some rare photographs, but also a copy of her book which Robeson had autographed.

Staging the exhibition in Wandsworth was not without problems. The borough was Tory-run and Robeson's politics were definitely to the left. The assistant director of libraries, who was also in charge of the arts, decided that the exhibition would have to be 'checked' before it went on public display, his reason being, 'I don't want the members to be offended by the exhibition'. The list of guests I had given to his secretary was censored, and many leading Labour politicians like Michael Foot were never sent invitations to the opening.

But nothing could check the success of the exhibition, which advanced from Battersea to a central London home at the Royal Festival Hall. By coincidence Peggy Ashcroft, Marie Seton and Paul Boateng came to see it at around the same time. Paul Boateng, now a Labour MP, was at the time chairman of the Greater London Council's Ethnic Minority Unit: 'We must have it at the GLC,' I remember him saying. Parminder Vir, head of the GLC Race Equality Unit, helped secure funds for the move, and a memorial concert and film tribute were arranged to complement the exhibition. Organising the concert and exhibition left me with little time for anything else, so Stephen Bourne, whom I had met when I staged the exhibition in Wandsworth, organised the film tribute.

31   Paul Robeson at a CND meeting in Trafalgar Square, early 1960s.

31

Preparing the expanded exhibition meant that better photographs had to be located and bought, and the originals of newspaper articles which were torn, yellow or unreadable, had to be located and photocopied. Album sleeves had to be photographed and laminated. The list of things to do seemed endless, but by the time the Rt. Hon. Neil Kinnock MP opened the exhibition at the Royal Festival Hall at 6 p.m. Wednesday 24 April 1985, London was set to rediscover Paul Robeson. Robeson's son, Paul Robeson Jnr, flew in from the US and many famous actors and several well-known MPs attended the opening.

The Paul Robeson memorial concert was held at the Queen Elizabeth Hall on May 6 1985 and featured two co-stars of Robeson, Dame Peggy Ashcroft and Elisabeth Welch. Also on the bill were the Welsh Choir, Cor Meribion Morlais, Martha Edwards, Willard White, Leo Wringer, African Dawn, Joe Marcell and myself. The film tribute on May 8 featured *The Proud Valley*, *Jericho* and *Song of Freedom*. John Akomfrah from the Black Audio Film Collective delivered a lecture entitled 'Paul Robeson, Film and Politics'.

After the exhibition ended it was taken back to Wales. Called *Paul Robeson, Honorary Welshman*, the exhibition is now permanently housed in Morgan Park, South Wales.

While Paul Robeson Jnr was in London we discussed the need for a second exhibition. Putting the second one together was no easier than the first. There were both practical and conceptual problems. The original exhibition had been laminated and making copies from boards measuring one metre by 70 cms was virtually impossible, not to mention costly. Stephen Bourne who had done most of the work on the films, began to talk about them as a separate section but I felt that too many people seemed prepared to compartmentalise Robeson's life and in so doing, detracted from what he stood for. I met Herbert Marshall who had worked with Robeson in his Unity Theatre days. We discussed aspects of Robeson's involvement with the Soviet Union, as Marshall had strong views on how the Stalin purges had affected him. I enjoyed meeting Marshall, but he seemed more interested in talking about his own role in Robeson's artistic career than keeping his memory alive, which was what I was trying to achieve. I increasingly felt that important aspects of Robeson's work had not been touched on in the earlier exhibition, for example his writings on Africa and particularly the racial problems of South Africa. Because I had spoken at length to many individuals who had known Robeson, I felt that it would be possible to organise a more comprehensive exhibition of his life and complete what seemed an impossible task. The quest took me to Eastern Europe.

32 Robeson at Heathrow Airport, 1958.

For some time I had been corresponding with Christine Newman of the Paul Robeson Archives in the German Democratic Republic. I would send her information for her doctorate on Robeson. A formal invitation eventually came from the Archives and I went to research the new exhibition. It turned out to be a memorable visit. My friend, guide and fellow Robeson scholar, Christine Newman, took me to the Paul Robeson school where I met the headmaster and then to Paul Robeson Street. That evening I stepped out onto the balcony of my apartment and noticed that the building directly in my sight was a library. Further inspection revealed that the library was called Bibliotek Pablo Neruda. For me the coincidence was too much: the great Chilean writer had written what to me was the best poem I had read on Robeson — *Ode to Paul Robeson*. The poem is also one of the favourites of Dame Peggy Ashcroft. I decided to call the exhibition, *Paul Robeson, Citizen of the World*.

The first public showing of *Citizen of the World* was at Swiss Cottage Library as part of the 1987 Camden Festival. Lord Pitt of Hampstead who was a friend of the great man opened the exhibition: 'Robeson was one of those who stood up to be counted,' he said. Robeson was an extraordinary man, and the inspiring comments by those who came to see the exhibition supports the validity of Black historial reclamation and the need to extend it to the numerous Black artists and figures who run the danger of being forgotten by history.

BLACK ARTS

TO BE SEEN AND HEARD

JIDE ODUSINA — STRUGGLING

This is an attempt at a critical review and discussion of the challenges, potentials and problems within the relationship of Black arts and the Black popular media. My experiences have been predominantly within the African-Caribbean community, so I will not attempt to extend the arguments to the South Asian communities. Radical Black newspapers and magazines like *Grassroots* and *Race Today* and arts magazines like *Artrage*, *Blackboard*, and *Race Today Review* have consistently supported Black arts. Their readerships are however by and large already tuned into the arts. It is the readerships of the mass circulating weeklies and the mass audiences of radio and television which Black artists need to reach to make their objective of arts by, to and for the people a living reality.

The major part of the Black mass print media operates with a misconception about the arts which is in diametric opposition to the actual arts practice of our cultures. As a reflection of bourgeois European ideology, the mass print media fragments our experiences and fits them into western arts categories — theatre, dance, literature, poetry, visual arts, music, textiles/fashion design and cinema. It also operates with a hierarchy of appreciation which reflects the racist stereotype of what Black people can or cannot do. Music is natural; the other arts come only with training. The ladder starts with visual arts at the top, then theatre, literature, poetry and dance in descending order. Music is the common 'art'. This hierarchy ignores the tremendous advances made by African peoples in these so-called 'high' arts over 4,000 years.

THE STORYLINE

The print media is the main mass media run by and for Black people; apart from some of the extra-legal radio stations, it is, in fact, the only Black-owned media. Black-orientated radio and TV programmes come from white-owned or run stations. The print media is dominated by two publishing houses: Hansib Ltd., which publishes *Caribbean Times*, *Asian Times*, *African Times*, *West Indian Digest* and *Root*, and Tee Vee Ay (Media Resources Ltd.) which publishes *The Voice*, *Weekend Voice*, *Black Beat*, and *Chic*. Tee Vee Ay is a relative newcomer, started up with help from the now defunct Greater London Council but with a robust independence from (some might say indifference to) community politics. There are a number of other Black periodicals of local and national significance. They are important as complementaries to the big two and as entries to smaller specialist markets. A full list is given at the end of this article.

I see four basic ways in which our media can help Black arts. One, editorial news coverage of activities; two, constructive/critical reviews; three, listings; four, features on issues, groups and personalities. In addition, there are human and material resources like journalists' writing and publicity skills, typesetting, photographic darkrooms and printing facilities which can be mobilised through collaborative ventures such as sponsorships, cross branding, advice and training. These resources are nonetheless inadequate to the level of demand in the Black communities. Even though our media is better resourced than Black arts, compared to white equivalents it is underdeveloped.

This state of underdevelopment, reinforced by racism, is shared with all peoples from the 'third world'. It has several ramifications, not least understaffing and pressure of work. I once asked a TV journalist why she did not go out and talk to groups in the community to report on what was going on at the grassroots. Her indignant answer was, 'I am not a social worker, and this is not a social service'. Whilst it is easy to question such trivialisation, it must be acknowledged that Black journalists work under very poor conditions. Newsrooms are inadequately staffed and supported and there is an undue reliance on the freelance and news releases from large organisations. Basic news-gathering and processing infrastructures are weak and compared to the white press the whole of the Black print media runs on a shoestring budget. These inadequacies do not however account for all its problems.

DIS IS DE RAPP

The Black print media is heavily relied on by Black arts organisations to get their message across to the public. Apart from recent improvements such as the launch of *Weekend Voice* and signs of an eagerness to support the arts, there has been a consistent tendency to trivialise and misrepresent significant sections of the Black arts movement. A choice example is the review in *The Voice* of a performance by Munirah Afrikan Women's Theatre Group (fig. 34). The reviewer spares no moment to trivialise the intentions of the artists and berates the show not for its artistic qualities, but for being too 'heavy'. The context in which reviews are placed is often problematic. Surrounding images negate or depreciate the intentions of the art, as in the flippant conflation of serious issues with hair straightening and face bleach advertising. It is not just little-known artists who suffer. The news item on Tina Turner (fig. 33) also reflects a flippant and sexist journalism, even though I'm not sure who comes out worse, Tina or the credibility of the newspaper.

33

Ball breaker Tina

Caption in West Indian News, September 24, 1986 reads 'Ms Tina Turner whose legs are a legend in the singing industry has just released a new album Break Every Rule. According to Vibration editor Mikey Massive, she 'epitomises the type of ball breaking black bitch that every middle aged ad agency executive dreams of catching up with any time he stops in a strange pub on a rainy

33 night.'

MS TINA Turner whose legs are a legend in the singing industry has just released a new album: "Break Every Rule".

According to Vibration editor Mikey Massive, she "epitomises the type of ball breaking black bitch that every middle aged ad agen-

cy executve dreams of catching up with any time he stops in a strange pub on a rainy night."

For more on Ms Turner, please turn to page 11.

This type of 'sunsational' tabloid journalism reflects an emergent and increasingly confident African-Caribbean petty bourgeoisie flexing its muscles. There is a sense in which it has to somehow undermine progressive community activity, in order to advance its thrust for private profit at the expense of collective gains. (Paradoxically, private profit includes lucrative advertising from radical left local councils.) There are close links between the privately-owned weeklies and periodicals and fashion/club/-music/hair commercial interests. The Afro Hair and Beauty Aids Institute (AHBAI) is pumping about three million pounds into persuading us to fry our hair, bleach our skins and paint up. A lot of that money will go to magazines like *Chic* and *Root* and newspapers like *Weekend Voice, Voice* and *Caribbean Times*. Such investments in the Black press encourage an exaggerated emphasis on 'jive' and the 'club scene', beauty contests and fashion shows and tend to undermine the challenging impact of Black arts. Black arts are about arming our people with a critical consciousness that challenges the history of cultural denigration and appropriation and provides our own models of beauty and life styles. They are also about alternative entertainments.

A comparison of column inches devoted to fashion, music and so-called beauty products with those devoted to the arts illustrates the tendency to ignore and trivialise. The Hansib papers, *The Voice* and *The Journal*, have arts pages. The *West Indian Digest* covers the arts, in line with its serious and mature image. In keeping with the pursuit of its image as a Black *Cosmopolitan*, *Chic* also provides in depth coverage, though it tends to focus on big names and rarely questions the dubious assumptions which underpin the practice of 'trendy' art in the community. As a public-supported magazine, *Scope* tries its hardest to reflect a commitment to youth and progressive community action.

Unlike the numerous collaborations between the Black press and hair products/fashion interests, there are few collaborations with Black arts organisations except for the occasional poetry competition and the sponsoring of concerts and carnival-related events. I see the latter as particularly soft options in which the Black press always indulges. There are only occasional signs of fruitful collaboration, as between OBAALA Poetry Theatre's Kwanzaa celebrations and the sponsorship by *The Journal* and *The Voice* of a national tour by Umoja Theatre Company and the Black Theatre Co-op.

The failure to promote Black arts as an integral part of community life reflects the elitism of petty bourgeois Blacks who perceive what they have constructed as 'high art' as being above the appreciation of the 'masses'; hence the failure to give them mainstream coverage with music and fashion. Having reduced the coverage of Black creativity to what it considers mass appeal, the Black press fails to provide an alternative to the Eurocentrism of the white media and its racist coverage of Black creativity. Consequently there has been little attempt to engage the arts in a constructive dialogue and explore common ground. A danger of this enforced separateness is the tendency for a small, self-satisfied and elitist art scene to perpetuate itself and pose as the enlightened section of the community.

ARTISTIC = VIRTUE   PUBLICITY = VICE

In the face of all this marginalisation and cynicism, you would think that your campaigning, anti-this, anti-that revolutionary Black arts movement would be up in arms. Not so. Everyone bemoans the situation, but few do anything to challenge it. The reason is not apathy but weariness at yet another obstacle, plus some reluctance to battle it out with a media which despite its sins has sometimes been our only public outlet. The point still remains that most Black arts organisations have failed to engage our media constructively on questions such as Eurocentrism, criticism, and collaboration, or to develop adequate publicity strategies.

Part of the problem is the lack of human and material resources. Few organisations and groups have specialist publicity workers or the money to buy in the expertise. Funding bodies rarely provide adequate money for publicity and marketing. The often-quoted figure for publicity is five to ten percent of the total budget. In the case of Black arts, this figure needs to be higher because of the extra problems of invisibility. If a proportion of the innovative creativity which informs Black arts went into devising publicity schemes and media strategies, Black arts would be significantly advanced. The absence of an overall publicity and marketing strategy is a severe impediment to development, particularly in terms of audiences and increased income.

The feeling among some arts administrators that media organisations and interests are too powerful to be interested in the Black arts is more imaginary than real if one knows how to tap into their methods of working and deal with their commercialism. The media's business sense tends to border on opportunism, since every day is a struggle for survival. Well-written news releases, sent on time with photos and a good angle, will usually be taken up and published. Visiting the editor and staff also helps. The media need news, but they don't have enough workers to go out and gather it. Even when they are not in agreement with the ideology of the arts group, the prospect of some advertising or of a lucrative collaboration will often be enough to get the media to help promote the group.

Occasionally the tendency to accommodate all interests and ideologies creates some interesting contradictions. In one issue of *Root*, there were two advertisements for skin bleaching creams and an article on skin condemning bleaching.

RADIO, THE BIG SOUND OF TOMORROW

In London, Capital Radio and LBC, the two independent commercial stations, and BBC radio have Black-orientated programmes. Capital's are limited to various types of Afro-music, soul, reggae, gospel, etc. In its presentations, the station strips the music of any relevance to the struggles of African peoples and reduces it simply to jive. Jive is an important weapon in the arsenal of a racist state. It defines a patronising attitude which revolves around the assertion that all Black people want, need and can handle is frivolity and escapism. Dialogues based on the social realities of being Black or on explorations of the issues which concern us are rarely encouraged. LBC, the all-chat, 24-hour news station, restricts us to one hour on Sunday. This programme, with the stereotypical name of *Rice 'n' Peas*, is hosted by amiable Syd Burke with his constant reminders to be 'positive'.

Only Radio London has anything approaching adequate programming aimed at the African-Caribbean community. The flagship is the nightly *Black Londoners* hour-long show, with a specialist arts programme on Tuesdays. Apart from these established stations, there is a multitude of extra-legal/private stations flying various flags of convenience, from those involved in outright commercial exploitation of Black music, to jolly buccaneers with hearts of gold and a passing commitment to the community and public service radio.

Radio offers the greatest potential for immediate development in spite of its drawbacks and problems. At present, the focus is on the debates surrounding community radio and the legalisation of Black-controlled stations. Community radio offers the arts the chance to gain access to wider audiences and to explore new and exciting avenues of presentation and communication. Ideally, community radio is run and controlled by the people. The station's programming policy is developed by its listeners who also choose the members of the management committee. The need to educate, entertain and facilitate a constructive community dialogue is put before profit maximisation.

The false dawn of a legalised Black community radio movement came with the defunct Home Office experiment in 1985. It failed to award the 21 experimental licences, pressurised into inaction by elements of the Tory party hierarchy who baulked at the prospect of Black people on the air waves, free of direct state supervision and control. Black people in particular stood to gain from 'community of interest' stations since they would provide a platform for the diverse and rich cultural, social and political interests of our communities.

The Tories replaced the experiment with a green paper on the future of all radio broadcasting. It came out at the end of February 1987 and was nothing but a charter for the demolition of public funded radio and its replacement by ear-to-ear pop commercial radio. Community radio would be nothing but a plaything for small business interests. There could be no public funding, strict control of political and religious affiliations, and no guarantee of democratic control and participation by the community. Progressive forces in the community radio movement are arguing strongly against the proposals, but the prime organisation campaigning for CR in the UK, the Community Radio Association, is in some disarray.

The leadership of the CRA made a feeble response to the betrayal of CR in the green paper's proposals, especially to the move to ban grants from local authorities and its pro-business bias. Many members would like to have seen a more vigorous rebuff. The Black Policy Advisory Group called for a more active condemnation of the paper, since the proposals would mean the stillbirth of true Black community radio. What we would get is 24 hours of ads, jive music, and inane deejay chat. Black arts would not get a look in. Radio would be in the pocket of the hair products manufacturers and the music business.

The dissatisfaction of the Black groups within the CRA boiled over into an angry emergency general meeting of the association. In a move reminiscent of the Black sections struggle within the Labour party, they called for the reaffirmation of the prioritisation of resources and licences for Black CR groups, strengthened representation within the power structure of the organisation, and a firm anti-racist stance. In what I can only describe as the most contemptuous, patronising, bleeding heart liberal fudge I have ever seen, the hierarchy of the CRA with the support of reactionary elements voted in a wrecking amendment which caused the motion to be withdrawn. This selfish and unprincipled move was made in spite of the professions of progressiveness made by the organisation. While the CRA has accepted social need as the most sound and principled basis on which to campaign for CR and the award of licences and resources, a large part of the association has baulked at the real implications of its commitment, unable to accept the loss of power and position that a progressive and vigorous anti-racist practice implies. In June 1987, the BPAG was

Review of Munirah Afrikan Women's Theatre Group in The Voice, March 15, 1986, begins 'As a Black person, when I go to the theatre to see a play I don't relish being confronted with the realism of life in a racist system because I encounter racism in my every day life.

34

Theatre

ON THE INSIDE (MUNIRAH TOUR)

As a black person, when I go to the theatre to see a play I don't relish being confronted with the realism of life in a racist system because I encounter racism in my every day life.

Theatre is about reality, entertainment and is a form of escapism. I think we as black people gather strength and courage from talking to one another about the brick walls society puts in front of our endeavours and how we can overcome them. We don't (I think) gain much comfort from leaving a play with a heightened sense of 'how bad our lot is', do we? Surely it's the racists in our society we need to educate?

In other words I'm fed-up of angry black plays. It's time to move on if they (theatre groups) want black people to attend and support black theatre. Some writers have overcome this by blending serious issues with humour. Laughter heals the soul after all -one has to laugh at one's self to survive. So it's a shame that there wasn't much laughter in *ON THE INSIDE,* a collection of hard-hitting poems written and performed by new Afrikan Women's Theatre Company Munirah, who were rightly anger about the shooting of Mrs. Gross *(sic),* Mrs. Jarret's death (Invasion), the riots, black men, the many fatherless children in our society, etc, etc. I don't

blame the cast, as they were playing roles they know and feel. But I know it too and I need more than a portrayal of heavy issues that I already know about to get me into any theatre.

All the same they had some nice pieces - like Talibah's portrayal of an old West Indian woman in a launderette who swore that her clothes were never washed clean enough by the machines, but changed her mind after she and the laundry-lady Hazel become friends when they share a feeling of incredulity as a 'woman of the streets' wiggles past them. The company did represent most types of women, but I felt the sketches were not given enough time to develop. Munirah are undoubtedly talented, but desperately need another vehicle.

Kamilla Nicol

34

made a sub-committee of the co-ordinating body. This move, coupled with the acceptance of its modified resolution, dampened its fires. Black members of the CRA have forsaken 'piracy' and blocked attempts to allow 'pirates' (anyone broadcasting outside the law) from gaining admission to the CRA.

The real lessons from that are one, we cannot play 'politricks' with our people's interests, in the vain hope of securing a few crumbs from the master's table; and, two, the issue of legality has to be critically examined because African-Caribbean people have made their biggest advances through extra-legal direct action on the streets. Each time, the state falls over itself to create opportunities, expand social provision and develop a community spirit; each time, the few concessions won are filtered away by the professional community workers and 'leaders' who supervise the pacification projects (temporary job schemes, new community centres, consultative committees, etc.). Why should legalised Black broadcasting be any different? If the state confers it, the state will control it.

Outside the CRA, Black people raid the airwaves every day and broadcast outside the law. Whether they are pumping out music for private profit, trying to bring underground sounds into the open or like community development radio, genuinely experimenting with the theory and practice of CR, at least they are doing it. Instead of piously offering jam tomorrow, they provide bread today for those who want to hear our music, understand what a go on, or reach the community with serious chat.

The CR purists in the CRA frown on this 'illegal' activity. The question for me is this: is there any use in refusing to talk to the music pirates like JFM, Solar, TKO, and RJR? These pirates have been going a long time, but the community has seen little benefit from their activities. They exist primarily to sell ads and promote deejays and clubs. There has been no attempt to deepen their listeners' understanding of the music or develop a critical awareness of the options. It is important to engage with them, especially with those which appear to be interested in at least some form of public service broadcasting. Their listeners also deserve to hear the arguments and issues surrounding community radio.

A number of Black stations are modelled on Dread Broadcasting Corporation (DBC), the first truly African-Caribbean run radical pirate. DBC was inspirational in that it broke new ground in Black broadcasting in Britain. It was the first to give women a chance as deejays (Miss P. of BBC Radio 1 is ex-DBC). It was the first to revive/popularise earlier forms of reggae, not just Studio 1, and pioneered a comprehensive programming of the broad spectrum of African people's music. The pressure of raids and the poaching of deejays caused it to give up the ghost in 1984. Its memory is kept alive by Leaky who sells DBC memorabilia (tapes and tee-shirts) on Portobello Road.

For Black arts, radio offers possibilities for radio dramas, literature readings, poetry performances and general discussions on art theory and practice. I look forward to listening to dramatisations of literary works by local writers as well as those by nationally and internationally known authors, to discussions, and to live broadcasts of concerts, plays and carnivals. More than this, radio offers artists the chance to seize the imagination of the people, to wipe away the cynicism that enters people's minds when they hear the words 'Black community' and 'art'. Genuine CR, with its commitment to full access, will allow innovative arts workers to fire the hearts of the people, by showing them that the arts can be entertaining, culturally uplifting and functional to their lives.

MAJOR AFRICAN-CARIBBEAN PUBLICATIONS

African Times
Part of the Hansib group, sells relatively few papers and has not captured the large continental African market which is dominated by **West Africa** and the other weekly magazines. Has been very supportive of community arts events with a strong African interest.

Artrage
Produced by MAAS (Minority Arts Advisory Service), it is the major arts magazine for 'Black and ethnic minority arts in Britain'. A quarterly review, it analyses major and topical events and issues in the field. Progressive in its analysis and critiques.

Black Board
West Midlands Minority Arts Service's version of **Artrage**: similar format, content and audience.

The Black Eye
Progressive community arts/news/listing monthly magazine. Produced as part of a community project, poor presentation and distribution (but it's early days).

The Black Voice
Paper of the Black Unity and Freedom Party. It has been going for fifteen years and has produced some very good articles on culture and struggle. Suffers from poor presentation and

distribution. A Black socialist perspective on the arts.

Caribbean Times

Flagship of the Hansib group, staunchly pro-Labour, though not consistently progressive in its coverage of national or world events. Has given extensive coverage to the arts and is strongly involved in sponsorship deals around Carnival.

Chic

The number one fashion, beauty and general interest magazine in the Black community. Professional layout, well-written features. Even advertised on TV. It tries to give the arts a look-in, though this tends to be from the point of view of strong individual interest rather than critical analysis. Pro-jive, attempts to be pro-women, but perpetuates some serious sexist and racist stereotypes. Is aimed at young working women and their partners.

The Federal

A weekly free sheet with strong links to London Labour councils. It is distributed to community/council centres for people to pick up. Black arts groups have not really started to exploit this new channel. The editorial line seems progressive, but it has yet to show its full hand.

Grassroots

'Organ of the Black Liberation Front' and the biggest and best-distributed revolutionary Black newspaper. It has passed through many phases, with arts coverage waxing and waning in relation to the dictates of finding space for the 'important' issues of the day. Recent arts coverage has been poor. Could provide the much-needed popular, socialist, realist critique of Black arts if it had adequate resources.

The Journal

This newcomer has done some pioneering work in focusing on community projects, workers, arts and artists. Originally quite progressive in its editorial line, though not without some inconsistencies. Has organised a wide range of collaborative deals and given advertising space to pirate radio stations for ads on the air and to Obaala, London's Black arts venue, for its logo on publicity posters.

Race Today and Race Today Review

Very important in the documentation of Black arts (at least those events they choose to grace). Progressive periodicals actively involved in the community's struggles, including the arts.

Root

Root was the first Black magazine in the **Ebony** mould in this country. In keeping with its up-market image, it originally gave quite a bit of coverage to the arts. Over the years, the direction of the magazine has drifted, and the arts have been given a low priority. With its incorporation into the Hansib empire, it seems to be gearing up to take **Chic** head on.

Scope

Started life as **Black Teens**, a sort of junior **Root**. It was part of the GLC's efforts to help develop a vibrant Black print media. It ran into problems and was relaunched as **Scope**, with an advisory committee of the good and great in our community. It has had to tread the fine line between popular fashion and beauty coverage and serious, informative, progressive journalism. For all its problems, it has done quite well, though it has not achieved anywhere near its market potential.

The Voice

Probably the most popular Black newspaper in this country, though this may have more to do with its extensive job section than its editorial content. **The Voice** has led the move into tabloid journalism in the Black press. It is aimed primarily at young Afro-Caribbean people born or brought up in this country. It has given a lot of coverage to Black arts, not always constructively.

The Weekend Voice

The Friday edition of **The Voice**, a cross between a listings magazine and a newspaper. Most of the arts coverage from the Buz section of **The Voice** was transferred to this venture. Definitely bumpy (Black Upwardly Mobile Persons) paper; jive, entertainment and upwardly mobile media pursuits.

Weekly Gleaner

The UK wraparound section of the famous Jamaican daily paper. It has given a fair amount of coverage to the arts. There is a bias towards events perceived to be of interest to readers who are by and large older Jamaican people, though the paper is trying to broaden its appeal.

West Indian News

Part of the old **West Indian World**. Most of its editorial lines and coverage are well to the left of many of the weeklies, but its attacks on the personalities of leading Black people in the Labour party are decidedly unfraternal. It has little space or time for the arts.

CEDDO

'THE PEOPLE'S ACCOUNT' AND IBA CENSORSHIP

It is not often that the Black community gets the opportunity to voice its position and respond to the many attacks levelled at it by an increasingly intolerant society. In recent times, media racism has become more blatantly overt and reactions to these attacks have been greeted with arrogant dismissals by those concerned. Television adverts are having a field day —caricaturing Black people as cannibals in the case of Ovaltine. And 'tropical' fruit juices, made in England, increasingly evoke images of drum-toting, hip-whirling, grinning natives beneath coconut trees. Critical response to these is dubbed 'over-sensitive'.

Where, before, accusing fingers were only pointed at programme producers and advertising agencies, it now seems that the Independent Broadcasting Authority itself has bared the ugly, offensive face of its own racism by seeking to censor Ceddo Film-Video Workshop's documentary, *The People's Account*.

JACOB
ROSS

CENSORSHIP

UPRISINGS

In 1985, a Black woman was shot by the police in Brixton. A few weeks later, another died in her home in Tottenham where the police entered, unlawfully, into her home to search. These two incidents were responsible for a series of powerful protests by the Black community. The authorities and the national press identified these protests as a 'riot', explaining it as the work of political 'agitators' and 'criminal elements'.

A DIFFERENT PICTURE

Ceddo's *The People's Account* seeks to paint a true picture of the Handsworth, Brixton and Broadwater Farm uprisings. Focusing largely on the Broadwater Farm community in Tottenham, it gives the people's account of the 1985 'disturbance', pointing out that it was one of self-defence and resistance to racist oppression. The documentary uses interviews with people from Broadwater Farm and Birmingham and dissects the historical and contemporary re-lationship between Black people and the police, their social and economic predicament, and the role of the media in distorting and undermining the fundamental reasons for the reaction of the Black community to the death of two of its members within such a short space of time.

CENSORSHIP

Ceddo received financial assistance from Channel 4 TV which is more than happy with the production. Channel 4 lawyers and legal representatives of Ceddo are satisfied that nothing is legally wrong with the programme. Why then, can the Independent Broadcasting Authority not make up its own mind? On three occasions the film was scheduled for transmission: July 20 1986; November 24 1986; and March 23 1987. On each occasion the showing was blocked on the grounds that too many anti-police programmes were being shown in the period. At the same time, Channel 4 was coming under pressure not to show too many 'unbalanced' programmes.

CONCERNS

A second reason was later put forward for not screening the film. The IBA pronounced that they objected to three 'things' in the content of the programme. When asked to explain the basis of the objection, the Authority did not seem ready or able to explain. They subsequently asked for a section of the film to be removed. Finally, to drive in the knife even deeper, Ceddo was informed that *The People's Account* would not be transmitted unless accompanied by a 'balancing' studio discussion programme, where a 'specially invited audience' would be planted to 'discuss' the film.

Ceddo's response is that *The People's Account* is itself a balancing programme for the numerous broadcasts that have previously been made on the same issue. The Film-Video Workshop affirms that its presentation gives voice to the legitimate concerns of the Black community and tells the truth about our relationship with the police.

EDITOR'S NOTE

The IBA subsequently clarified the contents it objected to and wanted removed from the film. These were the descriptions of Mrs Cherry Groce as 'a victim of police racism'; the disturbances at Broadwater Farm as 'a classic example of self defence by a community'; and the caption 'police terror raids continue'. In the following piece, Cecil Gutzmore, the commentary writer of the film, responds to these demands in an open letter to David Glencross, Director of Television, IBA.

CECIL
GUTZMORE

OPEN LETTER TO MR GLENCROSS

Director of Television, IBA

Dear Mr Glencross

Re: *The People's Account* and political censorship

My attention has been drawn to what, on the face of the matter, is your proposed censorship of the film, *The People's Account*, made last year by the Ceddo Film and Video Workshop. Ceddo, as you will know, is a collective of Black film makers.

Your act of evident censorship consists of your demand that three specific phrases used in the film be excised before it can be shown on Channel 4 — and presumably any other part of the Independent Television network.

I write both as the author of two of the phrases you wish to censor and as a member of one of Britain's Black communities. I hope it is common ground between us that the three phrases at issue would not, if broadcast either singly or together, break any law. What is at stake, therefore, is in the first instance your interpretations of your statutory rights over what is permissible for broadcasting on the TV network.

The People's Account presents a view from within the Black communities of the consequences in the domain of public order of the persistently lawless — not yet to say racist — policing we experience. This is a matter which is ignored or misunderstood at the peril of us all. How do acts of censorship of the sort you contemplate aid understanding? You are surely not intending it to be understood that a self-proclaimed liberal media will not allow Black people's experiences of life — including policing — in the UK to be talked about by us within the law without censorship? If so, we are going to have increasing difficulty spotting the difference between liberal and fascist media.

The further question must be asked: is your statutory duty being exercised in an even-handed and non-racist way where the broadcasting of material relating to the Black communities is concerned? Perhaps you will be able to recall for the benefit of members of these communities when the IBA last did something to prevent/mitigate the steady stream of racist TV programming —directly insulting as well as threatening to the well-being of Black people settled here — broadcast on radio and TV channels covered by your statutory responsibility. It would be tedious to cite the documentation upon which this assertion rests. However, if you take issue with it, I shall be happy to do so. Why is it that you appear to do so little against racist programming? Is it because it offends only Black people and anti-racists? Why, by contrast, your detailed interest in this small video by Ceddo? Does that interest derive from the fact that the Black people who made it raise some wholly legal questions about societal racism and, more particularly, about the racialism of that sacred institution, the police?

May I comment briefly on the particular phrases you say must be deleted before *The People's Account* can be beamed into the homes of our white and Black fellow citizens.

The description of Mrs Cherry Groce as 'a victim of police racism'. You may well be among those who take the view (based on a particular stipulation of the meaning of racism) that, since British police forces are self-evidently not racist, there can be no victims of their racism. If so, nothing will persuade you of the validity of holding that a Black woman shot down in her own home by a policeman who regarded her as no more than a menacing 'dark shadow' can be called a victim of police racism.

Alternatively you may be of the opinion that, since most of those recently shot 'in error' and 'in self defence' by policemen in England are white (these include a sleeping boy of five and a pregnant woman as well as Stephen Waldorf), the shooting of a Black woman cannot be 'racist'. Indeed, it could even be seen as an anti-racist attempt by the good Inspector Lovelock to include us in an area of national life from which — the case of Colin Roach notwithstanding — we had previously been excluded. If this is the argument on which you are relying for the censorship of the phrase concerning Mrs Groce, I invite you to take account of the fact that what Mrs Groce is suffering fits not only into the pattern of shootings just mentioned. It also fits into a pattern of police violence towards members of the Black communities, which has traumatised and angered individuals, families, and Black communities both locally and nationally. This pattern unwinds into a long history of police practices towards our communities, which we rationally interpret as racialism not unconnected to police and broader societal racism. Here also I refrain from citing the considerable body of writing which at least begins to document and speak of this history: but, of course, I should gladly do so if, indeed, you are disposed to dispute the matter.

In the light of the pattern of police violence towards Black people, into which we in the Black communities placed what happened to Mrs Groce, I find it incredible that you have discovered any laws, facts or tastes which render it wrong for *The People's Account* to refer to Mrs Groce as 'a victim of police racism'. Why do you wish to censor this phrase? I am sure you are a person of considerable imagination as a Director of Television for the IBA. This may be why you can envisage an armed police officer bursting into a Hampstead home in search of a person known to be white, failing totally to check out either the layout or the occupancy of the house, and then shooting down the white mother of the house as, in panic, she rushes from her bedroom, becoming a menacing 'fair shape' in the process. Why can it not be said in a film commentary on Channel 4 that racism, much more than any of the other fanciful factors, is what made it possible for such a thing to happen in Brixton with Cherry Groce — a Black mother — as victim.

The phrase 'police terror raids continue'. It may well be that the IBA has an unbreachable rule that the word 'terror' can never be used in respect of any conceivable action by British police forces. If so, what appears in this instance as censorship is in reality merely your way of securing compliance. One would hope that such rules could be notified in advance to film-makers.

If no such rule is in operation, the key issue becomes the accuracy of this phrase as used in a descriptive caption in *The People's Account*. Ceddo uses the phrase in the context of the presentation of direct evidence from Broadwater Farm residents of the ways in which police behaviour there, in the aftermath of the disturbances of late 1985, put them in terror. There is neither mystery nor mystique about this word: reliance is placed on the *Oxford English Dictionary*'s definition of it as 'the state of being terrified or greatly frightened; intense fear, fright or dread'.

The residents in question — young Black mothers — testified to being terrorised by Metropolitan Police raids in which officers armed with guns and sledge hammers, and uttering the most vile racial abuse, entered their homes in the early hours of the morning. Not all the evidence of this sort which Ceddo had at its disposal could be deployed in the video. A great deal more evidence of this sort was made available to the Broadwater Farm Inquiry chaired by Lord Gifford.

If Black people living on the Broadwater Farm Estate were in fact put in terror by the Metropolitan Police, why exactly does the IBA wish to censor a caption which acknowledges this?

The description of the disturbances at Broadwater Farm as 'a classic example of self-defence by a community'. It seems, at first glance, a difficult phrase to justify: a phrase waiting for the blue pencil, as it were. It is therefore important to understand the contexts in which it is used in *The People's Account*. Be assured, first, that its use is neither trivial nor deliberately provocative.

Self defence is not an easy notion. It is applied very strictly in *The People's Account* to the justified response of people put in fear by the threat and actuality of illegal physical force. There is evidence from the magistrates court hearing of the case against

Floyd Jarrett, from the inquest into the death of his mother Mrs Cynthia Jarrett, from the previously mentioned Gifford Inquiry into the Broadwater Farm disturbances and elsewhere, that those disturbances took place at the end of a long train of illegal acts by members — in growing numbers — of the Metropolitan Police. These include (a) the wrongful arrest and false charging of Floyd Jarrett, (b) the illegal use of keys to gain entry to his mother's house, (c) the obtaining of a search warrant for the search of that house no earlier than during or after it and (d) manhandling of Mrs Jarrett thus contributing to her death.

But the most important illegal act by police officers on the day was (e), their move to prevent a lawful and peaceable demonstration from going on its way from the Broadwater Farm Estate to the local police station. I know of no explanation as to why the Metropolitan Police sent a squad of riot-equipped officers to prevent that demonstration by seeking physically to confine those wishing to take part to the Estate. This action by the police was certainly of dubious legality. In the ensuing clash, the police were the aggressors against persons acting defensively. If the police had allowed matters to rest there, or pursued those they thought offenders over a more protracted time-scale, the real tragedies of the Broadwater Farm disturbances (which include the death of police constable Keith Blakelock, no less than the mishandling of those charged with his murder from start to finish, and the terrorising effects of the extended police follow-up operation) would never have occurred. This is not a trivial point.

It is a pity that the Metropolitan Police learn so selectively from Lord Scarman. They learned and applied his dictum about 'sterile areas', put forward following the Red Lion Square disturbances, in Southall in 1979 with deliberate and devastating effect. What they did not learn and apply at Broadwater Farm is Scarman's dictum — a re-emphasis of Kerner — that in civil disturbances it is wise to leave people an escape route.

By seeking to follow up the initial clash with demonstrators at one of the entrances to the Broadwater Farm Estate with an entry onto the estate with a larger and ever more menacing force, the Metropolitan Police obliged those on the estate to defend it against them. The view of the commentary of *The People's Account*, reflecting a widely held view in the Black community, is that those whom the police confined to the Broadwater Farm Estate on that afternoon were forced to defend themselves, which they did with such signal success as to justify the phrase 'a classic example of self defence by a community'. It was self-defence against police illegality and error. Yours sincerely,
Cecil Gutzmore commentary writer, *The People's Account*.

VALID CRITICAL COMMENTS

OUR RIGHT TO MAKE

SANDRA
ECCLESTON

The People's Account has effectively been banned by the IBA, unless we, the programme makers, agree to make 'small' editorial cuts. Clearly Mr Glencross wants us to forget our right as programme makers to make valid and critical comments. In his apparently unchallengeable position, he feels able to impose his moral and political judgement not only on us but on everybody. His discretion seems final on what is acceptable for transmission.

In his view, *The People's Account* is 'an angry and one-sided film'. He has even gone as far as describing the commentary on the police as 'racist', failing to understand that racism stems from and is perpetrated by an authoritative system which those in power direct to their advantage. In our view, the film gives a Black people's perspective and we did not feel it necessary to engage in liberal 'balancing' of views. The film itself balances much of the hysterical media bias which greeted the uprisings and it reflects the views of numerous women, men, the youth and elders of our community.

The struggle to transmit *The People's Account* is a contest of truth over control. The truthful representation and interpretation of Black people's experience is just one part of it; there are many other truths which need to be told.

35

INCIDENT ENQUIRY
COMMENCING
12TH OCTOBER POLICE
WILL BE MAKING
HOUSE TO HOUSE
ENQUIRIES ON THIS
ESTATE CONCERNING
THE INCIDENT OF
SUNDAY 6TH OCTOBER
1985

35 Police notice on the Broadwater Farm Estate.

IS AFRICAN MUSIC BEING COLONISED?

These four articles centre on the use and abuse of African music by white music enthusiasts and business interests. An example of this is an invitation from Capital Radio DJ and record company owner, Charlie Gillett, to the Dade Krama group to record music to a racist advertisement for Ovaltine.

We have been refused permission by Charlie Gillett to publish his letter of invitation to Dade Krama. We have also been refused permission by the advertising agency Lowe, Howard-Spink Marschalk to publish their original script for the advertisement. However, both the letter and script have been published in full in *West Africa* magazine, 8 December 1986, along with Dade Krama's reply to Gillett's letter.

In his letter to Dade Krama, Gillett said that he had been asked by an advertising agency to produce, using 'authentic' African rhythms, the background music for an Ovaltine TV advertisement. The script was enclosed with the letter.

In the script a white female character called Ovaltina saves a white missionary, seen stewing in a cauldron, from brown 'gooney type' creatures, as the script describes the natives who are planning to eat the missionary. After rescuing him, Ovaltina, like some female Tarzan, swings back into the jungle on a vine.

While a particularly blatant example of racial insensitivity to Black people generally and to African music and musicians in paticular, by media and commercial interests, it is hardly unique, as the following group of four articles shows.

DRUM POLITIKS

YUSUF
HASSAN

Like Africa's gold, music is a much sought after commodity. And like the glittering metal, it not only soothes the ears and wags the bodies of millions of people all over the world but is plundered by affectionate aesthetes. Unfortunately, the emphasis on the struggle for political freedom and economic emancipation has relegated the cultural struggle to a lower position. Perhaps this is because Black music has always been universally acknowledged as the king of music. Even the most racist societies have been influenced by African people through music. There is hardly any sound — be it jazz, soul, reggae or calypso — which is not rooted in Africa. White people in particular felt no contradiction in rejecting the Black race while unashamedly enjoying its aesthetic rhythms.

But there is a catch, and indeed a price. Remove the political

36 Nii Noi Nortey of Dade Krama.

36

sting and sever the traditional links, and Black music turns into a permanent pleasure, safe for old and young. The job to 'purify' African music falls on the shoulders of record producers who mint money out of the tongues and fingers of Black artists. Once 'refined' it is then made available to a mass audience. Music has made the transition to being a product and the artist is a commodity with a price tag. But those who thought they could depoliticise African aesthetics are in for a rude shock. Black people have used culture as a weapon in the struggle against imperialism. It has proved an effective tool to mobilise and raise consciousness.

The West is very much aware of this phenomenon and has tried hard to control Black arts. In the US, Britain and France, the establishment sees Black music not only as a threat to the neo-colonies but as a liberating force in the metropolis. For example, in the 1950s, there emerged a young Black artist who shook the music scene with his sensational hits. Little Richard was a rock-and roll pioneer who is best remembered for 'Tutti-Frutti'. Though a harmless song, he was never to make it to the peak of his promising career. The new superstar was attracting large numbers of young whites. This obviously worried powerful US politicians who could not stand their young idolising a Black man. Little Richard had to be stopped and that put paid to his ascent. The hitherto unknown Elvis Presley was promoted instead. Elvis made his way to the top on the success of Little Richard and rode on the back of many Black composers and artists. They were never paid properly or acknowledged by the white star who was given the key to the American media.

Since then Black music has made inroads in the US. Although there are Black radio, television and record companies, it is not easy for a Black performer to get exposed to a wider audience. In Britain, where the mainstream media is literally out of bounds to Black people, Black artists are more dependent on the good-will of European 'supporters'. As in the political and economic spheres, no independent stand is tolerated and dissenters are harshly punished by being cut-off or boycotted by patrons. Luckily, progressive Black artists in the community see their role within the on-going struggle for liberation waged in the diaspora. In the past three decades, Black artists have continuously fought to develop a free aesthetics which will sustain the creative spirit of the African people. Politically conscious artists have formed groups that have put the self-determination of Black aesthetics high on the list of the liberation process.

WHAT IS OURS

BUT WHO REAPS THE FRUITS?

BLACK VOICES, BLACK SOUNDS,

YUSUF HASSAN

The struggle for the liberation of Black aesthetics has been on the agenda for as long as Black people have walked the streets of Britain. But it ebbed and rose with the events of time. It intensified during the anti-colonial crusade, went down after the gains of politicial independence, and has since been given a new lease of life by the struggles in Southern Africa and the agitation for equal rights and opportunities in Britain.

The current stage is different from the past ones in two ways. One is the artist's assertion that culture is an integral part of politics and is, therefore, part and parcel of the on-going fight against imperialism. The second is the resistance to the attempt to 'peg hole' Black aesthetics and market it under the label of ethnic arts.

There are several groups who are actively involved in this struggle. Two of the most prominent are The African Dawn collective, a group of artists committed to the ideas of Pan-Africanism, and Dade Krama, four musicians from Ghana, who play instruments from different parts of Africa. There is also 15-year-old Tunde Jegede, the only kora player in Britain, whose attempts to promote the 21-stringed harp lute instrument in the Black community has been aborted by British promoters.

Dade Krama presents a committed cultural front which is 'impervious to compromise and resistant to decay'. In the words of Nii Noi Nortey, 'our music can only be part of the struggles of the African people wherever they are'. Dade Krama uses African music as a platform 'to transform our whole social existence' and reaffirm 'the inseparability of culture and politics'. The group sees cultural expression as a weapon for liberation. The ultimate aim is 'to determine our own future'. Ahmed Sheikh, a Senegalese poet and writer who is a member of African Dawn, believes this can be achieved by the artists controlling all aspects of their work. African Dawn's example of marketing, promoting, recording and owning the copyright of its works has courted the displeasure of the white cultural establishment.

Sheikh is particularly opposed to the middle men/women. These are the promoters who engage African musicians and bring them to perform in London. Through dubious arrangements, these artists lose control of their music. According to Sheikh, 'gaining control of copyright is an effective means used by the Europeans to appropriate African music'. African artists are also discouraged from making contact with Black artists once they are here: 'These musicians are considered private property and are pressured not to deal with us when they come here', said Sheikh. Tunde Jegede has first hand experience of this. On a number of occasions his joint performances with other kora players did not materialise. British promoters frustrated his attempts to forge links with players from The Gambia. Jegede, with the help of his mother, Galina Chester, presented his case in a book published in 1986, *The Silenced Voice: Hidden Music of the Kora.*

Kwesi Owusu of African Dawn condemns the exotic manner in which African art forms are generally treated in the West. Africa's finest artworks have become European collector's items and some of the best are hidden in the vaults of European museums. In late 1986, Lucy Duran, the curator of international music at the National Sound Archive, a centre which documents and records sounds and music of all kinds, organised and chaired a discussion on African music at the NSA entitled 'Crossovers'. This discussion ended in an acrimonious exchange between Black artists on one hand and a group of 'specialists' on the other. Among those specialists were Lucy Duran and two disc jockeys, Andy Kershaw of BBC Radio One and Charlie Gillett of Capital Radio.

The argument that erupted and the fallout that followed exposed the raw nerves of the 'specialists' or patrons of African music. Charlie Gillett, of Oval Records recording company, soon after wrote a letter to Nana Tsiboe of Dade Krama in which he made a passionate defence of Lucy Duran and commented that it seemed absurd to alienate Kershaw, whom he saw as the only disc jockey on Radio One to make a policy of featuring African records.

Deejay Kershaw is remembered for his famous utterance after returning from a trip in the Gambia: 'I am off with my tape-recorder so I can fetch back plenty more stuff like this.' Chester and Jegede comment on this sort of attitude in their book: 'When the gold-rush mentality erupts, new record labels spring up overnight to secure the spoils. Creating a boundary and then assuming a crossover is not exchanging resources — but taking them.'

Gillett told Nana not to bother to communicate with him. Nana, however, replied in an attempt to set the record straight. In spite of the sender's attitude, he was polite but firm.
'Your involvement in the "genre" of African music is . . . . . inconsistent. It seems to me you are primarily motivated by the success of Oval Records because on the one hand you claim to be the "friendly" disc jockey who is patronising African music and trying to do his best for its exposure, but the underlying tones suggest that it is all for the benefit of Oval Records and profit . . . . even if the Africans are portrayed as "coons" or jungle-

37

37 Members of Dade Krama.

bunnies and cannibals, all capped with a white Tarzan who saves the day.' Nana ended his letter by suggesting that 'It is a big shame if Charlie Gillett is the judge of Africa and the outlet for African music for British people'.

Another record company owner and editor of *Folk Roots* magazine, Ian Anderson, an associate of the other patrons, added his voice to the attacks on Dade Krama and African Dawn. In a letter to Dade Krama, Anderson expressed his anger at the accusations levelled against Duran and Gillett, calling them an 'unjustified' offensive against people who are amongst the hardest workers for raising the level of awareness of music from African countries in Britain.

Kwesi Owusu says Lucy Duran considers herself a 'music connoisseur'. The Gambia is her exclusive vineyard, where she makes regular safaris to sample the latest harvest of kora music. Her tastes are then recommended to the British public through radio shows on to which she is invited by her associates. These associates help produce records and write features and other promotion materials. They also have the special contacts to organise tours of African musicians from that part of the continent.

Black artists in Britain are challenging this unequal relationship. Chester and Jegede note that 'the changing role of the musicologist to international music promoter means that the dividing line between coloniser and colonised has subtly become the link between exploiter and exploited'. It is this link that Black artists are committed to sever and the self-appointed specialists have closed ranks to defend their turf. Ahmed Sheikh has no doubt which position will eventually triumph. 'Those who will change things are those who feel it and know it', he says. That force is gathering strength and 'will ultimately cut the middle man or woman out — it's a situation that can and will be changed'. Let us hope so.

WALKING AWAY WITH THE MUSIC

TUNDE JEGEDE AND GALINA CHESTER

After joining Friends of the Commonwealth Institute in early 1987 on the annual music trip to the Gambia and Senegal led by Lucy Duran of the National Sound Archive, Ian Anderson, the editor of *Folk Roots,* devoted the April 1987 of his magazine to kora music. This ran concurrently with the April/May tour featuring kora musicians Dembo Konte from the Gambia and Kausa Kuyateh, a 'new discovery' from Senegal, introduced to this country by Lucy Duran to promote the album *Tanante* recorded by her in the Gambia and released here by Rogue Records.

In the same issue of *Folk Roots,* the book, *The Silenced Voice: Hidden Music of the Kora,* by Galina Chester and Tunde Jegede, was reviewed by the editor. Mr. Anderson did not however apply the function of criticism, but instead launched a vindictive attack on the authors whom he had never met. While the level of abuse is beyond comment, we wish to correct certain errors and draw attention to the serious implications inherent in this piece.

Lamenting the absence of an 'authoritative' book on West African traditional music, Mr. Anderson overlooks such writers as J.K.H. Nketia, Francis Bebey and Kwesi Owusu. *The Silenced Voice* was not intended to be authoritative in the supremacist sense. It examines the role of the griot (poet-musician) in African tradition and in exile, and discusses with Ahmed Sheikh of African Dawn how cultural imperialism has silenced the political voice of the griot.

Describing the book as a 'preposterous and racist diatribe against the few people in Britain who have the enthusiasm, love, time, energy and desire to make this music available', Mr. Anderson goes on to say that it is a 'thinly veiled attack on the National Sound Archive's Lucy Duran without whom little kora music would have been heard here at all'. While failing to understand that racism stems from and is perpetrated by an authoritative system which only those few in positions of power can direct to advantage, Mr. Anderson demonstrates that the credibility of Britain's authority on kora music, Lucy Duran, apparently depends on members of the Black community here being branded as 'racists'.

Kora music is presented in the UK as a commodity art marketed to suit a consumer society which views African music as 'exotica'. Radio 1 disc jockey Andy Kershaw aptly summed it up on a recent show by describing African music as 'stuff to be fetched back from Africa on a tape recorder'. But while Lucy Duran and Capital Radio's Charlie Gillett may readily proclaim the generosity of musicians in Africa on *City Beats*, those in control of African music in Britain are at the same time walking away with the music.

Misrepresenting the griot's art has created a public ignorance of the true nature of African music, which as an integral part of society is of its nature political and concerned with change. It cannot be uprooted as an artefact. It can only develop when musicians come together seeking new dimensions. While the apartheid-style divide in British society denies the Black community here access to visiting musicians brought over on tour from West Africa, Lucy Duran's statement that Black people in the diaspora are 'culturally bankrupt' ('Crossovers Crossfire', *West Africa* Dec. 8 1986) perpetuates a deliberate divide which not only preserves the elitist concept of the griot's art, but also ensures that the African artist at home remains unaware that promotion in Britain can also mean exploitation in Africa.

The British Library National Sound Archive in South Kensington has over a million items of recorded sound on tape, disc and video. The International Music Section is described as the largest public reference collection in the UK of folk and 'ethnic' recordings, with an emphasis on traditional music. As well as possessing unique collections of ethnomusicological fieldwork, the Archive also makes recordings of concert performances and workshops in the UK by visiting overseas musicians. The invaluable function of a sound archive is to catalogue, maintain and preserve recordings. But custodial powers can be considerable. Significantly and uniquely, kora music is played essentially within particular families in certain parts of West Africa. This can be turned to advantage. Introducing a member of each family in turn with the emphasis on recording rather than performing not only secures the music, but also means it can be deliberately withheld in order to direct and control its availability through selected record companies and the media.

It has been said that any mention of the UK kora tour would be incomplete without crediting Lucy Duran of the National Sound Archive. Dembo Konte and Kausu Kuyateh were made available to Radio 1's Andy Kershaw (who also went on the Gambia trip), Capital Radio's Charlie Gillett and Radio 2's *Folk on Two*, and kora tuition from Dembo (but not from first-time visitor Kausu) was offered through Lucy Duran. Acknowledged as the 'prime mover' behind this and previous tours, Lucy Duran is presented as having championed the kora in Britain for nearly a decade. But because first-time visiting musicians introduced by her are often given just one performance at selected 'white' venues, kora music has remained exclusive and surprisingly little known here in comparison with anywhere else in Europe.

In his review, Mr. Anderson seems to be suggesting that Britain's Black community takes no financial risks promoting concerts by visiting musicians. Yet in 1984 the authors organised the visit of the kora player Sanjally Jobarteh to Britain and promoted, without funding, a series of London concerts and ILEA workshops.

Mr. Anderson continues: 'it is claimed that Jegede was the first pupil to study with kora master Amadu Jobarteh from outside the family tradition; in fact Lucy Duran did so for a much longer period some six years earlier and herself subsequently taught Jegede for two years prior to his brief Gambia visit.' In his haste to condemn, Mr. Anderson has not read the book very carefully. The authors in fact wrote, 'as a young person of African descent born in Britain, Tunde became the first pupil outside the family tradition', thus making the point that an important link had been made with the Black community here, an initiative which cannot be denied. While it is generally known that Tunde, hardly surprisingly, received lessons at one stage from Britain's 'authority' on kora music, he was not, as Mr. Anderson maintains, initially taught by Lucy Duran but by Bouly Cissokho from Senegal, who also gave Tunde his first kora. What Mr. Anderson is really insisting is that there is no such thing as Black initiative.

His final comparison between Tunde Jegede's only visit to the Gambia to study with Amadu Jobarteh in 1982 and Lucy Duran's regular visits to kora musicians in West Africa, has inadvertently but precisely made that point. In an appearance on Charlie Gillett's *City Beats* (Capital Radio, Jan. 25 1987), Lucy Duran discussed the music trip she led with twenty-two people to the Gambia and Senegal in January 1987.

While Charlie Gillett commended those who went round the Gambia cleaning it out of original cassettes as 'the more astute members of the group', Lucy Duran produced a recording of Kausu Kuyateh and introduced him as her 'new discovery' from Senegal. But the effusive, ingratiating tone . . . . left one wondering what will become of this artist when he, too, is ultimately discarded as culturally bankrupt. Describing herself as a patron of jalis (kora musicians), Lucy Duran demonstrated that they often sang her praises into their songs and even dedicated private recordings to her, which gave her 'kind of a nice feeling'. She added, 'I hope it doesn't seem immodest of me, but there is an awful lot of mention of Lucy Duran, Lucy Duran, Lucy Duran — in fact, another person who was in the group said at the end of the trip, "I think the only problem with this trip is that there haven't been enough songs about Lucy Duran!" '

Indulgent self-glorification is often the mark of cultural imperialism, and emphasises two extremes. While jalis in Africa queue to be introduced in Europe as the 'ethnic new find', it has been ensured that Britain's only kora performer, Tunde Jegede, does not play with visiting kora musicians and that the Africa Centre in London is rationed to one performance by Dembo Konte and Kausu Kuyateh.

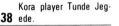

38 Kora player Tunde Jegede.

38

KOFI HAGAN

CROSSFIRE

'Crossovers' at the National Sound Archive in late 1986 was meant to discuss how the effects of increasing commercialisation were felt in the 'growing influence of traditional forms of Afro-Caribbean music' on European tastes. The panel included Andy Kershaw of BBC Radio 1, Charlie Gillett, Capital Radio, and Afari Aboagye and Nana Tsiboe of Dade Krama. Lucy and Andy left halfway through the programme in anger.

Having introduced the panel to the packed audience, and elaborated on the significance of crossover, Lucy Duran invited Charlie Gillett to comment. Charlie did so in the way he knew best, as a disc-jockey, with a record by the African Allos and his Zigzag Jazz Group which had made the British top five in the charts way back in 1957; he then analysed the link between this 'highly commercialised' South African music and its African roots. Deep-voiced Andy Kershaw coolly began by admitting that 'I don't like traditional African music', then agreed with everyone who had spoken before him.

Nana Tsiboe's comments were painfully ironic: 'It is interesting to note that as an African I am the last person you ask.' He questioned the selection by Charlie Gillett of the music just played and said that 'it is not fair to pull in that as representative of African music'. He explained correctly that in Africa, music served as a communal catalyst, reflecting all aspects of community life — sorrow, joy, social commentaries etc. — in order to create social awareness and a change for the better. Nana, with the support of Afari Aboagye, charged that because of this reality, it was best first to understand African music before exposing it, otherwise 'we consume it out of ignorance'. This conclusive point by Nana must have got under the skin of Lucy Duran and the other two panelists who consider themselves authorities on the presentation of African music to the white public. They were very defensive.

The discussion, which was recorded, was one of those democratic ones open to the audience. Kwesi Owusu was the first to speak from the audience. His intervention was an assessment of the cavalier and exotic manner in which African art forms are treated in the West. It was clear that he had rubbed it in too hard: Andy Kershaw engaged him in a furious argument, saying: 'There isn't just Africans, we got Czechoslovakians as well to play music to!' Owusu had not quite finished making another point when Charlie Gillett started playing a record of Zairean Franco. He protested angrily: more arguments and general free-for-all exchanges. Spartacus R, ex-Osibisa, was the next to make an intervention. He felt that the discussion was going off course.

What he thought must concern the panel was the politics involved in music, and the exposé of 'your system that you oppress us with'. The frontline of argument was by now clearly marked. A woman in the audience screamed: 'This is completely out of hand!'

Another woman wanted the music back on. She had paid £2 to come to listen to the music and not to be 'lectured'. Even when the programme was read to her stating clearly that it was a discussion programme rather than a musical one, she still clamoured stubbornly for music. The acrimonious argument between Kwesi and Andy had now taken its toll. Andy Kershaw left in anger, trailed by Lucy Duran. In the absence of the chair, things seemed to cool down. Nana Tsiboe, who had shown exemplary prudence in the question-and-answer session, took over the chair. Lucy returned later, stonefaced, and nervously introduced a new chair. 'We were doing alright before you came', was someone's brusque welcome to the new chair amid general laughter. An elderly women who sat in the 'argumentative' section of the audience made an interesting point: she criticised the radio stations in Britain for underplaying African music and music from the rest of the South (as opposed to the industrialised North), while the BBC External Services created a false impression to the outside world by doing just the opposite, adding that, 'I am attracted to African music because I feel it in my heart'.

A most embarrassing development had occurred before Andy Kershaw and Lucy Duran abdicated their roles on the panel. Nana Tsiboe, in stressing the extent to which even white liberals were sometimes just as bad or even worse than outright racists in both their social and economic dealings with Africans, said that his group Dade Krama had been insulted with an invitation to do the music score for an advertisement which insulted Blacks. He added that a member of the panel had been involved in the deal. Kwate Nii Owoo read the brief prepared by the Knightsbridge advertising agency, Lowe Howard-Spink Marschalk. While some members of the audience angrily advised that the culprit be reported to the Commission for Racial Equality, Lucy made the tactical mistake of furiously insisting, Iron Lady-style, that the dramatic revelations by Nana Tsiboe had nothing to do with the conduct of the discussion! More damagingly, Lucy Duran admitted that the title of the evening's discussion, 'Crossovers', was wrong in the light of its negative connotations of culturally bankrupt Black people who denounce their Blackness in order to succeed in the white world. Lucy Duran should have known. She is American, I am told. Whatever she is, or represents, good sense crossed over the hurdle of liberal control and misrepresentation of African music that night at the National Sound Archive.

THEORY AND PRACTICE

KEITH PIPER AND DONALD RODNEY

ON THEORY

In Britain's art schools, where the mythology of individual self-expression is held at a premium, collaborative activity is discouraged. Apart from throwing a spanner into bureaucratic machinery geared to assess the virtuoso, collaborative activities begin to counter many of the negative effects of an individualism which leaves the art student isolated and vulnerable. Supporting collaborative activity has therefore never been in the interest of the art school hierarchy, as many students expressing an interest in working collaboratively have learned to their cost.

Beyond the art schools, within the hallowed halls of the so-called 'mainstream', collaborative activity has to an extent been embraced, processed, and rendered commercially viable. Within celebrated associations such as Gilbert & George and Komar & Melamid, white male artists collaborate in order to indulge their racism and misogyny before an art world eager for voyeuristic titillation. Thus the claim of Gilbert & George that 'We want our art to speak across the barriers of knowledge directly to people about their life and not about the knowledge of art', is rendered hollow rhetoric. Their slickly executed consumer durables which come complete with fascistic inflections, are the stuff upon which the capitalist art market thrives. Nothing is challenged.

The radical potential of like-minded artists working collaboratively has yet to effectively challenge the established canons of an art history and practice founded upon the notion of the original genius, the 'old master'. The fact that this concept is not only sexist ('master' is by definition male) but also racist by dint of its unquestioned Eurocentrality, makes it all the more imperative that Black artists oppose it by all means necessary.

It is widely acknowledged that it has only been through a decade of concerted and united activity on the part of Black cultural activists that Black Art has secured for itself a modicum of visibility from which to challenge the racist assumptions of the mainstream. Piper & Rodney recognise that whilst loose association around the lobbying for visibility was necessary when the existence of 'Black Art' was often questioned, now, when many of our one-time comrades in struggle have found themselves coaxed into the claws of the capitalist art market through the private gallery system, a new level of collaborative activity is called for. It is a collectivity which roots itself at the very core of our practice, where work is conceived, researched, and constructed.

Along with the tactical advantages of collaboration, come its technical advantages. An African proverb says that 'Many hands make light work', and in a similar fashion collaboration, through the fusion of technical and creative input, renders increasingly ambitious projects practicable. Our work therefore spans media, fusing elements of disparate origin and technically outstretching the formal limitations of conventional gallery-based practice.

39

The Turn of the Screw, acrylic/mixed media, from The Devil's Feast exhibition, Keith Piper and **39** Donald Rodney.

ON PRACTICE

From the *Caribbean Times*, Friday March 13 1987:

The near blizzard that descended on Wolverhampton last weekend could not have picked a worse Saturday to strike. But it failed to deter 2000 people from marching through the Midlands town to vent their anger, not only at the killing of Clinton McCurbin, but at the all too frequent state-licensed attacks on Black people by police throughout the country.

'Police murderers' was among the popular chants as the march followed a route from West Park through the city, past the pedestrian shopping precinct where the killing took place.

Clinton's aunt, Mrs. Esther Mcvoy, laid a wreath outside the *Next* shop where her nephew was killed, but only after demonstrators persisted in the face of police objections.

There are several reliable eye-witness accounts as to what went on outside the *Next* store on Friday, and all conflict with the police reports.

Two teenagers had just come out from the nearby *Macdonalds* shop and were passing by the *Next* store on Friday when they saw McCurbin lying face down, one plainclothes policeman holding his legs, a uniformed policeman on his back holding his arms and another policeman with his arm around McCurbin's neck.

A Black woman went into the shop and shouted vehemently at a police officer, later identified as PC Michael Hobday, 'loose him back' because they were quite obviously hurting him.

PC Hobday continued to tug at McCurbin's neck, even though there was no movement in his body. The three policemen then got off the lifeless McCurbin to put handcuffs on his wrists.

They dragged McCurbin by the arms into the back of the store's woman's section on the first floor. They did not bother to apply first aid.

The strong arm of the state: Clinton McCurbin, Cynthia Jarret, Cherry Groce, are just a few of the names that come readily to hand when creating a list of recent state atrocities. There is an African proverb that says 'an injury to one is an injury to all'; there is also, dear reader, another African proverb that reads 'no next time, no next time'.

The Turn of the Screw,
acrylic/mixed media, from
The Devil's Feast exhibi-
tion, Keith Piper and
40 Donald Rodney.

The Turn of the Screw,
acrylic/mixed media, from
The Devil's Feast exhibi-
tion, Keith Piper and
41 Donald Rodney.

The Turn of the Screw,
acrylic/mixed media, from
The Devil's Feast exhibi-
tion, Keith Piper and
42 Donald Rodney.

The Turn of the Screw,
acrylic/mixed media, from
The Devil's Feast exhibi-
tion, Keith Piper and
43 Donald Rodney.

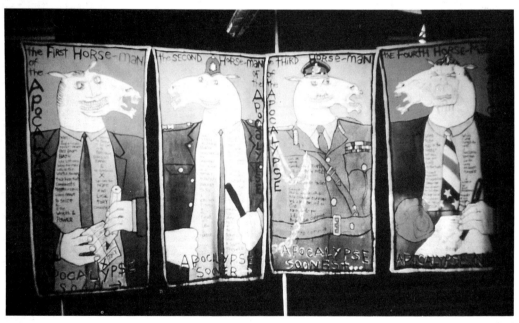

41

42

43

COME ON, CHEER UP!

ARAEEN
RASHEED

What is the point of writing if not to communicate with others.
But, who and where are the others? To begin with, how shall I get
rid of the feeling that I may in fact be wasting my time trying to
write these lines? One really needs a sympathetic — not
necessarily converted — audience to converse with. One could
though speak *to* people, but then it can often be a function of
power. An article for an art magazine? What for? Your name will
be in print again. And then you may one day come across a person
who would say that s/he liked your piece. What then? Is it
communication?

Could the fragments of one's personal experience be so
arranged that they may become meaningful to others? Is it
possible to intervene through a subjective level in a reality which
claims to be universally objective? Is it possible or desirable to
communicate through one's anger, frustrations, fear and anxiety?
Is it possible to have a dialogue with a world which is smug about
its presumed human values, which is Eurocentric, powerful and
privileged?

How to avoid a monologue? An abyss of madness! But, one
must talk; even if one has to talk to oneself. The alternative is too
gruesome: *silence*. Elena complains that I'm always talking to
myself. She can never get near enough in time to listen to what I
really say. She thinks I'm always grumbling about something or
other.

Why shouldn't we grumble? Are *we* living in the land of milk
and honey? We used to think that England's roads must be paved
with gold. My old parents in Pakistan find it impossible to believe
that one could be unemployed or a failure in England. They think
I'm somehow hiding the truth, in case they ask me for some
money. What the hell are you doing there, if you can't make your
living!

The *artist* shouldn't worry about the question of career. Art
should be dedication, performed in absolute seclusion and silence.
A commitment of the highest moral order, regardless of and
untouched by material forces! Those who are successful are so only
because of some heavenly act. They are blessed by gods! They are
rewarded because they have performed a unique function of lifting
the whole of humanity from primeval darkness to the bright light
of civilisation.

We are now living in an enlightened age when no artist of any
worth should suffer behind the walls of ignorance and obscurity. If
you can't sell your stuff in Bond Street, go to Bayswater Road.
Failure is the measure of one's unworthiness and insignificance!

Why this regardless commitment for the artist alone? Is s/he not also made of flesh and blood? How many art critics or historians write just for love of art or as a responsibility? What would one say about all those self-proclaimed radical art critics who made loud noises around the mid-seventies about the social responsibility of the artist? Where are they now? Have they all gone to the Himalayas? Maybe they are wandering in the desert looking for underdogs.

You must really touch the surface. Feel it — like this. You can feel the richness of texture, the *thickness* and variety of so many colours. You will indeed feel all humanity there. You will *feel* the *aesthetic dimension*. You don't need eyes!

'How about the three million unemployed?' 'You are changing the subject.' 'How would you sell your *aesthetic dimension* to those who are angry and frustrated?' 'It would give them hope to live.' 'How about racism?' 'But there is no racism in the art world.'

Art stands above social and economic realities of the time! It transcends racial barriers and conflicts and is really enlightened, with universal human values. Really! How about Henry Moore? How about Anthony Caro? How about David Hockney? How about Francis Bacon? How about... How about them? Which one of them is Black?

Unity in diversity. Human salvation can only be achieved by the unity of all four human races. How? Just look at the four chimneys of a fallen German house.[1]

Elena comes in, looks through the hatch in the kitchen wall and laughs. I look at her and feel embarrassed. I have been talking to myself again. Actually I was loudly swearing at a Bond Street gallery which could have taken me up about twelve years ago. The director was very impressed by the work; but, for some weird reasons he wouldn't show me. The art world has its own mysterious ways! He was though only showing English or American artists.

Meeting a white radical socialist artist in a pub; he says that G & G are not really racists. They are just stupid. They don't know what they are doing. I ask him if he or anybody else understands their work, in particular that which depicts Black people. He is somewhat lost. I try to give my own interpretation, based on an analysis of the structure of the work, social reference it contains and the nature of representation. He becomes apologetic: we shouldn't worry too much about that kind of mainstream art practice. We should concern ourselves with class struggle and the possible danger of fascism in the country.

Actually G & G are not the only people who *use* Black people in their work. While G & G are derogatory, many white liberals now turn their expensive cameras or attention towards the condition of Black people, with a self-righteous attitude of doing something *good* or radical.

In a pub again. P comes towards me smiling: 'I like your sculptures at the GF. You *had* the talent.' I don't know why my immediate reaction is to tell him to fuck off. I feel he is being sarcastic or patronising; and I hate being patronised. In either case he deserves it. He gets upset and complains about my aggressive behaviour. It's funny that he should complain. He is always pompous and rude to other people, in his writing as well as in public discussions.

A paradox or a dangerous symptom! The art world is supposed to be an embodiment of individual 'freedom of expression'. And yet people in the art world are so scared to speak up *openly* about certain issues. I come across so many people who say that they agree with me on many issues; but, they cannot and will not speak about them openly. They wouldn't like their careers to be jeopardised.

Only recently I met a person who was in Sao Paulo during the biennale, and he was very unhappy that G & G were sent there to represent Britain. He came across many other people there who were disgusted by racial elements or references to Black people in their work. I asked him if he would write something about it. He suddenly becomes evasive. He doesn't perhaps want to upset the people at the British Council.

Those who are in power are conceited and smug. Others are just scared of losing their jobs or positions. Commitments have become secondary to self-interest and cynicism: after all we all have to pay for our mortgages. We must worry about old age and pensions. Poor van Gogh!

The depressing thing is that most people are not aware of or couldn't care less about the oppressive atmosphere of the British art world today. New York looks different though, at least from here. When a white artist exhibits a series of charcoal drawings and calls them 'Nigger Drawings', a radical section of the New York art world comes out to protest against this blatant racism; while, at the same time, there are others who try to defend the individual's right to 'freedom of expression'. There is at least an open debate about the issue, unlike in Britain where such things are constantly swept under the carpet.

I agree 'that the practice, history and criticism of art must be open to conversation, that it must have some discursive, rather than merely liturgical, aspects in relation to others.'[2] But how is this possible *within* a controlled system? Can the question of conversation be dealt with effectively only at a theoretical level, without taking into consideration practical ways by which this may be possible or realised at a time when there is growing antipathy against the development of such a discourse? The question here is not about institutional mediation, which is inevitable. The point is: can we have a direct access to *basic* information about art practice or actual work on which serious art criticism may be based? How can we know that institutional control of art information has not reached the point where it is depriving even art criticism of its relatively independent function?

Art criticism has today become a function of the commercial gallery system. It bases its practice, radical or reactionary, on an assumption that whatever is shown in and promoted by the galleries, both public and private, it is a *fair* selection or sample of what is produced in a given time; and that only 'objective' considerations determine that selection. No wonder that almost all the critics who wrote about the recent Whitechapel show, British Sculpture in the 20th Century, took it for granted that it was a truly representative survey. Fingers were pointed at some absurdities, but nobody even suspected any possible significant exclusion. With the exception of Guy Brett, who pointed out the gross misrepresentation of the sixties in an article in *City Limits*, every art critic succumbed humbly to the falsification. And it was the falsified information on which most of the criticism was based. What is the validity of such criticism?

Apart from what Guy Brett dealt with, it would be interesting to take up a point here which is of historical importance. The official story is that there was a jump from New Generation sculpture to post-Minimalism in Britain, unlike in New York where there was a gradual move from the abstract sculpture of David Smith to the Minimal sculpture of Andre, Judd, LeWitt… and then to post-Minimalism. The story is true in a sense: a group of young students at St Martin's revolt against their teachers (Caro et al), lay down their tools and walk out of the school into the galleries. But how is this true history? We accept this as the history of art of the time because we assume that either significant art practice cannot exist outside the art-college/art-gallery axis, or that whatever significant art is produced necessarily reaches the promotional circuit.

This is indeed a dangerous assumption. It ignores the question of institutional/ideological control of art promotion and recognition. It ignores the fact that a falsification of information can *now* take place owing to factors other than normal recognisable factors. These *new* factors have to do with the changing nature of this society vis-à-vis its people since the last war, and these factors have not been able to enter into art historical or critical consciousness.

Walking home from Kilburn to South Hampstead, I suddenly come across some skinheads on the other side of the road. As soon as they see me they start chanting together: 'Paki, Paki, Paki'. I stop. I try to show my anger. I'm actually holding in one hand a big spanner which I have just bought. They stop chanting. I resume my walk towards home. They start chanting again. But I ignore them, and carry on walking. I'm really shocked. It is the first time in eighteen years in Britain that anybody shouted Paki at me (like shouting nigger at an African). I thought it would not happen to me personally. I'm often told that I look more like a Greek or Spaniard. I was really frightened when I was facing them, but I could have killed one of the bastards if they had come near me.

Meeting an old friend at the ICA. He advises me to be careful. 'If you want to be a successful artist, stop criticising the establishment. Try to make friends in the art world. This is a very sophisticated society and you must develop sophisticated responses to it. You can't bite the hand that feeds you, particularly when the hand is white and the mouth is black. Don't open your mouth too much.'

A few weeks later I'm walking with a white liberal friend, going home from the pub. He is actually an important person from the art world. There are some white kids (age about 10 to 14) around the street corner. They laugh and shout 'Paki' as we pass by. One kid comes near and tries to touch me. My friend laughs *as well*. He thinks it is very amusing. But I feel terrible and walk in silence. They are *only* kids, he says to reassure me.

An important West End gallery director visits me at home. I knew him in the late sixties, when he was very interested in my work. Somehow he later became reluctant to show me. Then we did not meet for almost ten years. Recently I saw him at a private view. He walked towards me and said hello, which really surprised me. He wanted to know what I was doing. So I asked him over for a drink. He now assures me that he still considers me his friend, still likes my work from the sixties. He is sorry he couldn't do anything for me. I try to show him some of my new work. But he doesn't really want to see anything. He just wants to talk. We talk about general things. He is sitting in a low-slung armchair and keeps on banging the floor with his left fist, trying to impress me with the importance of Carl Andre. I feel fed up: I know the work of Carl Andre and he doesn't have to tell me about him. He says that Carl Andre is the Michelangelo of this century. I try again to show him some of my earlier work which he had not seen: floating discs on water at St Katherine's Dock. After a few slides he stops me with a remark: oh, that looks like Daniel Buren. He is actually comparing my work of 1969-70 with that of floating paper boats by Buren, which I think he did in Berlin around the mid-seventies. How stupid! Anyway, the connection is altogether superficial. He again assures me of his friendship: 'I'm the most important dealer in Britain today; and I still have to come to see you. Leslie Waddington would never visit you like this.' He is now leaving, and I thank him for coming. He gives me friendly advice: 'Leave this country, Rasheed. Nobody likes art in this country. I have made it myself only because I have shown. You would have a better chance abroad.'

I'm puzzled and confused by his attitude. Why did he come to see me? It can't be just friendship. I occasionally see him around during private views. He always has the same cold, indifferent look.

'He would have become one of the most important sculptors in Britain today, if only he had carried on with his sixties work,' remarks a critic in a private conversation. Of course, I could have continued with that work, if only I could have seen the bright light ahead. But that's not really a true statement. In the early seventies my work changed because I myself changed. I went through a process of self-realisation, which gave me a new direction and context.

I still like that work. A lot of pieces still lie around unfinished; one day I would like to finish them. There was never a question of renunciation. Neither did I ever reject Bond Street carrots, since they were never offered to me. I did not have to denounce the sixties in order to become a socialist in the seventies. My earlier work has continued as part of my later work, but beyond and in opposition to stylistic concerns. The trouble is that we are so used to linear thinking, one style superseding another in a linear development, one style cancelling another in a frantic competition for supremacy, that even our radical concerns have become trapped in stylistic pitfalls.

'One can understand the doubts an artist from a country like Pakistan feels about producing purely aesthetic objects. Yet maybe the answer would be for Araeen to adapt his constructions to the design of light, colourful structures to house the homeless in the Indian sub-continent, where they would fulfil both physical and aesthetic needs,' says a critic who seems to have a great admiration for my sixties work. But, I have never produced *purely* aesthetic objects. Moreover, I cannot accept the other implication of the remark, although I recognise that it is well-meant. As far as homelessness is concerned, it is a utopian fallacy to think that it could be solved by an art practice.

Art cannot change the world! Why bother then? I myself do not think that art can change the world, in the sense commonly understood by many socialists. Art identifies with the world. Which world? In the early seventies I started using material from my actual social environment, from the actual world, in a specific way which relates to its (and my) contingencies and priorities. On the other hand, the bourgeois art world is obsessed with the notion of consistency in personal style. And the question of *style* has thus become a paramount concern for the artist. This is based on an ideology that I reject.

A white art critic passes through Railton Road, Brixton, on his way to interview a white artist who has his studio around there. The critic notices 'a lot of Black people in Brixton'.[3] He looks at young Black women admiringly, and he thinks it misleading to call them black: 'There are truly beautiful Asian women with fine, delicate features and skin paler than any Greek or Spaniard, and there are African girls with noble heads on long necks and skin the purple-black colour of aubergines.'[4] And the noble profile of an African head looks down from the roof. Brixton will burn again! Corrugated metal sheets will melt and leave no rubble. The white critic carries on to his destination to talk about the freedom and liberty we have to make abstract paintings.

I was not stupid or naive when I started doing work which explicitly alludes to my relationship with this society or Western culture. If a career was all I wanted I could have stayed in Pakistan, where I could have made a good career as an engineer. I'm now proud that I'm still an active part of the Black struggle, which again is part of a larger struggle in the world today against all kinds of determination and domination. And my work relates to this struggle, even when I do not paint propaganda pictures. I see no reason why I should change myself to become a successful member of this society. Or, for that matter, go back home. The problem in fact lies with the society itself which does not wish to see or recognise any significance in a position which looks at it critically.

A letter from Lewisham Borough about an artist-in-residence position. No joy. Perhaps the selection committee didn't like overt reference to racism in my work. People shouldn't be disturbed by or made aware of the reality of their society. They must have picked a dumb (white) artist who is an embodiment of love, harmony and happiness.

The middle class has the brightest arse in the world. No matter what you do, it would in the end highjack the whole thing. The Black middle class (of both Asian and African origins) has no moral qualms about its relationship with the white establishment.

It would collaborate with anybody and against the real interests of Black people. It plays all kinds of smart games, both on the right and the left, and gets the best out of everything for itself.

Ideas create space. But, they do not necessarily control or occupy the space they create. One could spend years and years trying to create a new space: a space which belongs to the contemporary world; a space which is critical in terms of its relationship with the world; a space in which it is meant to have a meaningful dialogue or conversation with others, so that it might help transform our consciousness and the world at large; a space which could be shared by all or different people as a result of a critical process.

But then one day a smiling young jackass is pushed into this space with all the power of the art establishment behind him. He places his archaic exotic shit, with a colourful covering to attract contemporary flies, all over the place. He then solemnly proclaims that the whole thing is religious and spiritual. The contemporary reality is thus masked over with phoney talk of harmony and unity, without showing irony or contradiction. The space is depoliticised: it is usurped. Hallelujah!

Are we living in a free society or fascist state? What is the function of art? Why shouldn't we Black people look at things critically and at the same time expect our perspective to be recognised as part of this society's transformational processes? It's said that the English don't like 'foreigners' to come here to live and then criticise 'their' country. Are we here then to play the roles of exotic monkeys, ethnic arse-lickers, or Uncle Toms?

I feel terribly depressed, which is not an unusual occurrence. I haven't talked to anybody for three or four days. I just sit in an armchair and gaze at the ceiling. Elena tries her best to cheer me up. But it doesn't work. She gets upset. But I feel numb, both in body and in mind. Van Gogh must have felt numb when he pulled the trigger!

A Pakistani friend rings. I go to his house. We drink and have Pakistani food (no curries or tandooris, please!). We listen to Indian/Pakistani music, every kind. Film songs, popular and classical music. It is very beautiful; but it is all about pie-in-the-sky romance or/and some kind of mysticism. It can give you instant nostalgia. We tell jokes, which are often sexist and stupid. We talk about Karachi. *Maybe we should go back home.* I feel better.

What do I hear? Britain is now a multiracial society! The favourite phrase is in fact 'multicultural'. We no longer live in the nineteenth century British Empire. 'People of different cultures' must now be allowed into the temple of high culture so that they may be blessed, and in turn they may 'add to the richness and variety of this country'.[5] The ancient gods have indeed descended on the high temple across the holy river. The message is: love & peace. The dissidents must be warned of their terrible fate.

Brixton shall shout: all we need is love! Southall shall chant Hare Krishna and dance exotic Bangra in front of the Royal Festival Hall! Bristol shall look to a new kingdom in Ethiopia! Bradford shall see a new messiah descending on the dome (which is likely to be that of the Playboy Club)! Come Mecca Dancing! We shall all rejoice. It is a moment of celebration.

Come on, cheer up! Isn't this what you have been struggling for all these years? At least something is happening. It is only a beginning.

London, summer 1982

NOTES

1   This paragraph refers to Caroline Tisdall's catalogue introduction to Joseph Beuy's work *dernier space avec introspecteur,* shown at the Anthony d'Offay Gallery, London (March-May 1982), in which she makes a totally absurd connection between Beuy's work and the various human races of the world: a blown-up photograph of what she calls 'Europe's chimney' is interpreted as 'an African head'. Instead of dealing with the actual significance of the work by placing it within its cultural context of postwar Germany, Beuy's work has often and deliberately been shrouded in the kind of mystification that turns a parochial European artist into a heroic world figure.

2   Michael Baldwin, Charles Harrison, Mel Ramsden, 'Art History, Art Criticism and Explanation', *Art History,* vol. 4, no. 4, London.

3, 4 Simon Vaughan Winter, *Artscribe,* 33, London.

5   This quote is from Mrs. Thatcher's famous speech about this country being swamped by people of a different culture.

EXPLORING

E X P L O R A T I O N S

THE FRONTIERS OF EXPRESSION

Their voices rise... the pine trees are guitars, strumming, pine-needles fall like sheets of rain. Their voices rise... the chorus of the cane is carolling a vesper to the stars.
Jean Toomer.

'Part of how we speak is musical. We are not alienated from our bodies, not resistant to respond to music, not inhibited by loud saxophones — our culture is visual, oral... Music is all our interactions, wrapped up in our person, in our children's games. Movement, music, dance have all got to be worked into the syntax of our language,' says Ntozake Shange in the opening interview with Jan McKenley and Suzanne Scafe.

Shange is one of the most significant Black writers of the eighties; together with fellow African-American women writers like Alice Walker, Toni Cade Bambara and Maya Angelou, she has become a torchbearer in the search to reclaim Black territories of expression. In this interview, she discusses the politics of writing and elaborates on the creative departures she is helping to chart. Carolyn Cooper in 'The Female Sensibility in the Poetry of Louise Bennett' and Merle Collins in 'Two Writers from the Caribbean' touch on similar themes. Cooper takes the poetry of Louise Bennett, the innovative craftswoman of what Edward Braithwaite calls 'nation language' and finds in it the basis of 'an indigenous feminist ideology'; Collins investigates

the differences in creative emphasis and strategies between two Caribbean writers, Joan Riley and Jacob Ross. Ross is a Grenadian who now lives and works in Britain; Riley, though not born in Britain, has a consciousness predominantly shaped here.

David A. Bailey explores the frontiers of expression through the image-making world of photography. He discusses what he sees as the theoretical and practical agendas for Black photography now, using his own work as an example. His approach is similar to that of Ruhi Hamid who is committed to demystifying the form and content of graphics. Photographer Armet Francis reveals how he creates a sensitive and refreshing profile of images of Black children.

The articles by Jatinder Verma and Amrit Wilson symbolise the internationalist nature of Black arts and the significance of the cultural gains and developments in Africa and Asia for Black artists in Britain. Verma summarises the lessons of the search for distinctive cultural expression in Indian theatre 'in an effort to formulate a crucial question for the future development of Black theatre in Britain.' Wilson gives a socio-economic, political and cultural profile of Eritrea to highlight the profound relationship between cultural and social transformation and to offer a vision of an alternative way of producing culture.

RODEOS AND RAINBOWS

WITH NTOZAKE SHANGE

AN INTERVIEW

SUZANNE SCAFE

AND

JAN McKENLEY

Ntozake Shange was born thirty-eight years ago in St. Louis, USA, and now lives in Texas with her daughter, Savannah. Surrounded by art and artists, she grew up in a very creative environment which also involved travelling inside and outside the States, observing different cultures and learning to feel their differences and similarities. In *Nappy Edges*, she recalls: 'my mother and father went to europe, cuba, haiti and mexico. They kept their friends around me from nigeria, togo, haiti, cuba, india, the philippines, france, mexico. i heard so many languages, so many different kinds of music. we used to have sunday afternoon family variety shakespeare, countee cullen, and t.s. eliot, my dad would play congas and do magic.'

Shange's poetry reflects these experiences and is full of vivid visual and oral imagery, the music of Oliver Lake and other jazz artists, the rhythms of doo-wop and blues and, particularly in her later work, cultural idioms from all the regions of the African diaspora. Her books include *For Coloured Girls...*, *Nappy Edges*, *A Daughter's Geography*, *Sassafras, Cypress and Indigo*, and *Betsey Brown*. This interview took place on her visit to Britain in 1987.

Your work, particularly *For Coloured Girls...*, and the collections of poetry *Nappy Edges* and *A Daughter's Geography*, are explorations of the relationship between the personal and the political and yet you state in *'takin' a solo'*, 'Writers are dealing with language/not politics that comes later...'.

The politics is in the art. The decision to write is itself a political act. But as Black women we are sensitive, we have wants and desires, we need to be cared for. Traditionally though, we have been the carers, the ones who are supposed to provide. That's not enough for me because that denies our rights as human beings to also receive love and care and be provided for. My characters want and need those things and there are people who offer them.

There's a paucity and scarcity which characterizes the life of poor people and spills over into our emotional lives. The political lesson in love is that it allows us to see that we each have enough to share, to soothe each other's wounds, but that does not make us weak; our strength comes from the mutual exchange of these things.

Is that way of expressing a politics, through the dynamics of individual relationships and with an emphasis on love and soothing, idiomatic of Black women's cultural expression?

Yes, but we have to be careful of not stereotyping the Black woman and her cultural production. We are individuals within a political or cultural grouping and we must not be inveigled by stereotypes. What I would say is definitive about a Black woman's culture, is that it is a culture defined by us. We assess what is beneficial and what is not and we get rid of the stuff that is not valid.

And what about feminism? Do you think it still is or ever was an adequate term to describe a Black woman's politics?

We cannot stop talking about feminism. We have children, we want equal rights, we want to be safe on the streets at night, and we have a responsibility to take on what is right for girls and women. Women have to act for and on behalf of women — ourselves. Those are all feminist issues but in its purest form it is about freeing people and creating possibilities for the things that seem impossible.

Sometimes it seems as if some of those issues are being hi-jacked. Publishing is an example of that. Could feminist publishers be accused of directing into the mainsteam what was/is radical and threatening, thereby depriving it of its potency? The result is that they 'establish' writers and then only publish those they have 'established'.

Here in America, I think the women's publishers have homed in on Black women writers but I do not see that as a bad thing. I mean, when I first wanted to go public or to 'publish' I used lithograph on cheap, cheap paper. I distributed my work to people I knew, to stores I thought would be sympathetic and would sell it. If you are serious about self-definition and presentation, that's what you have to do. The issue here is that we have to take responsibility for ourselves and if something out there is not working for you, you have to do something about it and that might mean a lotta hard work and determination. But at some point the buck stops, and it stops with us.

Is there a sense, though, that the market does manipulate? Are no Black men writing in America, for example, or are they just not being published?

Men dominated the Harlem renaissance in the 1920s and 1930s, and if there were women we were dancing girls in places like the Cotton Club, OK? No-one felt denigrated. That was all that was available, and the men certainly weren't saying 'Where are the women writers or artists?'

So now, for women, this is our era. We have had ten years of women's writing. It may be unfortunate for them, but in the cycle of things it's our turn now and it bothers me to have to apologise for this burst of women's work.

You seem increasingly in your work to be looking at ways of representation that cross the barriers of various nationalities within the diaspora. In *A Daughter's Geography*, for example, you draw quite heavily on the cultures of the Caribbean and Latin America. Is there a reason for this?

There are personal reasons for my interest in the Caribbean. My foreparents went on the Underground Railway to Canada and some of us came back to the United States and some went to Trinidad. I found descendents of those parents in Trinidad and Tobago and finding them and keeping contact with them has been part of the process of reclaiming my genealogy.

It is also politically correct to be concerned about the sons and daughters of the diaspora, to acknowledge the centrality of the Caribbean in our experience. To deny this is to deny the vitality of Toussaint L'Ouverture, Jean Jacobs Dessalines, Fidel Castro, all those who took part in the slave rebellions. It is important for us to defy the dispersal and divisions of the slave systems and to knock down state boundaries. We should have no respect for all the separations and false distinctions.

Is there a danger of thinking about a homogeneous 'Black' which denies differences?

No, it's not about referring to a reducible whole. As people who are poor we cannot afford to block one another from that kind of sharing. There are strong threads in the Yoruba music of Nigeria and Cuban merenge; there are links between Duke Ellington and Haitian music. All of us need to be closer together to enrich and respect each other.

Is your style of pushing language to the limits to express something of who we are as Black people?

Yes. In one sense we have an objective relationship with the Queen's English or the French of the Académie Française, but our Creole, our Rastafari, are ours; they express who we are and they are appropriations of the languages of the oppressors. We have taken what is useful to express our persona, our vision; it's our way of making that language free us.

It's crucial for all writers of colour who speak colonial languages to change that language to meet our needs. It's important to publish in our own forms. On the other hand, it is important to learn the oppressor's language as a foreign language.

Is using musical rhythms and contexts in your work a part of the process of expanding our linguistic expression?

Part of how we speak is musical. We are not alienated from our bodies, not resistant to respond to music, not inhibited by loud saxophones — our culture is visual, oral. I have to be true to where I come from. Music is in all our interactions, wrapped up in our person, in our children's games. Movement, music, dance, have all got to be worked into the syntax of our language.

What is the medium that for you best expresses those objectives of fusing our forms of creative expression within the spoken language?

I am most comfortable with poetry because it's the most immediate form — you have an idea and just write it down. I always go back to poetry in between writing novels and plays.

What are you working on now?

I am working on four plays and a novel. A musical version of *Betsey Brown*, a play about a Black beatnik and another about the sanctity of language called *Three Views of Mount Fuji*. The novel is called *Lianna: La Lutta Continua*, and is set mainly in the Caribbean and Europe. It's an investigation of the politics of love and art for Third World people. And finally I am doing a play called *Riding the Moon in Texas*, which is about a Black rodeo family where the mother dies, leaving father to bring up two teenage daughters, and how that community adjusts to his changes.

Rodeo? What are our connections with that?

We have always been part of that culture. In terms of my own history, after Reconstruction, part of my family on my mother's side went to the south-west to where people rode horses. I wanted to find out about the part of my family that was Black and rode horses. I got involved in it and I was good at it so I got an agent and I do oil barrel racing — not the bucking bronco type rodeo!

You see, some of our people play 'pan' and some us are riding over them. Reclaiming is not always fun, it's something I have to do. Discovering is sometimes to reveal painfulness, the pain that those same Black people had to work out to create beautiful harmonies. But you can work through that, and that's how you discover the connections in everything we do.

CAROLYN
COOPER

'THAT CUNNY JAMMA OMAN!'

THE POETRY OF LOUISE BENNETT

THE FEMALE SENSIBILITY IN

In the poem 'Jamaica Oman', the Louise Bennett *persona*[1] employs
an earthy metaphorical proverb to expose, with obvious relish, the
jinnalship (resourcefulness) and fortitude of the Jamaican female:

> ... Oman luck deh a dungle,
> Some rooted more dan some,
> But as long as fowl a scratch dungle heap
> Oman luck mus come! (SP, p.23)

In that body of Jamaican folk wisdom transmitted in proverb,
Anansi story, and riddle is the genesis of an indigenous feminist
ideology: the paradigm of a submerged and fated identity that
must be rooted up, covertly and assiduously. The existential
dungle, the repository of the accumulated waste of the society,
becomes in the folk iconography the locus of transformation. It is
the dungle, and the dehumanizing social conditions that allow it,
which is the enemy of woman.[2] Cunning, rather than overt
male/female confrontation is the preferred strategy for
maintaining equanimity.

This proverbial cunning of the Jamaican woman is one
manifestation of the morally ambiguous craftiness of Anansi, the
Akan folk hero transmuted in Jamaican folklore into Brer Nansi,
the archetypal trickster.[3] Folktales of the mighty outwitted by the
clever proliferate throughout the African diaspora: the shared
history of plantation slavery in the Americas consolidates within
the psyche of African peoples in the hemisphere, cultural
continuities, ancestral memories of sabotage and marronage,
systemic resistance to servitude. It is within this broader tradition
of neo-African folk consciousness — the Anansi syndrome — that
Bennett's elaboration of the Jamaican female sensibility can be best
understood.

This thematic/stylistic analysis of Bennett's rendering of the
Jamaican female psychology is organized under two broad subject
headings: 'Eena Yard' and 'Outa Road', to quote a Bennett
persona. I will examine domestic relations: male-female, and
mother-child; and extra-domestic affairs: women and work, and
women and politics.

EENA YARD

It is the positive, more so than the negative manifestations of the triscksterism of Anansi that Bennett affirms in her tribute to the resourcefulness of the Jamaican female in ordering her domestic affairs with the Jamaican male, amicably:

> Jamaica oman cunny, sah!
> Is how dem jinnal so?
> Look how long dem liberated
> An de man dem never know!
>
> Look how long Jamaica oman
> — Modder, sister, wife, sweetheart —
> Outa road an eena yard deh pon
> A dominate her part! (SP, p.21)

In the poem 'Jamaica Oman', the Bennett persona differentiates this tradition of indigenous feminism from 'foreign lan Oman lib', a more recent social movement:

> An long before Oman lib bruck out
> Over foreign lan
> Jamaica female wasa work
> Her liberated plan! (SP, p.22)

The legendary Maroon, Nanny, who 'teck her body/Bounce bullet back pon man', (SP, p.21) remains alive in Jamaican folklore because of her militancy against British soldiers. The allusion to Nanny situates contemporary Jamaican 'oman lib' within a long established heritage of consolidated male/female defence of cultural and political sovereignty.[4]

'Foreign lan Oman lib' is rejected by the Bennett persona because it fails to acknowledge the strategic differences between men and women:

> Jamaica oman know she strong,
> She know she tallawah
> But she no want her pickney-dem
> Fi start call her 'Puppa'.
>
> So de cunny Jamma oman
> Gwan like pants-suit is a style,
> An Jamaica man no know she wear
> De trousiz all de while! (SP, p.22)

This 'tallawah' Jamaican woman knows when to be appropriately 'weak' as the complementary poem 'Tan-Up-Seat' illustrates. The speaker there makes it clear that ritualized codes of decorum ought to govern male-female behaviour, particularly when a tired woman recognizes an able-bodied male seated on a crowded tramcar:

> Me doan sey man kean tired to
> But wen dem want show-off,
> Dem sey ooman is 'weaka sex',
> An ooman frail and sof.
>
> But wen man go pon tram and lef
> Dem mannas a dem yard,
> Dem gwan like ooman strong like man
> An cruff an rough an hard!
>
> An sometime when shame bun dem shirt
> Dem start gwan like dem shy,
> An sidung-man kean look straight eena
> Tan-up ooman y'eye! (JL, p.49)

It is the tenuous compromise that Jamaican women often make in order to live with their men which Bennett treats with such consummate craftsmanship in 'Jamaica Oman'. An excellent example of comic irony is the 'role reversal' by means of which women appear to have appropriated the male role as head of the household, but are indeed simply functioning true to nature:

> Some backa man a push, some side-a
> Man a hole him han,
> Some a lick sense eena man head,
> Some a guide him pon him plan! (SP, p.22)

Further, women will tolerate disparaging labels of powerlessness as long as they retain actual power:

> Neck an neck an foot an foot wid man
> She buckle hole her own;
> While man a call her 'so-so rib'
> Oman a tun backbone! (SP, p.22)

The speaker's disdainful allusion to the biblical narrative of origins, conveys her contempt for a sanctimonious patriarchal prejudice that dehumanizes women in the name of religion.

Bennett's portrayal of the cunny Jamma oman is not a solemn

study of manipulative female politics, or simpering subservience. Good-natured humour, decidedly shading into satire, characterizes her critique. For the poem ends on this ambiguous note:

> Lickle by lickle man start praise her,
> Day by day de praise a grow;
> So him praise her, so it sweet her,
> For she wonder if him know. (SP, p.23)

Two mutually ironic interpretations of this verse suggest that a) even when men concede the benefits of female power they may not be conscious of the jinnalship whereby women only appear to defer to conventional notions of appropriate behaviour, and b) men may indeed suspect the ruses of women, and simply allow them free reign. In this second reading, jinnalship would not be the exclusive perquisite of the female, as the poem 'Racket' illustrates.

The speaker there berates the wiliness of the Jamaican male who resorts to subterfuge to escape emotional and material indebtedness during the season of goodwill to all persons:

> As it come to Chrismus time
> Dem drop de gal-frien 'biff!'
> Becausen dem no waan fi gi
> De gal no Christmus gif! (SP, p.21)

The 'biff' 'gif' rhyme is particularly apposite. The onomatopoeic 'biff' — unlike a 'buff' — is lightweight; the rhyme thus carefully balances the weight of the negligent boyfriend's commitment against the worth of the missing gift. The deliberated drop is a temporary helping down of a burden to be assumed again, at a more convenient season:

> Dem bwoy dah gwan too bad, yaw mah,
> An smaddy haffi crack it!
> Las ear, two weeks from Chrismus Day,
> One po gal jus seh 'feh',
> Her bwoy-frien start mech nize an row
> An get bex an go weh!
> Him meck de nice-nice gal spen Chrismus
> Widout a bwoy-frien,
> An de las week a January
> Him crawl back een again! (SP, p.21)

In an ironic reading of the poem one begins to suspect the speaker of a bit of unconscious malice. The intensity of her righteous indignation on behalf of the victim, as expressed in the opening four lines of the poem, seems somewhat excessive for the offence:

> Tan! Oonoo know is what wrong wid
> De bwoy-dem nowadays?
> Dem is a set a raskill, cho!
> Dem got real dutty ways! (SP, p.20)

By the final three lines, when the speaker is prepared to obliterate the duly-punished-male-turned-duppy, one is sure that the critique of gross male negligence has been inverted. The joke is on the mourner who is bawling louder than the primary victim:

> Ef dat gal was like me
> Next ear him hooda haffi pick
> Quarrel wid him duppy! (SP, p.21)

The ambiguous nature of Jamaican male/female relationships, satirized in several Bennett poems, appears antithetical to the single-minded zealousness of divisive 'foreign lan Oman lib' which has its Jamaican equivalent in the predominantly middle-class women's federation movement established in the 1940s under the patronage of the governor's wife, Lady Huggins.[5] This kind of organized movement is essentially different from the perennial struggles of predominantly working-class women to root out their dungle luck. Bennett's treatment of the movement is equivocal. In the poem 'Bans O' Ooman', for example, one may detect satire, despite the speaker's laudatory intentions. In 'Mass Wedding' and 'Registration' tonal irony is even more readily apparent.

In 'Bans O' Ooman!' the female persona recreates the spontaneous excitement of the launching of the Jamaica Federation of Women designed to bring together women ' high an low, miggle, suspended,/ Every different kine o' class.' (JL, p.41). The comic use of the adjective 'suspended', which expresses the speaker's penchant for malapropism, also appropriately intimates the merely temporary suspension of ordinary class values which appear unimportant in the euphoria of the celebratory moment. Indeed, when the woman who finds herself on the periphery of the gathering in St. George's Hall, attempts to force her way to the centre of the event, she discovers that there is definite resistance to her upward social movement:

> Me was a-dead fe go inside
> But wen me start fe try,

> Ooman queeze me, ooman push me,
> Ooman frown an cut dem y'eye. (JL, p.41)

Undaunted, she resorts to subterfuge, the rear-entry politics of potential sabotage:

> Me tek me time an crawl out back
> me noh meck no alarm,
> But me practice bans o' tactics
> Till me ketch up a platform. (JL, p.41)

In the final two stanzas of the poem the satire becomes more pointed as one suspects a disjuncture of grandiose intention and actual accomplishment:

> Ef yuh ever hear dem program!
> Ef yuh ever hear dem plan!
> Ef yuh ever hear de sinting
> Ooman gwine go do to man!
>
> Federation boun to flourish,
> For dem got bans o' nice plan,
> And now dem got de heart an soul
> Of true Jamaica ooman. (JL, p.41)

The optimistic certainty of the last two lines seems premature.

One of the many plans of the Federation of Women, to ensure that women enter into properly legal relationships with men, is the subject of 'Mass Wedding'. Rex Nettleford's gloss on the poem is succinct:

> The late Mary Morris Knibb of Kingston was a
> pioneer in the fight against bachelor fatherhood (taken
> up again in 1965 notably by the Soroptomist Club of
> Jamaica led by Edith Clarke, the anthropologist and
> social worker). One solution offered by Mrs. Knibb
> was the mass wedding, organised at little expense to
> the marrying parties, many of whom might have been
> living in common-law relationships for years. (JL, p.30)

The speaker who is hastily trying to secure 'one boonoonoonos man' (JL, p.30), whom she has just met, seems on the surface to advocate the idea of the mass wedding. But when one notes the imagery of coercion she employs, one concludes that even she is aware that the frantic speed of the enterprise may be matched by the unwilling bridegroom's prowess at escape:

> Dat lady Mrs. Married Knibbs,
> She is a real Godsen'
> For every man now mus tun husban,
> Dem kean be noh mo' bwoy frien'.
>
> Ah she meck nine-toe Berty
> Wed kaas eye Sue you know?
> An she force awn Mary Fowl-head
> Pon Miss Biddy cousin Joe.
>
> So fine a good man dat yuh hooda
> Like fe stan up beside,
> Den see Miss Knibbs an yuh will be
> Mongs de nex mass wedden brides. (JL, p.31)

The speaker's vacillation between the redundant 'Mrs. Married Knibbs' and the contextually deficient 'Miss Knibbs' seems unintentional and thus reinforces the poem's irony that ultimately the legal distinction is functionally unimportant.

The class values of the Mary Morris Knibbses, as evidenced in 'Mass Wedding', go against the grain of a long established Jamaican folk conviction that one ought not to marry, unless one can do it in style; they also violate the well-documentated Jamaican superstition that the legal marriage ceremony can itself undermine the vulnerable balance of extra-legal male/female arrangements.

In the poem 'Registration', Bennett satirizes yet another campaign of the well-intentioned Federation to coerce the working-class Jamaican male into conformity to the demands of middle-class propriety: the drive to register all fathers. The Bennett persona gleefully advocates the plan, citing three Jamaican proverbs to confirm the unequivocal authority of the proposed law:

> Every sore foot got him blue-stone,
> Every tief got him las' deal,
> Noh care how smaddy dah-gwan bad
> Sinting deh fe spokes him wheel. (JL, p.42)

Despite the apparent commonality of folk and middle-class values, what the speaker proceeds to do, apparently unwittingly, is to draw satirical attention to the social distance between the respectable middle-class women of the federation, who have decent responsible husbands, and the unfortunate, husbandless, working-class women whom the new legislation will seek to elevate.

Upstanding middle-class women, with thom the speaker empathizes, can afford to antagonize delinquent males because their own houses are in order:

> Guess how de man dem gwine bex wid
> De ooman Federation
> Me glad mose o' de lady dem
> Married an got dem good husban.
>
> For like how somuch bwoy gwan weh
> And Jamaica short o'man,
> Dem ooman wat pass de law gwine have
> De dickans fe hook one! (JL, p.42)

In a delightfully ambiguous line the speaker allows that unmarried middle-class women might themselves have a hard time hooking a man of their own in this period of social turbulence.

Long-chin James, who understandably objects to the legislation is cursed by the woman: 'go weh, man a debil!' (JL, p.42). But his quick repartee is: 'dat is not no cuss, /For ooman a debil-mumma/So we kean tell which is wus'. (JL, p.42). James is indeed perceptive. For what is evident from Bennett's wide-ranging portrayal of male-female relationships is that working-class men and women have much more in common than do middle-class and working-class women.

But there is also evidence in Bennett's poetry of the internalization of the values of middle-class domestic order by working-class women who believe that the state of wife, however transitory, is intrinsically superior to that of 'baby-mother' or girlfriend. In the words of one woman, who praises the war for its side benefits:

> Soh me wi help de war, an ef
> De war shoulda help me
> Fe get married, me husban can
> Gwan fight fe him country.
>
> An ef my husban even dead,
> Me don't seh me won't cry,
> But de joy dat ah was married
> Wi meck me satisfy. (JL, pp.100-101)

Similarly, the speaker in the poem 'Praises' expresses great joy that with the establishment of the Sandy Gully American base, and the attendant employment opportunities it offers, her status changes:

> Look how me an Joe did live bad.
> But praise to Sandy Gully!
> As him get de fus week pay him do
> So baps — married to me.
>
> An now him meck love sweeter mah
> Him style me now as 'Honey'
> Hear him — 'Ah dat way bout yuh Hons
> Ah hopes yuh goes fo' me.' (JL, pp.98-99)

There is the inevitable irony that the 'ten-poun baby pram' (JL, p.99), bought in the first flush of prosperity, has to be converted into a fish cart when Joe is laid off and must revert to his usual occupation. Even though he is later recruited for the migrant labour scheme to the US, his wife's anticipation — 'Wat a way we dah-go bruck sport/Wen we ketch a U.S.A.' (JL, p.99) must be tempered by the advice of yet another Bennett persona:

> Betta yuh tan home fight yuh life
> Than go a-sea go lose i.
>
> De same sinting wey sweet man mout
> Wi meck him lose him head,
> Me read eena newspapa sey
> Two farm-man meet dem dead! (JL, p.94)

But the new wife's optimism is unshakeable:

> Me still love me Jamaica mam,
> But like a tenkful wife
> He haffa praise American
> Fe put me eena life. (JL, p.99)

It is this aspiration that their families be 'put eena life' which governs the child-rearing practices of Bennett's vocal women. The proverbial ring of James's uncomplimentary observation that 'ooman a debil-mumma' reinforces the fact that women — married or not — are largely responsible for the socialization of children in Jamaica. Though there are very few Bennett poems that deal specifically with mother/child relations, there is a group, the theme of which is the aggressive ambition of mothers that their children, particularly their sons, acquire education, the entrée to middle-class culture. Fluency in the English language is an important rite of passage, which must be accomplished whether by formal schooling or as a consequence of living 'in foreign' or 'in town'.

The male persona in the poem 'Writing Home' expresses retrospective gratitude to his mother for her attention to his education: 'Ah did soh glad yuh did force me fe teck de zamination/Far now, ah can demands a job fe suit me edication'. (JL, p.117) There is pathos in the disparity between the young man's expectations and what he appears equipped to do. Indeed, the muted humour in the poem derives from the fact that though unemployed, he has joined a trade union and is 'on strike':

> I is not workin now but ah
> Jine in a labour set
> An ah 'ope to keep awn strikin
> Tell some esteem jab ah get. (JL, p.116)

A satirical portrait of an indulgent, self-congratulatory mother is given in the poem 'New Scholar'. The mother's misguided concern for her son's well-being is apparent in her words of advice to the boy's teacher, on his first day in school:

> No treat him rough, yaw, Teacher;
> Him is a sickly chile:
> As yuh touch him hard him meck nize —
> Some people seh him pwile.
>
> Teck time wid him, yaw, Teacher —
> If him rude an start fi rave
> Dis beat anodder bwoy, an him
> Wi frighten an behave.
>
> For nuff time when him rude a yard
> an woan hear me at all
> Ah just beat de bed-poas hard, mah,
> An yuh waa fi hear Jack bawl! (SP, pp.8-9)

A similarly satirical poem is 'Uriah Preach', which holds up to comic scrutiny the self-incriminatory pride of misguided maternalism. Rhonda Cobham-Sander's gloss on the poem is accurate: 'Bennett recounts the vicarious pleasure taken by a Jamaican mother in the accomplishments of her children and especially in her son's ability to use his occasional ascent to the pulpit to lambast the family's enemies':[6]

Fi-me famby is no peaw-peaw,
Me daughter Sue dah teach;
An when rain fall or parson sick
Me son Uriah preach.

. . .

Him climb up pon de pulpit, him
Lean over an look dung,
Him look pon all we enemy
An lash dem wid him tongue.

. . .

Him tell dem off, dem know is dem,
Dem heart full to de brim;
But as Uriah eena pulpit
Dem cyaan back-answer him. (SP, pp.60-61)

The general tenor of the mother/child relations described in
Bennett's poetry, is aphoristically expressed by the perceptive
speaker in 'Bear Up': 'Noh mock mawga cow, him a bull muma.'
(JL, p.53)

OUTA ROAD

The majority of Bennett's women are engaged in traditionally
female, working-class occupations: domestic labour and higglering.
Both are low-paid, higglering far less so in recent times, with the
rise of the internationally travelled female merchant class. The
supply of prospective domestic labourers far exceeds demand, and
employer/employee relations often reflect the market-value of the
domestic servant. But a definite shift in the balance of power
occurs when domestic servants come to recognize that their labour
is essential to the smooth functioning of the middle-class
household.

The female servant in the poem 'Seeking a Job', for example,
makes it clear that domestic labour is not her preferred avocation.
She will only descend to certain quite specific tasks, stated in her
job description:

Ah cook an wash, but sake o' me nails
Ah doan clean floor again
But a can get a gal fe do
Dat fe yuh now-an-den. (JL, p.192)

Furthermore, if antagonized, she will simply withdraw her

services:

> ... the las' ooman ah work wid
> Didn' have no fault to fine.
>
> Doah wen she start tek liberty wid me
> Ah lif up and walk out,
> For as ole-time people sey 'yuh play
> Wid dawg dem lick yuh mout'.
>
> Ah hooden stan har facetiness,
> Far we wasn' company, (JL, p.191)

A humorous example of class antagonism resolved by the conjuring up of a fictitous male relative occurs in the poem 'Me Bredda'. The speaker, a vociferous domestic servant, cows a middle-class women into submission in a dispute arising from the servant's tardiness in arriving for work — the very first day.

The housewife attempts to fire the woman on the spot, but is bombarded by a spate of abusive rhetoric:

> Oono call me bredda fi me!
> Beg yuh tell him come yah quick!
> Tell him bring him pelt-yuh-kin cow-cod
> An bus-yuh-open stick!
>
> Me naw meck no joke wid you, mah!
> Quick an brisk an pay me off,
> Or ah call me bredda in yah
> Meck him beat you till yuh sof! (SP, p.18)

One is seduced into admiring the daring subterfuge of the outrageous servant:

> Yuh would like fi know me bredda?
> Me cyaan help you eena dat.
> Me hooda like know him meself,
> For is me one me parents got! (SP, p.19)

Yet one senses the moral impropriety of her victory; this trickster sabotages the very economic system she pretends to enter, employing Anansi tactics to accomplish pragmatic goals. She is a remarkable contrast to the uncharacteristically submissive domestic servant in 'My Dream', who does not openly rebel against her truly exploitative cousin/employer. She displaces her aggression on the clothes that she is forced to launder:

> Ah swear ah mus fine a way
> Fi wounded cousin Rose,
> An ah tink it hooda hut her
> If ah start maltreat de clothes. (SP, p.112)

She consoles herself with the proverbial certainty that moral rightness will inevitably be restored:

> Dog a sweat but long hair hide i,
> Mout a laugh, but heart a leap!
> Everything wha shine no gole piece. (SP, p.113)

This sublimatory use of proverbs in a potentially explosive context of class antagonism is an excellent example of linguistic subterfuge, indirection as a strategy to preserve psychic wholeness. These apparently divergent responses to domestic labour/economic exploitation — overt and covert sabotage — are essentially manifestations of the Anansi syndrome.

The Anansi mentality is also evident in the behaviour of the higglers who speak in 'South Parade Peddler' and 'Candy-Seller'. Their dramatic monologues counterpoint open cajoling of potential customers with sotto voce invective:

> ... Come here nice white man
> Don't pass me by soh sah!
> See me beggin by de roadside
> Come buy a nice wangla.
> Wen w'ite people go fe ugly
> Massa dem ugly sah.
> Koo 'ow dat deh man face heng dung
> Lacka wen jackass feel bad. (JL, p.29)

Another higgler who eloquently affirms the importance of her trade for the well-being of her family, is a single parent, whose market basket is causing offence to fellow passengers on a bus:

> Yuh can cuss me, yuh can beat me,
> Yuh can call me all de 'it';
> Do anyting yuh want wid me
> But lef de basket.
>
> For dis basket is me all-in-all,
> Me shillin, pence and poun;

> It is me husban an me frien,
> Me jewel an me crown.
>
> Me ha six pickney — an sence me
> Stop teck dem Pa to court
> Dis dutty, brucksy basket yah
> Is dem ongle support. (SP, p.92)

Attempts by women to support themselves in non-traditional occupations is the theme of 'Footworks'. The speaker lauds the first female recruit into the Jamaica Constabulary Force:

> We haffe do we bes, tun eas,
> Tun wes, tun right about
> We kean afford fe meck de man
> Police dem beat we out. (JL, p.70)

The choice of 'afford' appropriately emphasizes the increased wages that women will earn in a traditionally male occupation and which they dare not relinquish simply because they cannot manage the heavy police boots:

> Lif up yah foot gal, practise up
> Fe tun ooman police.
> Oonoo mus bring two clothes-iron
> Fe tie pon oono foot.
> So we can practise how fe wear
> De heavy police boot. (JL, p.70)

The clothes iron selected to assist women in their new field of work is a comic reminder of the domestic labour force from which they have now graduated. The final verse of the poem humorously suggests that there is no essential difference in the capacities of the male and female recruits:

> Go outa jail an watch good wha de
> Man-police dem do
> Yuh mighta fine nuff o' dem wid
> De same trouble as yuh. (JL, p.71)

Women's engagement in the political process is similarly motivated by the desire to share with men the benefits of increased economic opportunities. Pragmatism characterizes the attitudes of Bennett's women to politics. In an interesting pair of poems, 'New Govanah' and 'Mrs. Govanah', it is evident that affairs of state are acknowledged as important only to the degree that they guarantee perceptible material benefits. Mervyn Morris's gloss on 'New Govanah' is lucid.

> The poem ridicules the fuss made over the arrival of a new governor (Sir John Huggins) in 1943. People, it says, are behaving as though the Governor were really valuable and worth worrying about, like steak, or white rice, or condensed milk — commodities scarce during the war... Unlike those people who have dressed up, the speaker is not in awe of the Governor, and she wonders whether (in accordance with a common Jamaican decency) he has brought any message or parcel from her boyfriend Joe... There are courteous ironies within the final stanza. The Governor is implied to be irrelevant and out of key with ordinary needs and values: he has brought nothing for her, neither material things nor values. (SP, pp.130-131)

Similarly, in 'Mrs. Govanah', the speaker mistakes the commotion caused by the ritual passage of the Governor's wife through Nathan's department store, as being precipitated by the distribution of 'free ile or green banana' (JL, p.126). Images of oral gratification are frequently used by these women in cynical reference to organized politics. In the poem 'Rightful Way' the persona gives advice on the proper way to vote, noting that politicians, the main beneficiaries of adult suffrage, would be deprived of nourishment if the system were sabotaged:

> Yuh know how de genkleman dem
> Weh dah-gi speech all bout
> Hooda bex fe know yuh help fe teck
> De pap out o' dem mout. (JL, p.135)

Female politicians are not exempt from ridicule. The speaker in the poem 'Which One' questions the competence of all the candidates up for election, including the female representative:

> Pose we try a ooman an she
> Teck it put eena her lap
> An go get up absent-minded
> Meck we constitution drop! (JL, p.136)

A more sympathetic, though equally problematic image of a female politician is given in 'Big Tings', which documents the in-fighting between two high-powered male politicians, the Hon. Sir Alexander Bustamante, and the Rev. E.E. McLaughlin:[7]

> De po' woman councillor nevah sey a ting,
> She stay quiet like lamb,
> She watch all de man dem antics
> An shet up her mout 'pam'.
>
> Me noh blame de po' ooman mah,
> Becausen is she one,
> And de po' ting mus feel frighten
> Mongs dem blood-t'irsty man. (JL, p.151)

The female politician's silence is as eloquently damning as the verbosity of the American consultant in 'Distinguish Merican', imported to assist in launching the 'Be Jamaican, Buy Jamaican' campaign.

> But wen speakas leggo speech
> An Amy ask wha dat,
> Hear Me: 'Wuds, wuds, dem deh is wuds,
> Is pure wuds dem a-chat.'
>
> Hear Amy: 'Wuds? Wha kine o' wuds?'
> Me sey: 'Gran wuds, me dear,
> Wuds can' express de wuds,
> Dat man mout full o' wuds yuh hear!' (JL, p.158)

The empowerment of the Jamaican woman, as portrayed in Louise Bennett's substantial poetry, is not accomplished by mere dependence on the flatulent rhetoric of politicians — though participation in the political process is essential for all:

> Everybody got a vote, an
> Every vote gwine swell de score;
> Missa Issa, Missa Hanna,
> An de man wat sweep de store. (JL, p.129)

What is of equal consequence is that meta-political conviction of intrinsic worth, validated by the proverbial wisdom of the folk, that 'ooman day wi come at las'. (JL, p.93) Out of the compost heap of history the cunny Jamma oman, in her maternal role of mother hen, must root up for herself the prophetic certainty that 'oman luck mus come!' (SP, p.23).

NOTES

1. For two accounts of Bennett's use of persona see Mervyn Morris's Introduction to Louise Bennett's *Selected Poems* pp. xvii-viii and Lloyd Brown's *West Indian Poetry*, Boston, Twayne, 1978, p.116.
2. See, for example the poignant description of the dungle in chapter 1 of Orlando Patterson's *The Children of Sisyphus*, London, New Authors Ltd., 1964.
3. See, Laura Tanna 'Anansi – Jamaica's Trickster Hero', *Jamaica Journal*, 16, 2, May 1983.
4. See, for example, Lucille Mathurin's *The Rebel Woman in the British West Indies During Slavery*, Institute of Jamaica, 1975, pp. 34-37.
5. For an autobiographical account of her career in Jamaica, see Molly Huggins, *Too Much To Tell*, London, Heinemann, 1967.
6. Rhonda Cobham-Sander, 'The Creative Writer and West Indian Society: Jamaica 1900-50', Diss. U. of St. Andrews, 1981; Ann Arbor, UMI, 1984, p.241.
7. For an abbreviated description of the affair, see Rex Nettleford's gloss on the poem, JL, p.150.

REFERENCES

Bennett, Louise, *Jamaica Labrish*, Rex Nettleford (ed.), Kingston, Sangster's, 1966 (references cited parenthetically in text indicated by **JL**. The orthography of this collection differs from that of the later, more readable **SP**).
Selected Poems, Mervyn Morris, (ed.), Kingston, Sangster's, 1982, (references cited parenthetically in text indicated by **SP**).

MERLE COLLINS

TWO WRITERS FROM THE CARIBBEAN

JOAN RILEY AND JACOB ROSS

In *The West Indian Novel and its Background,* literary critic
Kenneth Ramchand states that since 1950 most West Indian
novels have been published in the English capital. At least 162
works of prose fiction have been produced by a total of 56 writers
between 1903 and 1967. Since then, many significant works have
been added to the list by writers of Caribbean parentage who have
either been born in Britain or spent most of their early life here,
resulting in new and different explorations of concerns other than
those reflected in the works of say, Claude McKay, George
Lamming or Merle Hodge, whose works focused on geographical
and socio-cultural realitites in the Caribbean. Samuel Selvon's
novel, *The Lonely Londoners,* digresses only slightly in that it
examines the experiences of Caribbean newcomers to British
society.

This essay focuses on the works of two young writers — Jacob
Ross's *Song for Simone* and Joan Riley's *Waiting in the Twilight*
— in order to point out the differences in emphases of the
'Caribbean' writer born or growing up in Britain and a writer such
as Ross who came to Britain at a much later stage, conforming to
a trend of Caribbean 'exile' writing since the 1950s.

Jacob Ross is one of the writers who came to prominence in
the wave of social and political upheavals which transformed
Grenadian society in the 1970s. Better known in Grenada for his
poetry, *Song for Simone,* a collection of thirteen short stories, is
his first work of prose fiction and the first to be produced by a
writer from Grenada.

Song for Simone details experiences of life within Grenadian,
and in a broader sense, Caribbean society. The title story is an
exploration of the life of a girl, Simone, her mother, Nita, and Mr.
James, Nita's lover. The three move and grow independently of
each other. Yet each is profoundly influenced by the other's
exploration of the surrounding social reality.

The story begins with the sound of Beethoven's *Minuet in G*
wafting down from the big white house on the hill to disturb
Simone's early-morning sleep. The music is pervasive. It
preoccupies the girl's adolescent mind. To her, 'something was
missing in that music', to the extent that she feels compelled to
search for the missing element. The music introduces the central
symbolic theme of the story: that of search, discovery and cultural
affirmation. Simone's quest is assisted by Mr. James, a player of

steelpan music. Both the instrument and the kind of music that Mr. James is associated with are significant because they represent the opposite end of the social-cultural spectrum with which Beethoven's *Minuet in G* is normally associated. The first exchange between the young woman and Mr. James sets the stage for questioning the perceived relationship and status of steelpan. Their conversation reflects their own search for cultural identity and echoes the domination of popular traditions by European cultures. Mr. James asks:

> 'You call steelpan music, music?'
> Simone frowned, considering, 'Well... erm — Why not?'
> 'No-no-no! I want a straight answer. Yes or no?'
> He placed the rest of his breakfast on the table and rested both elbows on the rough surface. The fingers of each hand were clasped together in a curiously comic, yet dignified posture.
> 'Yes,' the girl answered, somewhat irritably. 'Is music, oui.'
> 'Then,' the man said, 'I'z boss musician.'

From this hesitant acceptance of steelpan music as 'music', the young woman moves to a state of obsessive involvement with it. An accomplished player now, she is equipped for the final, decisive struggle between Beethoven's *Minuet in G* and all that it represents to her, played on the piano and trumpet in the big house on the hill where her mother works as a servant, and the pulsing music of the steelpan which she is preparing to play on the streets on carnival day. The story climaxes when, in defiance of her mother, Simone leads the players of the band in a devastating calypso rendition of Beethoven's *Minuet*. Hers is a challenge rooted in the need to define and assert her own social and cultural reality. The writer's language becomes the language of assault:

> The drums went first. In rapid waves the tenor pans reacted. Then the rest of the band. Simone picked up the rhythm with a vengeance. The crowd moved forwards, dancing and ad-libbing to the fierce calypso rhythm. She pounded the music out in hot flushes of anger. Catching her spirit, the players sent their notes riding high above the houses and the night. The church clock struck the half-hour and that too became music. The girl was grimacing, her eyes closed. There were the tenors screaming, majestically; the enraged

congas, stammering; the scraper, teasing; the steel-rim clamouring; and her bass drums belching thunder.

Simone has discovered that with her own music she can not only challenge but also reshape, give relevance and new meaning to an alien reality which until then had assaulted her young mind. The band shares in this discovery. Her triumph is the band's triumph in the same way that her awakening points to the awakening of an entire society's consciousness of its cultural worth and potency.

Jacob Ross explores the idea of having to destroy in order to build; of having to fulfil that other self which can vaguely sense something missing; of gaining the resolve to discover what is missing and using that as the basis to create.

In a sense, the central theme of *Song for Simone* belongs to the entire collection. In 'A Game of Marbles', a little boy is forced by circumstances to find meat for an ailing grandmother. Soldiers patrol the road in jeeps, breaking up the game of marbles the children play in the road. Food is scarce. There comes occasionally the sound of gunshots. The boy goes out into the night to find meat, armed with a slingshot and some steel marbles. The quest and its pointedly triumphal end reveal to the youth some hitherto unacknowledged dimensions within himself. In 'The Gun', an ex-policeman who had probably used his gun to kill people during the Big Riot, takes his daughter to hunt monkeys in the mountains. The child wonders about the rumours of his brutality. The moment of truth comes when he fires on a troupe of monkeys and becomes transfixed by the sight of a mother holding her young monkey up before him, 'its gaze direct, its eyes imploring'. 'Cold Hole' is a story of self-discovery. Ian responds to a challenge to go to Cold Hole, the place where the river met the sea and children's souls were sold. He goes alone and the experience makes him less afraid and stronger.

Though not overtly stated, 'Oleander Road' carries echoes of the US invasion of Grenada. A tired soldier returns after facing 'the terror of an incoming army who'd claimed they came to save'. Damon is tired, not only from his confrontation with the soldiers but also because of the emotional trauma resulting from a sense of betrayal 'by his own'. He is walking home, wounded. The long unending road he marches on is symbolic, representing more the need to go on than the certainty of getting anywhere. If he stops the physical movement, Damon fears, he might never find the will to start again. Perhaps Ross is speaking metaphorically of a deeper need to continue believing in the possibility of attaining the dignity and pride destroyed at the period of the US invasion of Grenada.

'Oleander Road' occasionally contains a style of writing not utilised in the other stories. Damon, the central character, is a soldier and a poet. The unfolding of his thoughts provides us with some intriguing flashes of poetic expression as Damon surrenders himself to the road, an unfinished poem turning in his head, and the reader is left with echoes of the unfinished poem that is the struggle of the Grenadian people for national pride.

Always it is the voice of the peasantry and the working class of his society to which the writer introduces his readers. In 'The Room Inside', a group of women come together to deliver a child themselves because the doctor has refused to attend the mother, his wife reminding him that they only have enough petrol to take them to a friend's wedding the following day. Both are representatives of a class which seems untouched by the deprivation existing among the working class.

'The Return' takes the form and structure of a folk tale. Through the voice of an old man, Uncle Dan, is described the relationship between a brother and sister. This relationship can be falsely perceived as incestuous because of the uncanny closeness of the two characters. In fact, the girl and her brother are one and the same person 'only she wuz de woman part o he; or her, the man part o she'. The themes of love and search and above all alienation are raised in the context of the girl's attraction to a white stranger living on a small island not far from the mainland. Her relationship with the stranger leads to an undisclosed situation which may have been her pregnancy. The stranger leaves, and both Bella's and her brother's dreams are destroyed. They eventually find a solution by plunging naked into the sea and swimming out in search of their dreams. We are left sharing the conviction of Uncle Dan that they are not dead but swimming still. For the past fifteen years, Uncle Dan has been going to the little hill over the sea awaiting their return, because, as he explains,

> Is not a long time if you check how big de world is... You see, de world is round like a orange... Dat mean, if you start swimmin from here an continue right on widdout stoppin you must come back to de same place after a time... A man mus believe, you know, else it don make no sense livin.

It is because of this belief that the two young people plunge, significantly naked as at birth, into the sea to begin the long swim back to their origins. The writer reveals an almost self-conscious intent to touch the inner consciousness of his women characters.

They are powerful in the collection, not merely a token presence, but often determining the direction of events and therefore the character of the stories. This is true for Bella in 'The Return', for all the women in 'The Room Inside', for Sis in 'The Canebreakers' and for Simone in 'Song for Simone', despite Mr. James's occasional intervention as Simone's 'guide'. There is an exploration of the fact that, as a girl, Simone faces resistance to her joining the male band of steel players. Her membership not only introduces an awareness of a rebellion against this attitude but also provides answers to her questing mind.

It is perhaps the debates of the eighties, the ongoing struggles of women and Jacob Ross's own experiences not only of growing up within the region but also as part of a revolutionary movement within Grenada, which make him conscious of the need for male writers to address and explore these issues.

It is interesting to consider *Song for Simone,* the work of a writer shaped by his experiences of a geographically Caribbean reality, alongside that of another Caribbean author moulded, at least partially, by experiences of life in England.

Joan Riley is concerned with the condition of women within personal relationships and the impact of the wider society on their lives. Her second novel, *Waiting in the Twilight* employs the cinematic technique of flashbacks to trace the life of Adella, born and bred in Jamaica and crippled in her latter years in England by a stroke brought on by the pressures of home, family, an uncaring male partner and a demanding job.

Perhaps the most powerfully written section of *Waiting in the Twilight* is when Adella, who has spent her life believing in Stanton, expecting his return and ignoring all evidence and opinions to the contrary, lies on her deathbed and conjures the vision of a Stanton reformed and repentant.

> He had not changed at all; he was still the same and he was smiling the same smile she had always loved. 'A did say you would come back,' she said triumphantly. 'A did say you wasn't goodfanuting.' ... Stanton was here now and nothing mattered. She knew she was dying, that was why he was at her bedside, smiling encouragingly at her.

Her mind has gathered all of the family to her bedside: Mada Beck, Granny Dee, Aunt Ivy, Aunt May and even Jini who she could swear somebody had written and said was shot dead somewhere in town — all of them were smiling. The children were there also 'all the children smiling at her ... All dat respect, she murmured to herself, and this time her eyes smiled as they closed.'

The world has failed Adella. But she dies happy, recreating in her mind a fantasy that ignores the neglect that has killed her. Adella has had nothing but disrespect in the end, from Stanton and from society. The doctor has failed to reach her deathbed. The love and care from her daughters are the redeeming factors which enable Adella to perceive love where there was only neglect.

The conclusion of the novel is intriguing in that Adella's fantasising leaves us sad, but not hopeless. This might be because neither Carol nor Audrey, her daughters, are fooled. Each is, at least marginally, more equipped than their mother to deal with the difficulties thrown at them by society.

Joan Riley's first novel, *The Unbelonging,* also concludes powerfully. Hyacinth returns from England and makes a trip up the hill in a taxi to visit her grand-aunt. But whereas the power of that final scene in *The Unbelonging* is diluted by the negativity of Hyacinth's reaction to the poverty and drabness with which she is confronted, the anger and sadness we feel as Adella dies in *Waiting in the Twilight* is paradoxically more positive. Her experience must, we feel, have some influence on the lives and attitudes of her two daughters.

Significantly, in *The Unbelonging,* the immigrant returns to the Caribbean which she had romanticised. When confronted by the reality, she cannot cope with it. In *Waiting in the Twilight,* the immigrant refuses to return and dies an obscure death, neglected by the doctors in the English hospital, forgotten by some of her children. The children who are with Adella protest against the hospital's neglect of their dying mother. Audrey cannot accept that they can 'just leave her here all day, and they haven't given her some things to make her feel better.' Although it is a painful end, the girls' recognition of the injustice of the institution is a basis for their struggle against such injustice.

Both novels focus on issues with which the Caribbean community in Britain continues to be concerned, and it is perhaps because of the debates surrounding these issues that Joan Riley's powerful, agonising conclusions are successful. While the negativity expressed at the end of *The Unbelonging* is unpleasant, it does reflect what must be the feeling of any person of Caribbean parentage born or bred in Britain, who has been given a 'touristic' view of the Caribbean and is unaware of the historical effects of imperialism, colonialism and neo-colonialism. *The Unbelonging* should therefore lead us to focus on the historical and socio-political content of the education of young Black people in Britain. Just as an elitist education system can alienate young people from their working class origins, so existence in British society which claims economic and cultural superiority to the so-called developing world can create a Caribbean community which exists in deprived conditions yet feels superior towards the Caribbean communities at home. The very title of the novel draws attention to this issue. Significantly, in *Waiting in the Twilight*, the immigrant who refuses to return seems in the final analysis to be no happier in British society. In a society which discriminates both against her blackness and her disability, Adella's one source of hope is her children.

The novel goes some way towards exploding the myth of a life of care and wealth in Britain, a myth prevalent in the Caribbean because of glowing reports from immigrants anxious not to reveal that life in the host country is not a bed of thornless roses. For Adella, people at home cannot be allowed to discover that her house, which is a mark of her success, is derelict.

The men in the novel, Beresford in Jamaica, Stanton, Mr. Thomas, have little to redeem them. Yet one can see their contemptible meanness and crude neglect as the products of a society which demands little of them. Stanton, we learn, did love Adella at first, during the early days in Jamaica, taking on the responsibility of caring for the children she had before meeting him. His character progressively declines as he finds himself increasingly lacking the means to cater for his tastes and vanities. He becomes more and more dependent on and abusive of the more creative, dedicated and hardworking women.

Why are the men portrayed by Riley in *Waiting in the Twilight* and *The Unbelonging* so abusive and uncaring? Since they do reflect some aspect of the reality of the Black man's attitude, is this a function of race, or class, or both, since capitalism and its vehicle, colonialism, has made of Black people a collective underclass? Whether Riley intended it or not, we cannot but wonder how much a part is played by wealth and comfort in the maintenance of decency.

Considering Joan Riley's novel alongside Jacob Ross's collection of short stories, one is left with the feeling that, whereas the Africans have after three centuries and more fashioned a culture and a home away from home in the Caribbean, the land to which they followed their captors in search of the wealth which the latter flaunted, is still a hostile one.

The works of both writers focus attention on the use of Caribbean languages in literature. Attitudes to the languages of the region have evolved from the days when Creole (Caribbean nation languages) was employed for humorous effect and regarded as the uncoordinated mouthings of lesser beings. Ramchand quotes the

English historian, Edward Lange (1774) as saying: 'The Negroes seem very fond of reduplication to express a greater or less quantity of anything; as walky-walky, talky-talky, washy-washy, happy-happy... In their conversation they confound all the moods, tenses, cases and conjunctions without mercy.'

Today, the Caribbean has its own language specialists examining the origins and development of Caribbean languages. In *Language and Liberation* (Karia Press 1986), Hubert Devonish analyses the dimensions of the political struggle for recognition of a language rooted in the African thrust for survival in a region dominated by European languages and cultural norms. In *Caribbean and African Languages* (Karia Press 1985), Morgan Dalphinis explores the cultural aspects of this political and historical experience.

The two works of fiction discussed here provide, through the use of language, important indications of the cultural and linguistic differences between British and Caribbean/Grenadian society. Adella's use of the Jamaican Creole situates her in terms of economic status and educational and social attainment. Her daughters, born in England, consider their mother's language 'bad English', and are more consistent in their use of standard English. In *Song for Simone*, the author acknowledges that regardless of social status or aspirations, the nation language is spoken in varying degrees by everyone. Mr. Celestine, the teacher in *The Understanding*, talks to his class in English, but when with the student Skinner, shifts comfortably back to Grenadian: 'Next year, I will be teaching scholarship class... when I finish, you-all will be as sharp as cutlass on grindin stone.'

The two books reflect the continuing influence of Caribbean experiences on Black writing in Britain and are an important source of the linguistic innovations that are an exciting characteristic of the growing body of Black literature in Britain. Both writers explore their societies intimately, presenting us with a wealth of issues and challenges that are transforming the agendas of writers in both societies.

BLACK PHOTOGRAPHY

DAVID A. BAILEY

IDENTITY AND SUBJECTIVITY

This article explores Black photography, raising questions about subjectivity and identity, using my own work as an example. The Britain of the eighties has seen a significant development of Black photographic practices, with more Black people entering photographic colleges and Black intellectuals beginning to tangle and untangle debates around Black representation within post-modernist theories. Within the Black communities there are critical readings of the popularised photographic image for it is these so-called 'naturalistic' or 'realistic' images that reinforce exotic and animalistic stereotypes of Black peoples. The activities of Black cultural practitioners signify important interventions within the sacred frame.

Critically analysing the complex processes within the acts of taking and looking at photographic images has always fascinated Black cultural practitioners. By trying to decode, articulate and re-articulate the dominant meanings within the image, it has often been stressed that there is not one meaning to a photograph but several. These are constantly being articulated and re-articulated within different historic and spatial situations.

The histories/herstories of representations of the Black communities in British society are those of struggle over meanings, some dominant over others. Exhibitions such as *The Black Triangle; Testimonies: Three Black Women Photographers; Darshan: An Exhibition of Ten Asian Photographers; Aurat Shakti; Black Edge* and *Reflections of the Black Experience,* highlight a new era in Black photographic practices in the struggle for visibility within the photography sector and positive image-making within British culture of the eighties. This article attempts to go beyond the debate on visibility and explore some of the issues around representations.

Photographic history has been dominated by the content and textual quality of the visual image, with little status given to the arena of representation. However this arena is crucial because it is within the context of identity and subjectivity that we can begin to ask questions about the role of photography in creating Black images and stereotypes.

Since its invention, photography has played a major role in articulating our identities and subjectivities. We only have to look at our passports, bus passes and membership cards to understand how important it is in social systems of identity. Without it it

44

could be difficult to exist legally and socially, because we could not prove our existence or identity to people outside the arena of family and friends.

The actual photographic process, the taking of the image, is the terrain on which photography makes statements about our identities and subjectivities. The idea that photography captures the 'real' is a myth. Unlike the sensitivity of the human eye, the camera fixes an image or appearance, removes it from the context of other images, and preserves it. The image is taken out of its social, historical and spatial context and reproduced within others.

For example, a photograph of the British Museum is only a mere image of the British Museum. The reality of the British Museum is in its history, structure, the forces and relations of its production, its political and financial power. It is the combination of these factors which constructs different universes of meanings. The diversity of practices, the production process, the consumption of images and the historical situations within which they happen, make photography an important arena of ideological struggle. It is a prime site where ideas and ideological practices are articulated and transformed within spatial and historical contexts. Its history reflects this.

45

In the nineteenth century, photography was seen as a natural science because of the way photographic images represented the real. Within a short time, the agencies of the state, notably the police and medical and anthropological institutions, began to use it as a means of surveillance and for subject analyses and research. The police used the camera to photograph social deviants, reinforcing theories of deviancy and criminality and related physical and psychological stereotypes. Images of criminals today, especially Black criminals, are a legacy of this earlier use of photography. The medical profession worked on similar lines to the police. It was particularly obsessed and fascinated by images of physical and mental disability.

PHOTOGRAPHIC PRACTICES AND IDENTITIES

The popularisation and mass circulation of photographs makes photography a crucial means by which we develop our own social identities and those of others. When we look at photographs we are articulating and re-articulating identities within different photographic discourses. These discourses (like our identities) are not fixed but are shifting and changing all the time. Photography

46

No one can hold you back because of your colour or race.
The law says that you must have equal treatment in jobs, housing, education and in shops, pubs, clubs and restaurants.

Get a free guide to the Race Relations Act from the Commission for Ra

is therefore a significant arena of intervention in the reproduction of meaning and representation.

In the process of taking pictures, there is an element of spectatorship. Looking down the lens or within the frame, an illusionary barrier separates the photographer from the subject. The photographer stands outside the arena to be photographed and looks in as an observer. From this location he/she positions the subject within the frame. Since it is virtually impossible to capture everything we see within the frame (unless we use an ultra-wide angle lens, which distorts the image) the photographer has to decide what aspects of the image she/he wants to capture. The decision may be based on a number of ideological factors as we saw in our analysis of the social construction of the image. The strategic forms of positioning which differentiate one photographer from another and one practice from others, enable us all to make visual statements on our experiences informed by our gender, social and cultural backgrounds. They enable us to engage with the subject, thereby drawing us into the frame from the spectator/voyeurist position. Through these processes we articulate our own identities and subjectivities and our place within society.

The above outline of the relationship between identity/ subjectivity and photographic practices is by no means the total picture but only part of the frame, so to speak. Within the dominant discourses, Black identities are predominantly articulated on the basis of skin colour and nationality. Through the process of positioning, Black photographers are constantly redefining Black subjects within the dominant discourses and exploring alternatives. It is through the process of articulating the elements of the dominant discourses differently that we produce new meanings and break the ideological chain within which they are currently fixed. Ideologies operate and are transformed through struggle.

In Britain an important form of ideological control is the racial stereotype. Large numbers of people come to share an over-simplified image of Black people and believe it to be true. Understanding the complex mechanisms involved requires an examination of the ambivalent forms by which it operates. These forms reflect a certain desire/fascination with the subject, or/as well as an underlying fear/threat. The ambivalence is illustrated in most newspaper and magazine images which popularise the Black stereotype. Images of Black people rioting or as muggers and rapists are examples of the Black person as a feared/threatening object to the stability of white British society. As dancers, musicians, singers, comedians, athletes and people deemed to possess a rampant sexuality, we are constructed into objects of

47

48

49

50

desire/fascination for white society. The naturalism or realism of these images needs to be questioned, for they have been 'fixed' by the camera, taken away and placed within ideological discourses which confer on them negative imagery and meanings. The images have specific political meanings within the ideologies of the Black experience in Britain, in the same ways as those of African and Asian rituals. The transformation of the images from their own contexts into racist discourses results in a constant bombardment of the Black community with images that negatively affect its identities and subjectivities.

There is no doubt that dominant photographic practices have a vested interest in the process of stereotyping in the way they fix and preserve images through social construction. Black photographers therefore face the challenge of confronting this interest, dismantling stereotypical images and re-articulating them. Through processes of re-definition the Black communities make statements about their own identities and subjectivities which challenge dominant practices.

To conclude, I would like to make the point that Black photography is not a homogeneous or monolithic practice obsessed by documentary/community practices. It is a diversity of practices contextualised by historical conjunctures in which Black images are produced, circulated and deployed. My work reflects a part of this tradition and is thus not representative of the whole movement. Exhibitions such as *Positive Images of Black People* (1984); *Appropriation and Control, A Photographic Exploration of Black Images* (1985); and *Exploring The Meaning of Desire* (1986), were attempts at creating positive images of the Black communities as well as tackling the issue of visibility in this society. They represent a certain stage in the gradual development of my ideas on Black photography and representation.

My preoccupation with debates around semiology, structuralism and post-structuralism has also identified for me two fighting fronts which frequently overlap. They are the arenas of independent photography and representation, particularly identity and subjectivity.

As human subjects, we are socially constituted and the way we talk, look and form relationships is governed by the agencies of representation such as photographic imagery. The consumption of images is significantly the consumption of signs, messages and codes of behaviour. It is through the penetration of the visible that we begin to uncover the invisible and underlying social rules and laws. To engage in this arena of representation, whether it is in the production or consumption process, should not be considered a mere academic pursuit but a form of political struggle.

51

52

57

53

56

54

55

58

PHOTOGRAPHIC EXHIBITIONS

SOME RECENT BLACK

Aurat Shakti

The aim of the exhibition is to show the lives, expectations and experience of Asian women. The purpose, say the organisers, is to create 'nana chaubi' (different pictures) and 'we want to do that in a way that is determined by and controlled by ourselves. The exhibition will reflect various aspects of our lives in this country.' The exhibition was organised by Manjula Mukherjee, Vibha Osbon, Amina Patel and Mumtaz Karimijee. For further information contact the Cockpit Gallery, c/o ILEA Drama and Tape Centre, Princeton St., London WC1.

Black Edge:

Afro-Caribbean Photography in Britain. This exhibition was selected by Errol Lloyd and focuses on the work of Afro-Caribbean photographers: David A. Bailey, Vanley Burke, Newton Brown, Ahmet Francis, Madahi, Horace Ove and Terri Quaye. Contact the Mappin Art Gallery, Weston Park, Sheffield S10 2TP.

The Black Triangle

An exhibition by Armet Francis, the result of many years photographing the people of the African diaspora in the Triangle, geographically defined as Africa, Europe and the Americas. Contact Derek Bishton, Triangle Media Centre, Birmingham B4 7ES, for touring details.

Caribbean Labour in Revolt:

The 1930s and Its Aftermath. An exhibition of photographs, contemporary newsprint, books and documents. The 1930s — the main focus of this exhibition — was without doubt the most crucial decade in the history of the Caribbean since the end of chattel slavery in the nineteenth century. It was a result of the resistance put up by the Caribbean people in the 1930s that new institutions and new forms of rule had to be brought forward by the outside powers. The exhibition was organised by Cecil Gutzmore and Lance Watson. For further details contact the Caribbean Visual History Project, Institute of Education, 20 Bedford Way, London WC1 0AL.

Check This

An exhibition by the Blackwomen's Creativity Project. Women of African and Asian descent from all over Britain explore their creative potential through a spectrum of media including paint, clay and textiles. Contact the Lenthall Road Workshop, 30 Lenthall Rd., London E8.

Darshan

The exhibition presents the work of ten Asian photographers in Britain: Zarina Bhimji, Prodeepta Das, Ashwin Gatha, Sunil Gupta, Sunil Janah, Mumtaz Karimijee, Abida Khan, Samina Khanour, Sarita Sharm and Padma Shreshtha. A unique exhibition reflecting the breadth of vision and creativity of a group of prominent Asian photographers. For details contact Camerawork, 121 Bethnal Green, London E2 0QN.

Forces and Figures in Asian History

This exhibition includes such figures as M.K. Ghandi, non violent political activist, and Afia Begum, anti-deportation campaigner. It indicates that although the motor force of the struggle has been the community itself, the role of individuals in these struggles cannot be under-estimated. The exhibition was organised by the Southall Afro Caribbean Asian Arts Collective (SAAAC). Contact SAAAC, Unit C16, Charles House, Bridge Rd., Southall, Middlesex.

From Resistance to Rebellion
The exhibition shows how the various strands of resistance were 'set on the loom of British racism' and looks at the rich mosaic of struggle and organisation thrown up in the process, in such areas as policing, immigration control, education, housing, welfare and racial violence on the streets. The exhibition was organised by the Institute of Race Relations, 2-6 Leeke Street, London WC1 9HS.

Reflections of the Black Experience
Ten Black photographers were commis-sioned, for the first time in London, to document Black people's presence in Britain today. The photographers selected were: Mark Boothe, Vanley Burke, Ahmet Francis, Sunil Gupta, Mumtaz Karimijee, David Lewis, Madahi Sharak, Zak Ove, Ingrid Pollard, and Suzanne Roden. The exhibition was organised by Monika Baker and can be reached through the Triangle Media Centre, Birmingham B4 7ES.

Starring . . . Mummy & Daddy
An OBAALA exhibition (Organisation for Black Arts Advancement & Leisure Activities). Twenty Black photographers present a unique and poignant exhibition featuring portraits of their parents. These are the people who we sometimes see in old footage arriving from the Caribbean or Africa, referred to as 'our coloured friends' by the British media. For further details contact the Black Art Gallery, 225 Seven Sisters Rd., London N4.

DEMYSTIFYING GRAPHICS

RUHI
HAMID

The Palestine Liberation Organisation based in Zimbabwe asked me to design a solidarity poster. I explore the theme of African solidarity with the people of Palestine in visual terms, using the spear, a basic fighting weapon, as the symbol of solidarity. The Palestinian scarf is tied to the spear; it is embracing and intimate, epitomising readiness, a common struggle, and a shared destiny. Solidarity is not passive, it is an active love and commitment. I use the cut-out to intensify and accentuate the power and dynamism of the spear.

PEOPLES OF SOUTHERN AFRICA

SOLIDARITY

PEOPLES OF PALESTINE

60

A poster to promote a book. South Africa is a stark reality of oppression, so I utilise a series of prison bars to comment on the dimensions of social experience and emotion. They are partly splashed with blood for it is a war situation, though an unconventional kind of war. The liberation struggle intensifies and the all-seeing eyes remember and reveal all injustice. They see the future and it belongs to the people.

The massive buildup of nuclear arms allows for no complacency. We must make this issue our responsibility and challenge the superpowers. We must take control of our destinies and those of our children and not leave them in the hands of comedians who sit in 'White' Houses. This is a personal statement on the nuclear arms race. I chose to do it as a screen print in two colours, red and black. A third varnish overprint creates an ambiguous smoke cloud in the background, only visible with the play of light upon the surface.

61

A call for entries to an exhibition by the newly-formed Zimbabwe Artists Union. The exhibition aimed to encourage and mobilise Zimbabwean artists to produce solidarity works for the liberation of South Africa. The medium was screen-printing and I collaborated with Chaz Maviyane-Davies to produce it as part of a union workshop for school children at the National Gallery in Harare.

62

These postcards, 'Passport to Survive' (the pass laws) and 'Fruits of Labour' (sanctions-busting by western companies) were the result of outrage after watching a TV documentary on the South African regime's aggression on front-line states. They later became part of a three-minute audio-visual show on South Africa in which I used a montage of graphics and images to depict the lives and conditions of South African gold mine workers. The idea of integrating text with image and sound was important

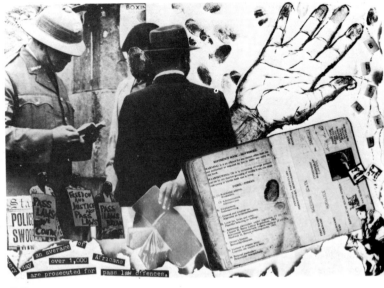

63

64

to me, so I chose a multi-media form of presentation. The colours, voices and sounds of the liberation struggle give credibility to the lives of the Black mine workers and people of South Africa, lives weighed down by oppression and exploitation but always resisting. A selection of 300 slides was projected on to a wide screen from twelve slide carousels through four main bank projectors, computer-programmed and synchronised to the sound track of Hugh Masekela's 'Gold'.

Part of a project to design a poster, catalogue and invitation for an exhibition on the Spanish painter Velasquez and his seventeenth-century contemporaries. The Velasquez painting was chosen as the main image of the poster to reflect his stature as a painter and strength of style as a portraitist. We used the title on the supporting material for the exhibitions. The type was selected for legibility and to complement and enhance the image.

65

6

67

68

69

Moto is a Zimbabwean monthly magazine, one of the few African magazines to publish in pre-independence days. Subjects are wide-ranging, with a special feature every month. The role of a magazine cover is to be eye-catching and striking in its image and clear and concise in its message. Design deadlines are short so working with speed is important. A wide range of income groups buys **Moto**, so the image is clear, simple and sensitive to local cultural traditions and patterns. In designing **Moto** covers I aimed to contribute to a popular visual discourse that informs as well as awakens the conscience of the readership. In a country like Zimbabwe, which has been bombarded with negative racist images for so long, this is crucial.

70

These pictograms were part of a project at Studio Dumbar in The Hague to design the signage system for the Rijksmuseum in Amsterdam, one of the world's largest and busiest museums. The challenge was to communicate essential information to visitors from all over the world. We used two languages, Dutch and English. The limitation of using just two languages in such an international venue meant that the use of good pictograms was imperative. They are often made up of stick-like figures and are not very effective. Also, different cultures often interpret them differently. To achieve something new and exciting, we made a careful selection of details of paintings in the museum and used them as backdrops to the depictions of the various functions. 'Like bringing Mozart and the Beatles together,' commented the head of painting.

The Rijksmuseum project involved designing a ground plan to function as an aid to the signage system. We set out to simplify the complex architecture of the museum by producing a 'pop-up' to clarify the different floor levels. We used four European languages to give information on the contents of the various departments of the museum and made three isometric plan drawings of the floors, using the colour systems of the museum's main boards to differentiate the departments. The flip side of the plan illustrates the pictograms in the sign system.

71

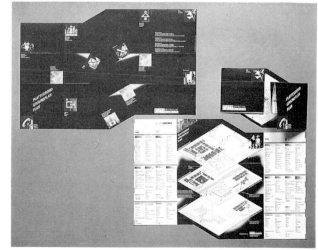

CHILDREN OF THE BLACK TRIANGLE

AN INTERVIEW WITH ARMET FRANCIS

How do you work as a photographer in the street? Is everything posed or grabbed?

There's a respect which is very necessary for me when I take photographs, because I feel that the camera is a massive imposition on people's existence. You can either walk into a situation and feel that you can work and not impose or there are times when you have to reason. I have to reason with a lot of people I photograph, maybe for hours. You know what reasoning is? *Reasoning* is an understanding or trust that the images you are going to capture will be used correctly and you can either do that through the eyes, or just through the way you are. People can just look at you and say 'Ah, a person I trust' or 'a person I don't trust'; when you travel it's even more like that.

73

What do you hope people will see when they look at your work?

If you look at my work and you see that all the images are Black and you say to yourself, 'I can only relate to these people to a certain degree because they're not my colour or my race', you are completely missing the point. The point is that I'm just using my people as a format to say something to the world. If you see them simply as Black people then you have closed yourself off from the common human condition, which is not just for Black people — you only have to go out in the street and see that it's a common human condition we're looking at. That's fundamental in my work.

74

You photograph children a lot. Is it difficult?

When you're working with children, you first have to become
visible to them, because adults are quite invisible to them other
than as people that represent authority. So what I do is become a
child, which is pretty easy for me. Kids like to do things and
they're fascinated by the camera because it points at you, right?
And anything you point at a child, is dealing with them, so they
want to know. So if you try and take a picture of a child, they will
walk up to the lens and poke it, right? So either you say, 'Oh, you
mustn't do that', or you say, 'Come around and have a look
through this end', and the next thing they want to do is take a
picture. So what I do is let them take pictures of anything they
want to take pictures of —they might want to take a picture of
me, or their mates. Between, say, three or five, that's about as
much as they take in.

Why do you work that way?

The importance of it is they're communicating with me and they don't see me as this strange thing coming into their secure environment, and I introduce them to myself and they introduce themselves to me; in other words I'm saying to them, look, I'm alright really, and they start telling me things: kids either tell you things or they ask you questions and from there the whole dialogue begins and then you have a load of kids, doing things. I don't work, I function, I live with people. Children are, have an innocence, which overcomes.

75

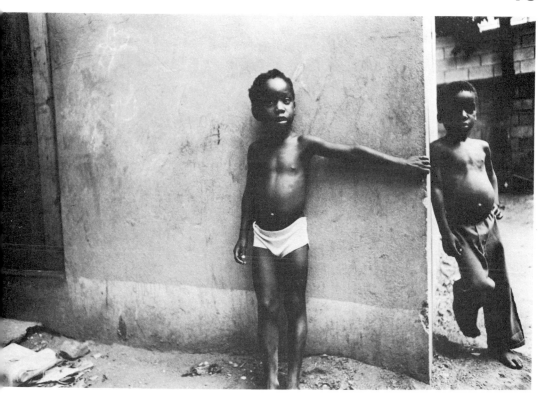

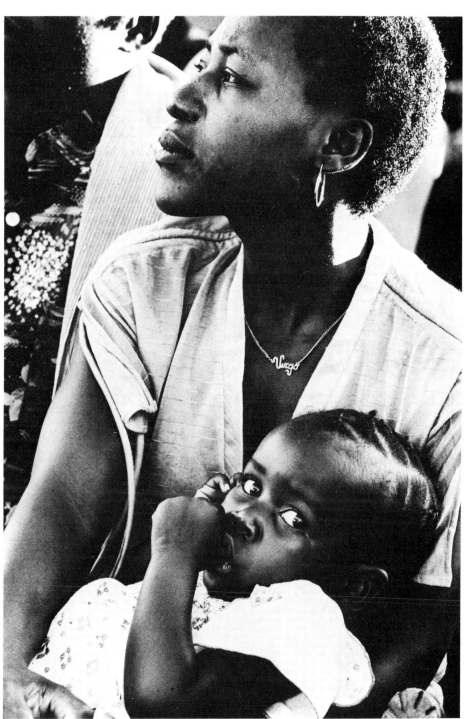

When you function with them, or when you join together to create something, what are you giving them?

We learn from each other, basically. If you get rid of all the crap that adults have and stay with kids, you can find the really basic energy that transpires right round the world, and that's what I see, that's what I look for in children. I mean some children have already grown through their childhood, you can see it. Hence you have four-year-old geniuses and stuff like that. But there is an innocence with clarity that most children have. They don't have any prejudices unless they're presented with them. There is a certain age, and it's nothing to do with one, two, three, four, five. When I'm talking about children I'm talking about anyone up to a hundred and five, and it's something that I look for and you probably see in some of my pictures, some of them. Innocence but not naivety is what I look for.

78

How do you encourage them when you're doing photography with them in a workshop?

It's amazing how visual children are. They will look at you and decide very quickly what you are, who you are and where you are coming from and then they will either go away from you or come towards you. That's where you have a dialogue of learning, that's where it starts to happen. It's really communicating with each other.

How does the camera come into it?

The camera has the ability to do what we cannot do, which is to stop a moment, a moment of truth if you like, a moment that we can all look at and understand, because nothing, unless it's inanimate, stays static. So the camera keeps that moment, the moment I'm talking about, that conscious moment.

79

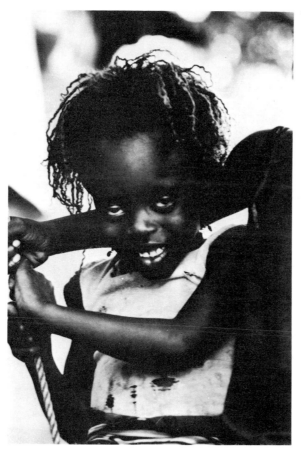

How do you explain that to kids?

You don't have to. When you're really communicating with someone, you don't have to explain things like that. You know, kids are not really into photographs, the camera is not crucial for them. What they want to find out is how you play. Are you fun? They don't really want any heavies. If you go with a group of kids, they've mostly got a game going already, and if you can't bring anything into them, into their game, into their play, they'll soon walk away. Children have a time limit on how long they're going to put up with you before they say, alright, I'm going over there to play football.

So the camera is part of the game?

There is a fascination. The reason I came into photography is to do with the fascination with seeing images. I think everyone has a fascination about images. Because we like to look at ourselves. Everyone likes to look at themselves to see how other people see them. I'm not talking about narcissism or images of self, I'm talking about the fact that we all, children included, are fascinated by images that are out of the norm. The first thing a camera does is it makes everything a lot smaller, so already it's different, and it puts it on a flat plane, so there is already a fascination. If you look at a child watching television, there's very little realism for that child; if somebody walks into a room when they're watching television, they're completely engrossed, they don't notice the person who's come in.

Do kids get anything from taking pictures?

Oh yes, because there's that fascination. I can set it up so they can take a picture of themselves, I mean how many three-year-olds get to take a picture of themselves and take it home to Mum and Dad? Then they can do something they think they can't do, and there's no fear in it. That's what I hope they get out of it — kids are very basic really, very straightforward.

THE SIGNIFICANCE

FOR BLACK THEATRE IN BRITAIN

OF DEVELOPMENTS IN INDIAN THEATRE

JATINDER VERMA

When the 'return to the source' goes beyond the individual and is expressed through 'groups' or 'movements', the contradiction is transformed into struggle (secret or overt), and is a prelude to the pre-independence movement or of the struggle for liberation from the foreign yoke.
Amilcar Cabral, *Return to the Source.*

One of the less-documented aspects of the struggle against imperialism has been the search for distinctive cultural expression by the colonised peoples. In various parts of Africa, the Indian sub-continent and the Caribbean, this search for a distinctive voice as a response to imperial/western 'ways of seeing' offers, for Black theatre in Britain, some important hints for the future. Reference to such post-imperial cultural movements can help locate Black theatre in a wider critical framework.

This article draws upon the specific situation of one such society — India — in an effort to formulate a crucial question for the future development of Black theatre in Britain.

Since Independence in 1947, Indian theatre practitioners, reacting to the centuries of colonial rule, have striven to develop a distinctively Indian theatre: a contemporary, mainly urban, theatre aesthetic that draws upon the rich corpus of traditional performance arts still practised in rural areas throughout each region of India and at the same time reflects the realities and concerns of a post-colonial society.

This search was signalled initially, though briefly, by the Indian Peoples Theatre Association (IPTA), which between 1942 and 1948 chose to take the issues of anti-imperial and anti-fascist struggles to the towns and villages of India. In its attempts at formulating a popular or people's theatre, members of IPTA turned to traditional, popular forms such as the burra-katha. This folk form of Andhra Pradesh, south India, usually involves three people, one of whom is the lead singer. He begins the narrative, while his two companions provide the chorus effect, all of them using the long Andhra drum as accompaniment. The mode of narration is punctuated by significant pauses to heighten the dramatic effect of the story while the musicians employ simple movements to emphasize certain emotions or to round off certain phases of the narrative. The narrative traditionally consists of heroic tales or folk parables such as the *Ballad of Venkataramani*, the boy who ate his mother's ears. Burra-katha performances in the open air can have audiences of up to 30,000 people. IPTA workers employed potent popular forms such as this to tackle contemporary themes of social reform or issues such as those raised by the great Bengal famine of 1943.

Despite its relatively brief history, IPTA's influence on modern Indian theatre is incalculable; for it was the progressive artists involved in the Association who first articulated the call for a distinctively Indian theatre, and set up the signposts for its search.

This search elicited the exciting period of the sixties and seventies (contemporaneous with Britain's own theatrical Angry Decade), when new dramatists like Girish Karnad and Vijay Tendulkar wrote *Hayavadana* and *Gashiram Kotwal* respectively. The former transposed a short story by Thomas Mann, which had originally been inspired by an ancient Indian story, to a South Indian theatre idiom (yakshagana), while the latter employed the bawdy folk form of maharashtra (mamasha) to present a critique of high-caste society during the Raj. This period saw also the establishment of the National School of Drama, India's first, and to date only, professional drama school, under the direction of E. Alkazi. Alkazi drew upon the rich vein of traditional Indian theatre to mount spectacular productions like *Tughlag*, performed on the ruined ramparts of an old fort in Delhi. Alkazi's successor, B. V. Karanth, continued the process, staging a Hindi version of *Macbeth* in the yakshagana style, using only a hand-held curtain and elaborate face-masks and costumes. In addition, theatrical pioneers like Habib Tanvir worked with villagers from one of the most backward regions of India to produce biting social satires like *Agra Bazaar* and ancient classics like *The Little Clay Cart*. We in Britain have had the pleasure of admiring some of these productions (or being inspired by them) in the last few years.

But what of the eighties in India? Increasingly, with the proliferation of officially-sponsored Festivals of India, the State has begun to make a decisive intervention in the articulation of theatre aesthetics. Backed by substantial financial resources, the Government of India has projected the 'Folk' on to world consciousness. By seeking to make political virtue of India's traditions, the state has begun to affect modern Indian theatre, polarising developments as Folk/Tradition versus Urban/Modern.

Perhaps the most significant concern, and the challenge for the future Indian theatre practitioner, is that in making a commodity out of the Folk and projecting it as the mark of the non-western, attention is being diverted from developing a non-western *methodology* for the craft of Indian theatre. Theatre students more often than not have voice projection techniques taught them which owe more to Cicely Berry than to, say, the ancient Vedic system of chanting which is more appropriate to the performance techniques of traditional theatre forms. Or else they concentrate on characterisation exercises that are premised on the naturalistic tradition of Western European theatre, rather than on the archetypal modes of depiction which are at the root of Indian theatre traditions.

For Black theatre in Britain, the aesthetic quest of many Indian theatre practitioners since Independence can be paraphrased in the question, What is Black about Black theatre? In other words, does the fact of Black performers on the stage, or of Black content, constitute the totality of Black theatre? The form, the 'way of seeing' theatre, I would argue, is just as important, indeed constitutes the challenge which has been insufficiently addressed by contemporary Black theatre. To challenge Eurocentrism without challenging Eurocentric modes of perception and evaluation is a contradiction, a contradiction which will eventually nullify the potentially subversive impact of Black theatre in contemporary Britain if it remains unaddressed by Black theatre practitioners.

The significance, then, of developments in Indian theatre for Black theatre in Britain are threefold:

1   An active research into (and thereby reappropriation of) alternative performance art traditions of Asia, Africa and the Caribbean. Eurocentrism is characterised, in its relation with non-European arts, by a particular 'way of seeing'. It is by such modes of perception that 'non-Europe' has been characterised as the 'third world', as 'underdeveloped', as the 'other'. This mode of perception cannot be confronted on its own terms.

2   The development of a methodology for the training and production of Black theatre that is premised on our own traditions of performance arts.

3   The development of a distinctive Black aesthetic that is premised on (a) our own traditions, which provide models for scriptwriting, stage settings, production and performance techniques as well as the *purpose* of theatre; and (b) the need to make our work accessible in contemporary Britain, that is, accessible to *all*.

The current debate in Black theatre — as far as it exists at all — is centred on opportunities: on greater access to venues, theatres, critics, funds, etc. While this issue is of great importance, it cannot be addressed out of the context of a debate on what Black theatre *is*. Without such a conscious search for distinctiveness, the contemporary experience of India suggests that the state of its attendant orthodoxies will ineluctably impose its own definition. To put my question another way: how 'Black' is Black if we are producing what amount to white plays, with their Aristotelian notions of the unity of time and place and a psychological realism that owes more to Kodachrome than to the artifice that is theatre?

ERITREA

OF CREATING A NEW CULTURE

THE EXPERIENCE

AMRIT
WILSON

'Everything new comes from the forge of hard and bitter struggle,' wrote Mao in the middle of the Chinese revolutionary war. 'This is also true of the new culture which has followed a zig-zag course in the past twenty years, during which both the good and the bad were tested and proved in the struggle.'

Today the same process of creating a new culture as a part of revolutionary struggle is going on in Eritrea. It is significant for Black arts in Britain. For 25 years the people have been fighting for self-determination against a coloniser who has been helped in turn by the United States and the Soviet Union. Without help or arms supplied by any outside power they have succeeded in liberating most of their land, and in these liberated areas, in the face of famine and drought and of course the continuing war, are transforming an essentially feudal and nomadic society into a country free of exploitation and oppression. As the old culture's property relations, feudal institutions and social values are being

81

swept away, a revolutionary Eritrean culture created by the struggle itself is taking its place.

Briefly, the history of this struggle is as follows: Eritrea was colonised by the Italians in 1890. In 1942, after the defeat of the Italians, it was taken over by the British. Ten years later as a result of pressure from the United States, it was federated to Ethiopia because, as Secretary of State John Foster Dulles put it, 'The strategic interests of the United States in the Red Sea basin make it necessary that the country has to be linked to our ally Ethiopia'. The 'strategic interests' at the time were mainly the establishment of a military base and control of the Suez Canal route. As for Ethiopia, it was indeed in that period a staunch ally of imperialism. Haile Selassie's regime intervened on behalf of the West in Korea and in Zaire to support Mobuto against Lumumba. Federation was followed by increasing violence against the Eritrean people. The Ethiopian regime banned trade unions and political parties, closed factories or moved them wholesale to Ethiopia, and broke up strikes and demonstrations with the utmost violence, injuring and killing hundreds.

1961 saw the beginning of armed struggle. The Ethiopian regime responded with indiscriminate attacks on the Eritrean population. Thousands of men and women were imprisoned on suspicion of being sympathisers of the guerrillas, villages were burnt down and in the towns arbitrary arrest, rape, torture and killings became commonplace. In 1962, the Emperor simply annexed Eritrea and sent in the Ethiopian army, helped by the Americans and Israelis, to suppress the people.

Eventually Haile Selassie's regime was overthrown but the effect on Eritrea of the policies of the so-called Marxist government which followed remained the same. Today the only difference is that Ethiopia is supported by the Soviet Union and not the United States and that the region's strategic importance has vastly increased with the importance of Saudi Arabian oil. Although a prime area of super power rivalry, the US does not support Eritrea; the reason is that the US (and also the Soviet Union) sees a genuinely independent and socialist Eritrea as the biggest threat of all.

Since 1970, the Eritrean struggle has been led by the Eritrean Peoples Liberation Front, EPLF. Its policies are based on the principle that military success and the transformation of society are entirely interdependent. One effect of this is that women's lives have been revolutionised in the highlands which are essentially feudal, in the semi-desert areas inhabited by nomads and on the front line of battle where 35% of the fighters are women. The EPLF also identified right from the start the need to

Women in training, Eritrea. Photo: Network.

'organise, politicise and arm the masses' and there are now well-established organisations representing women, peasants, workers, youth and so on which make mass participation in decision-making possible. In the process of changing property relations and feudal institutions, traditional structures have not necessarily been

82

discarded; instead, wherever possible, they have been built on or transformed. For example, the old village judiciaries which represented only the male feudal upper classes have been transformed to elected village assemblies which represent the interests of the people as a whole. This in turn has enabled the existing feudal land distribution system to be changed to one where every adult in a village has a right to his or her own land.

Electrical department at the garage at Sheb repairing starter motors and dynamos for EPLF trucks, 1983. Photo: Mike Goldwater, Network.

82

At the same time, the EPLF has introduced new marriage laws which forbid dowries and forced marriages. But they, too, are not enforced from above by harsh dictatorial methods, because what is involved is the removal of a feudal culture which is extremely deep-rooted. Instead, the people have been, and in some areas are still being, gradually educated and convinced of the need for change. These changes in social relations have been crucial in the creation of a new culture. I asked women in the EPLF what life and feudal culture used to be like in Eritrea. They told me about their lives: 'My family belonged to the middle level of peasants; we had a pair of oxen, about 40 sheep and some land. We were always conscious of Ethiopian oppression. There was an army camp near our village and we had to face constant attacks and humiliations. In the extended family the woman's work was very hard and exhausting. Rearing the children, working in the fields, weeding, cleaning, cutting, carrying water, sometimes from very long distances. After the day's work the woman would of course have to come home and cook. My mother would warm the water and wash my father's feet. Most girls would be engaged before they were nine and be married before fifteen. They had no right to say anything and very few met their husbands before marriage. A dowry had to be paid to the husband's family. If it was considered too low the girl's life would be a misery; she could be beaten and insulted, told "you came empty handed".' This is the culture which is being changed. In some areas it has been swept away. In others the process is not complete.

What motivated women from this feudal background to join armed struggle? Their sufferings at the hands of the Ethiopians had given rise to an anger and determination to fight for freedom and to die if necessary. Meza, a woman of 21 now wounded in the back but eagerly waiting to return to the 'field', told me how she had joined the EPLF at the age of 14, the day her grandmother and grandfather had been killed while praying in the village church. Another woman, Asmaret, now a pharmacist, described how she had joined immediately after escaping from a house where her sisters were being tortured and interrogated by the Ethiopians. Many of them had lost touch with their families but in the struggle had found a new, profound and unpossessive love. Reflections of this were everywhere: in the way comrades greeted each other; in the testimony of a surgeon: 'Any facial deformity does have a psychological effect. But I can say that our fighters are different from others. They don't care much about external appearances — maybe because they are accepted by society or because they are dedicated to the struggle — external deformity does not cause psychological disturbance'; or in this description of his new life by a young fighter: 'When I was 14 my father was murdered by the regime. Two years later I myself was imprisoned and tortured. This lasted till I was 20, then I escaped and immediately joined the EPLF. I found others who had suffered like me. Almost every single person had lost someone close to them, or faced prison and torture themselves. Now memories of those early days of my childhood seem very dim. If someone who knew me when I was young reminds me, "Do you remember you did this or liked that?", then I can vaguely remember something. I am not in touch with my family, though I know that my mother is in the US with what remains of the family. But although I still love them, I do not miss them. Here I have found a deeper more complete love and support... here you are encouraged at every point. Whatever you achieve, however small, people encourage you, they say "Ajoha". On the frontline we are all together, old and young, men and women. We think of each other, specially those who are young and don't feel tired. We are ready to die if necessary.'

In this framework of revolutionary relationships, people have come to identify culture and their own liberation with national liberation. As Maa'za, a fighter taking a break for pregnancy, said: 'For us nationalism is a food for the mind.' This nationalism is of course a nationalism of resistance, but it is different in many ways from the cultural nationalism of some Black groups in Britain which looks back constantly to the 'glorious past' as a defensive response to the ridiculous racist assertion that Black people have no history. Eritrean nationalism looks at the present and the future with all its exciting possibilities. The past is not necessarily to be glorified or mummified; it is brought right down to the present where people can question it and learn from it.

There is also no moralistic dualism or sense of revenge. Ethiopian prisoners of war, whose existence is not acknowledged by the Ethiopian government but some 12,000 of whom are currently in Eritrea, are treated for their wounds and given basic education, including literacy classes where needed. Many eventually join the EPLF, and their cultural troupe is popular with Eritrean fighters on the front line. In fact they are accepted whole-heartedly because 'they did not know who their real enemy was'.

Everyone who joins the EPLF receives both military training and political education. Chuchu, now a teacher in the Revolutionary school in the liberated zone told me about her experiences: 'When I joined I found 400 women in the training school. I was just surprised and I cried. I was so happy to see that so many women had come to join. A few were Eritreans from abroad, some were from Ethiopia, there were peasants and factory

83

workers. The youngest were 15 or so and the eldest were 45 or
more. Some of these older women had come with their children to
join the struggle. Women were taught to put into practice that
they can do what men do. Because it is better, more convincing, to
practise this than to learn it in theory.' Revolutionary culture in
Eritrea is not just words; it grows out of revolutionary practice.

After training, the EPLF women like the men are assigned
specific jobs as mechanics, as barefoot doctors in the liberated
zones or in the medical mobile units which go behind enemy lines,
as pharmacists, as teachers or of course in combat. Are they really
accepted as equals by the men? Although the EPLF leadership took
women's participation extremely seriously, I was told that during
the early seventies when the women joined the men thought,
'What can they do these women? But then the men saw what
women could do. In the clinics, as dressers, and then when they
were assigned to the frontline, they saw them fight, take prisoners,
capture tanks, they saw them when they lost their legs, their eyes.
And then they stopped speaking about women that way. Now we
have women company commanders commanding men and women

84

Ethiopian prisoners of war, Eritrea. Photo: Mike
84 Goldwater, Network.

and there are squad commanders and platoon commanders. This is
not done for the sake of women's rights. Eritreans are fighting for
freedom. But to fight for freedom you have to have your rights.'
Fundamental changes like equality for women bring to light new
priorities. These in turn change other deeper cultural values of the
society. At the same time the needs and strategies of the war
inform the practical demands of a society in transformation. For
example, sanitary towels were identified as a priority if women
were to be effective fighters but the factory set up to supply the
fighters also supplies women all over the villages and towns of
Eritrea. EPLF members, male and female, are proud of these
developments which have not only helped the struggle on a
military level but have affected the cultural consciousness of the
people as a whole. It is one step towards liberation from the
particular feudal ideology (also shared by capitalism) which makes
a woman's physical needs a matter of shame. (In Britain, although
sanitary towels are commodities they still cannot be mentioned in
polite company.)

The cultural change which has come out of revolutionary struggle has released an astonishing collective dynamism and creative energy. What visitors to Eritrea realise with shock is that when people are united in their commitment they can work miracles. The hall which seated 2000 people at the second congress of the EPLF with its magnificent stone podium, vast doorway and simultaneous translation facilities was built secretly (for security reasons) and almost overnight. When the congress was over it vanished almost immediately and without a trace, bulldozed to the ground.

In the bases of the liberated zone, everyday life is like a series of wonders. An area may be so well-camouflaged that the casual observer would think it unpopulated, and where thanks to MIG and Antonov bombers it is not safe to be active during the day, nightfall brings the rumble of massive Soviet trucks captured from the enemy (like almost every other item in the war) and reconverted as fuel or water carriers. Total self reliance is a crucial aspect of Eritrean culture. Nothing is wasted. In converted containers, surgeons perform the most highly skilled operations: faces half blown off by shrapnel are reconstructed, artificial limbs are made and fitted, essential drugs and intravenous fluids are produced and major industrial machines are manufactured. All these advances have occurred in the last ten years. Those who are performing these tasks are not foreign experts but people who a few years ago may have been rural housewives or nomads. They are armed not only with skills but with revolutionary determination and optimism.

Here the confidence of the people makes for an atmosphere of security. But the signs and effects of the war are everywhere: the daily early morning sorties of the Antonovs, the gashes in the hillside where bombs have landed, the arrival of the wounded in hospital or the comments of children whose school had been hit with many pupils injured and killed.

It was in a place like this in 1987, Orota, that I witnessed and took part in the celebration of International Women's Day and encountered Eritrean revolutionary art. The main national celebrations were being held at the Solomona refugee camp where thousands of people, refugees in their own land, forced to leave their villages by the bombs and napalm of the Ethiopians, are rebuilding their lives. There, I was told, the audience lined an entire hillside for a spectacular display of revolutionary music, dancing and plays. Although I was unable to go there, there was no feeling of being left behind. In Orota, despite the war and the constant shadow of food shortage, there had been for several days an air of excitement and expectancy. Rooms were cleared, halls prepared and constructed, stages erected, suwa, the local millet wine, brewed in large quantities. I was to realise that Eritreans had made International Women's Day their own, a people's celebration of its revolutionary achievements.

Around midday, on happening to pass the local bakery, a building camouflaged like so many others into near invisibility, we are invited in. To our surprise, a play is going on inside. When our eyes get accustomed to the darkness we see men, women and children, many in traditional dress, sitting in rows watching the show, commenting and drinking suwa. I catch sight of Maa'za, the woman who yesterday had been talking to me about nationalism, and she comes and sits with us and interprets.

In this workplace, with a space cleared for a stage and floursacks as curtains, the workers perform for themselves and their community. The spirit of such an event with the commitment and resourcefulness of the participants is hard to imagine in Britain.

One play is about the role and sufferings of a mother. A woman is harassed by two Ethiopian spies who demand information about her sons. They beat her and throw her to the ground, but she refuses to break down. The security forces move in and she is imprisoned. Her sons, freedom fighters, return and kill the spies but the woman dies in prison. Women holding their babies brush tears from their eyes. It is a story close to everyone's lives.

Unlike bourgeois theatre where individual characters represent themselves, here the woman represents Eritrean women as a whole. Their deaths, their willingness to die, are not a sign of defeat or passivity, but a reaffirmation of the strength and continuity of the struggle. Another play is about a poor couple in a village who have little to eat. When the man comes home from work he refuses to eat and asks his wife to have what little there is. She refuses, but does not speak or explain why. While the husband is at work the next day, his wife goes to a wizard who lives nearby. She pays him an exorbitant sum and brings him to the house. He exorcises her, shouting, 'Ask what you want! Ask what you want!'. Only then can she speak. Maa'za explains that this play is both representational and educative. It shows the position of women in feudal society in which they were unable to express themselves, state their needs or make certain types of demands. It also demonstrates how superstition makes people vulnerable to feudal corruption, represented by the wizard.

After the plays there are poems, one by an Ethiopian prisoner of war turned EPLF member: 'Here in Eritrea I found the river of revolution. Its branches will go all over the earth.' Then there is

85

dancing in which we, the visitors, join to everyone's delight. Soon almost everyone has taken to the floor, men and women, old and young, fighters and nomads. Maa'za says, 'Look at the older women, the mothers, look how they move, so proudly and gracefully'. Then someone shouts out, 'You have so much happiness, take it, live it!'. Here in the people's happiness, revolutionary art can be seen as one with revolutionary culture; the individual and collective become united and inseparable.

I N T E R ǀ O R S

CREATING THE LANGUAGE OF FREEDOM

**Listen more to things
Than to words that are said
The water's voice sings
And the flame cries
And the wind that brings
The woods to sigh
Is the breathing of the dead.**

Birago Diop

Interiors continues the explorations of the last section. It highlights the issues and commitments which inform the search for new languages of creativity and gives examples of the work of artists attempting to do this. The concept of language utilised here demands an acknowledgement of the extensive processes of communication implicit in most Asian and African cultures. In his discussion of the African paralanguage of gestures, expression and ritual, Jacob Ross writes: 'By language I do not mean the mere concatenation of words to signify some sort of meaning. I am talking about the form, structure, gestures, music, rhythm, the silences, the way space is organised in order to define, nurture and underscore relationships in the process of communication.'

In Asante culture, drum orature makes communication possible without verbal expression. At durbars, issues are articulated and debates conducted through drum language and the varying interpretations of dancers. Since Columbus set sail and ushered in western domination of the rest of us, this understanding and aesthetic sensibility has been subordinated within a European culture which has progressively undermined and depreciated its qualities. The specific field of study devoted to Africa and Asia by the west was anthropology. Heavily influenced by nineteenth century racist ideologies and methodologies, it failed to examine Black cultures on their own terms and stigmatised their values as inferior and primitive.

The work of Black artists in modern culture, using dynamic languages in which thought and feeling collide with a world of objects and people, represents a significant departure from western ways of knowing, seeing, and producing truth. Perhaps Jean Paul Sartre was not exaggerating when he observed in *Black Orpheus* that 'the Black is closer than we to the great epochs in which, as Mallarmé says, "the world creates the Gods'".

It can be difficult for Black artists in the west to sustain the inspiration and aesthetics of orature in our work because we create in a landscape that is essentially unaccommodating and silent to our voices and the mark of our hands. However, the difficulty of producing artistic syntheses which articulate our cultural histories and experiences of being part of western reality, is not necessarily negative (however much such concepts of assimilation and appropriation as 'ethnic', 'minority' and 'Black British arts' try to make it so). In fact, this difficulty gives Black arts a creative tension and dynamism which spurs on the search for new languages.

The paintings of Gavin Jantjes and Sonia Boyce should be read as visual essays, with the captions and poems as additional layers of interpretation. The poetry which goes with Jantjes' paintings comes from the trilogy, *The Arrivants,* by Edward Kamau Braithwaite, a leading Caribbean poet. Jantjes' paintings represent his search for a new visual approach after his dissatisfaction with the realism of his earlier work, based on photography. Boyce has created a sensitive visual language that excavates the buried memories of Black experiences in Britain, detailing moments of solitude and remembrance.

The essay on the Notting Hill Carnival offers a reciprocal relationship between image and text

and attempts a way of seeing and writing which gives credibility to the creativity of the event as well as to its historical and political significance. The background to this exploration lies in the misrepresentation of Europe's biggest street festival as a mere hedonists' jump-up or an excuse for multi-racial gesturing (hence the photograph of a policeman kissing a Black woman which graces the front pages of almost every London daily the day after).

Ngugi Wa' Thiong'o, leading African writer and critic, discusses his decision to stop writing in European languages. In the paper translated from the Gîkuyû, he argues for the importance of writing in African languages to the 'process of decolonising the mind'. The paper was originally delivered in Belgium at a conference organised by the Institut Marie Haps on the 'Promotion of African Languages and Literatures'. Paradoxically, African writers discussed their own languages and literatures in European languages. Ngugi Wa' Thiong'o however spoke in Gîkûyû and Swahili with simultaneous translations into English and French. The experiment worked well and for translator Wangui Wa' Goro marked the beginning of a new approach and attitude to African languages.

Gail Thompson describes the struggles of her musical career and her constant search for new languages. This search has been affected by a muscular condition which makes it impossible for her to play the saxophone.

'The Flexed Foot' is Shobana Jeyasingh's attempt to explore the aesthetics of Indian dance in the often narrow confines of western structures and ideologies.

Cecil Gutzmore's 'The Image of Marcus Garvey in Reggae Orature' discusses the power of meanings, symbolisms and political imagery inspired by Garvey, a significant Black historical figure and cultural icon. As a study of a popular cultural tradition, it brings to light the types of ideological battles which characterise the search for and affirmation of particular languages.

Pitika Ntuli opens the section with a self portrait as an oraturist, searching to create the language of freedom. His journey is charted on a canvas which stretches from his birthplace, the shantytown of Blesbok Masakeng in Azania (South Africa), to the Britain of the eighties. A sensitive fusion of ideas and practice, it provides an insight into the joy and excitement of creative experience: 'In the midst of poverty, constant racial harassment and daily indignities, I was infinitely consumed by a voracious appetite for love, beauty and self-expression.'

ORATURE

A SELF PORTRAIT

In my art I seek to express myself in a manner most appropriate, lucid.
The self I attempt to express is a collective self.
Ideas are not born in isolation
The brain or body responds to the external world,
Builds a storage of facts and feelings to be touched, triggered, cajoled...

In a dialogue with others I am a capsule of love and anger
A memory cell of oppression, repression
And a violent struggle within me to be free
To express my dream.

My body is a centre of colliding forces
My brain a matador, a gored bull sometimes
My brain is a film, an art gallery, a war zone.
I try to externalize it
To make comparison with other canvasses
To confirm, contradict, to contribute to a debate
A confirmation, denial.

The brain is the mirror that reflects itself
Feelings are copiers that reproduce themselves
Self programmed. Time programmed.
Rebelling against programming
I am a free agent moving in the sky in ever widening spirals of love and hate
War and peace...
In a state of **BECOMING!**

PITIKA NTULI

Photo: Graham de Smidt.

In the midst of poverty, constant racial harassment and daily indignities I was infinitely consumed by a voracious appetite for love, beauty and self expression.

'Tell me what you do not have; I will teach you how to make it or how to do without it.' My grandmother.

I have been asked to write brief autobiographical notes about my life, my relationship to/with art, my attitude to orature in particular. It is a difficult task. I must journey back in time to trace strands of my formation. I remember the shantytown of Blesbok Masakeng. My parents' house was made of corrugated iron. On

87

87 Photo: Graham de Smidt.

sunny days light cut through the corrugated iron describing beautiful patterns: crocodiles, musicians, birds. On windy days or nights we heard flutes blow. On rainy days we used buckets to trap water from the leaking roof. The sound was like piano notes! We tried to create orchestras by adding our own sounds of saxophones and trumpets.

During holidays I visited my cousins in the rural areas. I admired the colourful mudhouses with geometric designs made of earth colours. My aunt had a reputation for making the most beautiful murals. I remember one afternoon when tourists came along dangling cameras and extra lenses. They were American. I was eleven years old. It was on such days that I felt proud of myself. I acted as interpreter!

'Ask her,' a tall man boomed, 'why does she use earth colours that wash away so easily when the rain falls? Why does she not use Parthenon Paints?'

My aunt, who is not known to laugh, shook with laughter. 'Your friends are strange. They always dream of creating little forevers. Our pleasure is in creating new designs all the time, in forever creating!'

It took years for me to grasp what my aunt had said. Much later, in response to events the same day, I wrote the following poem 'Our Beehive Huts':

> When
> they saw our beehive huts
> doors very low
> they said we'd suffer from backache
> using them
> they tried to move in
> to evict us
> doubly bent as they entered
> they were vulnerable
> leaving us in our huts
> they bowed out at the door
> head high
> we told them
> > our beehives
> > are our castles!

It was when I came to the West that what I took for granted (the fusion of art-forms, an Afro-centric view of life) was fundamentally challenged.

The Ndebele people of Azania. People of the rainbow. Colourful mud houses, colourful beads around the neck, the ankles, and the wrists, blankets with all the colours of the rainbow worn daily.

Bright plumed birds, wild flowers in a riot of colour, brindled cows, breathtaking sunsets and exhilarating sunrises. With so much colour around me I did not need to paint! It came late, very late, in London, as a protest against grey skies, smoky houses and monotonous terraces.

Art is the highest expression of a given culture. It is a flower of which the community is the tree, branches, leaves, stem, bark, roots. To understand the petals, the flower, we must first understand the roots.

When I was born, my umbilical cord was cut. Then it was buried in the soil. A tree was planted on the spot. The tree of my life has more meanings to it, figurative and metaphorical. Planting a tree with my umbilical cord also involved the act of implanting ideas of conservation in me. Respect for nature. The organic link between me and a tree requires me to have that special respect.

In many African societies, even in Sri Lanka I learn, you cannot cut a tree without first speaking to it, or its ancestors, asking for permission. You must have good reason! To make a drum for a particular function you need a certain type of tree. Nowadays, whether or not we still follow our custom, knowledge of this fact is an implicit acceptance of the idea.

88

89 Photo: Graham de Smidt.

The umbilical cord is not only a link between mother and child, it is also a link with those of the nation who for time immemorial lay underground; whose spirit nourishes us in our struggles for survival, beauty and heightened living. My sculptures in organic materials are a celebration of this fact.

I collect branches, roots, stems, leaves of different shapes, grains and sizes. I leave them lying about for months, sometimes years, to re-establish a relationship with them. I do not try to 'tame' or 'alter' the wood or nature. I work with it, to heighten the hidden forms and messages, to interpret them.

It is a partnership.

Each type of wood, each shape or grain is like a fingerprint. Each piece of wood embodies millions of possibilities. To carve, define, name the piece of wood is to render it finite. It is a serious responsibility. The infinite forms I destroy are not totally destroyed. The finitude of the finished work invokes them. If a piece of wood is so complex, has so much potential, what then of the human being? A human society?

I grew up in a society where our culture was denigrated and white culture exalted. A culture that permitted a privileged class of Black people (amazemthithi, the exempted ones) certain privileges — to buy and drink whisky!

I made my first sculpture when I was eight. Polish tins, wires and strings. I constructed a toy car that I drove to and from destinations, using my lips to produce engine sounds.

In class, bored with biased history classes that presented our heroes and heroines as 'thieves' and 'bloodthirsty savages', while exalting the virtues of Francis Drake and William the Conqueror, we placed our rulers on desks, pressed them hard on our left hands and strummed them with our right, producing music like that of a string bass.

Later we used plywood boxes (originally intended for carrying Ceylon tea) and affixed planks and strings to make an instrument. These acts were always communal.

In the evening we would sit around our Welcome Dover Stove No. 8 with cousins, brothers, sisters and friends, cracking jokes at each other's expense, indulging in repartee. We did not know at the time that we were sharpening our minds to produce poetic images. We would make that connection years later.

THE ARTIST IN EXILE

To be an exile is to be nurtured outside the womb of your culture. It is to be placed in a situation of perpetual readjustment. To be a battleground of suspicion, stubbornness and a desire to belong. Let me put it differently, to be an exile is to be a transplant. How you survive, live, or die artistically depends on what kind of tree you are and whether you escaped or were forced to leave your own culture or country with, or without, a fistful of soil to nourish you.

In my country, and in Swaziland, my country of adoption, the fusion of art forms, to be a poet, painter, sculptor, musician, actor, all in one, can be just a matter of course. Ceremonies, rituals, fuse all art forms to allow for a cross fertilisation within the same setting and time. Arriving in Britain I found myself living, or half living, in different compartments simultaneously. Each compartment seemed hermetically sealed. Each so stiflingly private. I was plagued by a state of permanent impermanence. Each handshake or greeting of a new neighbour was at the same time valedictory. I was beginning to feel like a deserted man in an arid desert or wasteland of ice. In 1981 an oasis materialised before me. I came into contact with the members of the Pan African Orature Collective, The African Dawn.

An echo of Swaziland; a combination of poetry, drama, music and visual artistry. My transplanted soil begins to mingle with others, to share nourishment, to feast. My dehydrated roots are watered and spread, Festival of Progressive Arts from Africa, Black Artists for Azania, Monti wa Marume, Inkaba Pan Root

Cultural Festival. Celebrations of creativity, spontaneity, unity, hope.

The preparations are harrowing, battles for resources, funding, space. Art critics and journalists seeking answers to questions that are meaningless to our events, demanding 'central' figures from our collective. Brain cells die in the process. Nerves fray. Only a vision of the future (or is it a memory of my past?) keeps me going.

Opening nights, art forms in co-existence, co-mingling takes over, artists swim in their sea, the heartaches and frustrations are shelved.

To be an artist is to be especially aware and appreciative of one's environment. To be able to utilise it creatively. I use my environment both physically and metaphorically. What is my environment in Britain, in London? It is the media whose lips drip racism, violent cartoons, shit and petrol bombs through letter boxes, the ever-contracting boundaries of progress for Black people and Black culture, punctuated by occasional meadows of love. Scrap yards, skips, derelict buildings, my rose gardens. I salvage weapons of war against ugliness. I attempt to humanise objects, exhaust pipes, gearboxes, saucepans; curses, insults, appreciation, grey clouds, monotonous terraces, odd patches of colour in parks, human touch, frustration and hopes... my raw materials. Orature is more than the fusion of all art forms. It is the conception and reality of a total view of life. It is a capsule of feeling, thinking, imagination, taste and hearing. It is the flow of a creative spirit. Within sculpture alone it is stone, wood, found objects, metal, shells. In poetry it is not only the images but also their presentation. Orature is the universe of expression and appreciation and a fusion of both within one individual, a group, a community. It is a weapon against the encroaching atomisation of life. It is the beginning come full circle on a higher plane. It is a gem, an idea, a reality that beckons us to be part of it.

REFLECTION

To live up to the ripe age of thirteen in my country is a miracle, to paraphrase Steve Biko. We are born into a violent world. Organised terror tactics are realities of the state. Bottled up fury of my people that almost always explodes at the nearest target — a brother, a sister, an aunt, uncle or friend.

When I was eight years old I tried to save money to buy my own 'three star' or 'Okapi' knife. At thirteen I needed a tomahawk battle axe, not against the state, but against my neighbours, my people. I knew I was like so many others, marked for an early grave. My body is a ploughed field of scars, my brain a battleground. I am a survivor. That I still smile, love, embrace, create, is a bonus, a freak bubble within a miracle. Nowadays thirteen year olds do not arm themselves against each other. They take on the might of the state. They call themselves 'comrades'.

How time moves. Things change. Images change. Life is a sea of images. Shantytowns grow into matchbox houses, self images develop, sometimes undergo a metamorphosis. Imperceptible changes. I wake up one morning. I no longer need a knife, a tomahawk, but a book, a world of ideas — of colour, form, line, movement, organised sounds, rhythms — to know those that encapsulated me since birth — anew.

90 Photo: Graham de Smidt.

90

POSTSCRIPT: AN ARTIST'S CRISP MORNING

When I woke up this morning, I turned on the TV set to watch the news. The first thing I saw and heard was an advert for KP crisps: 'He came. He saw. He sat down.' There was a Roman Legionnaire sitting on a pile of huge bricks eating crisps. Later, as I drove along the North Circular Road to Dalston, I caught myself whistling the tune from the same advert. I immediately snuffed it. I consciously whistled a tune from Dade Krama's album *Ancestral Music Of Africa*. Two miles later, I was back on my KP crisps tune! When such tunes catch you, it is a battle to finally defeat them.

You would argue that this has nothing to do with art. Well, that's the matter we have to determine. First, let us admit adverts are very persuasive, but more importantly, we must also admit our own sensitivity. An advert lasts only a few seconds, comes on TV perhaps a few times a day.

I am an avid news watcher. The State of Emergency in South Africa, shootings and bomb blasts in Ulster, US increases support for Contras in Nicaragua, US attacks Libya. In all of these countries, it is not the question of he came, he saw, he sat down. It

91

91 Photo: Graham de Smidt.

is the case of coming, seeing, destroying human lives. It is events and issues like these that occupy my day-to-day existence. Reading newspapers and magazines, listening to speeches every day about the future of 'mankind', 'man', 'masterpieces', 'chairman', watching and listening to the abolition of women. To be silent about this would be a political act.

The Conservative Government has introduced new stringent immigration laws to affect, directly, people from India, Pakistan, Bangladesh, Ghana and Nigeria. Sir Woodrow Wyatt stated in the *News Of The World* that Black immigrants are 'lawless, drugtaking, violent and unemployable'. John Carlisle, British Minister of Sport, was let loose to defend the massacre of Azanians. There is daily brutalisation of Black people and acts of exclusion of other cultural 'minorities'. To be silent about these would be another political act.

It is such political acts that white institutions call upon Black artists to perform. They always do find some Black artists who oblige. This is a crowning political act.

For me, as an artist, to be silent about these issues would be an act of political suicide.

92

92 Photo: Graham de Smidt.

TALKING IN TONGUES

SONIA
BOYCE

93

93 Cricket Days? Domino Nights! Young arrivals/ new home/homeless. The streets are paved with gold in this green and pleasant land. Mixed media on photocopy and paper, 9 by 4 feet, 1986.

Missionary Position 1–
lay back. Pastel on paper
94 3½ by 2½ feet, 1985.

94

95

95 Missionary Position II–
position changing. Pastel
on paper, 6 by 4 feet,
1985.

Conversational Piece: kitchen table talk, strange
dreams. Mixed media on
photograph, 3 by 2 feet,
96 1986.

Mr. Close-Friend-of-the-Family Pays a Visit Whilst Everyone Else is Out. Charcoal on paper, 5 by 4 **97** feet, 1985.

Ring of Confidence — encouraging ideas, encouraging dialogue, imaginative man and his two nieces, who both dreamed of being Sleeping Beauty or maybe Queen would do. Mixed media photograph, 7 by 4 **98** feet. 1986.

LITERATURE IN AFRICAN LANGUAGES

Translated from the Gîkûyû by Wangûi Wa'Goro

NGŨGĨ WA'THIONG'O

A debate has been raging around my book *Decolonising the Mind*, which deals with the politics of African language literatures. Some participants in the debate are clearly in support of the challenge in the book, that African writers should stop serving foreign/colonial and neo-colonial languages, such as French, English and Portuguese, and turn to the development of African languages, by writing in them. Other participants in the debate form a group which feels embarrassed at even the slightest mention of African languages. Why does Ngũgĩ want to plunge us back into darkness? Essentially their arguments are based on false assumptions which ignore or downplay the wealth of African languages. They also ignore the lessons taught by the history of other languages.

If we turn to history and look at a language like English, we note that most English writers wrote in Latin during the fifteenth century, because they considered their native language barbaric. It could not express philosophy or religion, they argued, and lacked the vocabulary to create stimulating literature or compose poetry. Writers like Chaucer and later Shakespeare refuted these claims. Today they rank amongst the world's most renowned writers. John Milton wrote his early poetry in Latin but later changed to his own language, English. His Latin poetry is today hardly mentioned. The patriotism of these writers enabled them to have a better appreciation of the wealth of their own language. In Italy, we cannot forget the role played by Dante who rejected Latin and chose instead to write in his own Italian, then the 'common everyday language'. The important *Divine Comedy* was a by-product of this decision. Other significant writers such as Boccaccio joined Dante in refuting the arguments against Italian and developed the language to the same stature as Latin in terms of quality of vocabulary and richness of concepts.

If we move eastwards, we note that as recently as the eighteenth century, the Russian language was considered inadequate for the expression of scientific ideas and not good enough for diplomacy. French and German were used to fulfil these functions. Again, writers such as Pushkin and Tolstoy refuted such arrogant assumptions and developed their creativity within their own languages. It is clear how significant a contribution they made to the language when today Russian carries some of the world's most advanced ideas. Finnish writers had to save their language from the domination of Swedish.

Yet another example comes from the experience of Vietnam, a country whose history is closer to that of our own. Like most African countries, Vietnam has passed through the phase of colonialism and later of neo-colonialism. When the French dominated Vietnam, they promoted writers who wrote in French. The reasons they gave for promoting these writers was that Vietnamese languages did not have as adequate a vocabulary as French. Later, during the period of their domination of the South, the Americans, too, tried to impose their own language and culture on the people. What of today? Since the defeat of the French in the fifties at Dien Bien Phu and of the Americans in Saigon in the seventies, the writers who wrote in foreign languages have become mere footnotes for the writers of today. The struggle of the Vietnamese people to liberate their languages went hand in hand with their struggles against imperialism.

I believe that we as African people have a lot to learn from these histories. I shall draw upon the Kenyan experience, mainly because Kenya epitomises all the contradictions of a neo-colony. English is considered the first language of Kenya. It is the language of administration and instruction and is given first place in effecting all matters of national life. Kiswahili is the national language of communication for the country's nationalities and promotes the unity of workers and peasants. Each nationality also has its own language: Masai, Somali, Baluhya, Luo, Gîkûyû, Turkana, Oromo, Kamba, amongst others.

The attitude of the neo-colonial regime towards these languages is one of contempt. It uses English to repress workers and peasants in their creativity, education and culture. English is also used to suppress struggles for unity and against oppression. The intention of the regime is to suppress African languages and make difficult effective dialogue and communication amongst the people.

I have written novels, plays and essays. Between 1960 and 1977, I wrote books such as *The River Between, Weep Not Child, Grain of Wheat, Home Coming, Petals of Blood, The Black Hermit, This Time Tomorrow* and *The Trial of Dedan Kimathi* (co-authored with Micere Githae Mugo). All of them were in English. In 1977, however, I decided to do most of my writing in Gîkûyû, one of the languages of Kenya. I wrote a novel whose translated title is *Devil on the Cross*, and a play, *I Will Marry When I Want* (co-authored with Ngugi wa' Mirii). I continued to write essays in English, such as 'Writers in Politics', 'Detained', and 'Barrel of a Pen'. But after writing *Decolonising the Mind*, I decided to say a final farewell to English and do all my writing in Gîkûyû and Kiswahili. These are two languages amongst many other African languages.

I believe that using our languages in this way is an important part of the process of decolonising our minds. It will go a long way to contribute to the democratic struggles that will bring meaningful change in Africa. All democratic-minded people and revolutionaries must use all possible means to struggle against the forces of reaction. Using our languages to express our creativity and against corruption, dictatorships, neo-colonialism and exploitation is a first step towards liberating Africa's wealth and labour.

It is important to stress that every language has the potential to develop. It is only through constant use that the European and Asian languages mentioned earlier have developed. What the speakers and users have done is to add new vocabulary to embody new concepts as they encountered them. There are various ways of introducing new concepts and ideas into a language. One of the most common is to explore existing linguistic structures as the basis of forming new words. Sometimes language throws up entirely new words to form new concepts. Borrowing words from other languages and leaving them in their original form or authenticating them is also quite common. The latter is evident in the way African languages have developed, with the interaction with oppressive cultures as well as those encountered as a result of trade and geography. To illustrate this, I will draw examples from the Gĩkũyũ language. The words have their roots as indicated. The root language may also have borrowed the word from other languages.

GĨKŨYŨ	FOREIGN WORD	DERIVATION
Ngeereci	garage	English
Kabiaru	coffee	English
Kareendi	Lady (+ Gĩkũyũ diminutive ka-)	English
Thabari	Safari	Kiswahili
Metha	Meza	Kiswahili (derived from Portuguese)

Most African languages have common roots as for example Twi,
Fantsti and Akwapim in Ghana which belong to the Akan
language. This special quality enables the languages to borrow new
concepts and vocabulary from each other more easily. Language is
also best developed by those to whom it belongs. In other words,
charity begins at home. Pushkin, Dante and Shakespeare had to
lead the way in the liberation of their languages from foreign
domination and contribute to their development. All African
artists, writers of poems, novels, story-tellers, song-writers,
performers, educationists and media workers, have the task of
developing African languages and forging a vibrant interaction
between them as the basis of a new culture.

At this juncture I would like to respond to some of the false
assumptions and arguments of those opposed to the use of African
languages. I elaborate on them in my book, *Decolonising the Mind*.
Firstly they claim that writing in African languages will divide
people and promote what they call 'tribalism'. This is an old
argument. They would have us believe that division is caused solely
by language and by implication that a single language in a country
is synonymous with a unified nation. The experience of Ireland for
example, refutes this. It highlights the complex schisms of politics
and religion which divide Catholics from Protestants, republicans
from unionists, revolutionaries from reformists. Countries like
Switzerland and the Soviet Union also prove that numerous
languages and nationalities can co-exist and interact within unified
political units.

I do indeed see the specific and significant role and function of
language in efforts towards unity, but there are other fundamental
issues which determine it. These relate to the economy, politics
and dynamics of the peoples' history, amongst other factors.

The irony of the position which argues that a single language
can bring about a unified nation, is that it sees foreign languages
as best qualified to achieve it. The very languages which have been
used to oppress and balkanise us! If they were not so bent on
discrediting and playing down African languages, they would at
least, according to their own rationale, look at a case like Tanzania,
with its use of Kiswahili. This denial of African languages is an
expression of a colonial mentality and self-hatred.

In any case, it is only a very small percentage of African
people, approximately 5%, who speak French, English or
Portuguese. The assumption that unity will be brought about by
these foreign languages implies that the unity of the nation is
complete with 5% of the population. The argument does not
consider the unity of the peasants and workers who comprise the
remaining 95% of the nation. Where does their unity come from?

These people have always spoken their own languages and always lived in their own nations. How is it that it is only now that their languages are suddenly dividing the nations? They have spoken their own languages, and significantly forged a unity strong enough to dismantle colonialism.

My belief, one which history has proved to be true, is that unity can only be forged in struggle, as for example when people fight against a common enemy. At present, the greatest enemy of the African people is neo-colonialism. This is the cause of division amongst those trying to build a new society today.

There are various ways of building unity in a nation. The first step towards building this unity is to struggle against imperialism, and especially imperialism in its neo-colonial form. The struggle against exploitation of labour, and the constant drain of our wealth from Africa to the West, is also very important. The third vital factor is the struggle to maintain and protect people's democratic rights. This involves a struggle against neo-colonialism and its caretakers, the small comprador clique who have sold out Africa to imperialism. We need a new breed of leaders who are committed to a democracy which would enable the equality of all the nationalities of our countries to thrive. Democratic development should also be looked at from the perspective of the working class and the peasantry of each nationality. It means that smaller nationalities have to be respected, and not feel intimidated and oppressed by larger ones. The fourth factor necessary for the building of unity is dialogue between the African languages. We should strive towards finding different ways and means of learning from each other's languages. The promotion of translation and interpretation skills in our languages is a crucial factor in the struggle towards unity. By writing our literature in our languages, and by developing the skills of translation and interpretation, books can then be more easily published in the different languages. Breaking the barrier of communication between different nationalities, would mean greater understanding of the cultures and languages. It would facilitate the borrowing of values and of vocabulary. In orthography, different languages can designate similar characters to represent similar sounds, borrowing from already existing forms. These processes facilitate economic and political exchange between different nations and states as well as between different countries. I also believe that no patriotic African would be opposed to the promotion of one or a few languages such as Kiswahili and Hausa as continental languages provided this did not mean the suppression of other languages. The fundamental condition for such a promotion is democracy.

We should be proud of our languages. We should write in our

languages. We should talk to our people about the unity of the masses of our continent. Let us sing of the victories of the workers as well as those of the peasants, especially in this final stage of imperialism, namely neocolonialism.

I end this paper with a poem written by Wangûi wa' Goro, one of the many young people who shoulder the responsibility of the future of our continent, Africa. Her poem, *On Language*, originally written in Gîkûyû, calls all African patriots.

> Come you intellectuals
> let us hold talks
> Speaking in our tongues
> Speaking of our thoughts
>
> Come you child
> Let us hold talks
> Speaking in the tongues
> Of generations past
>
> Speaking in the tongues
> Of history of our land(s)
> Speaking in the tongues
> Tongues of many shades.

Yes, let's sing of a new United Africa in our languages!

THE TIMELESS VOICE

FOR THE NEW LANGUAGE

REFLECTIONS ON IMPERATIVES

JACOB ROSS

Late evening. The wooden homes perched like spiders on the hill stand gaping, door-mouth-wide, at the crackling fires in the open spaces of the yards below. The smell of cooking, the pepper-sweet stench of wood-smoke. Voices in the wind, returned and returning from the day-long toil on soil and sun-parched cane plantations that stretch, century-long, beyond the mute mountains, the river and the sea. The children wait while inner storms, reflected in adults' eyes, abate. Food is solid, nourishing. Tiredness is shed in sighs; oppression warms and melts in smiles. And then it comes, sure as the sickle moon that hangs above the mountains. An Old Voice sings: 'Tim-Tim.' The chorus comes in cataracts: 'Ba-sheh!'

The Old Voice sings a song in French patois while expectant eyes settle on the withered face. In the centre of the circle, the fire burns, shedding light and warmth on all, containing the group, defining space. The 'Nancy' story that follows comes in chant song and choruses and gestures:

> Once 'pon a time,
> It had a lil' peeny-weeny spider name, Anansi...

The story rides the quiet night, one of thousands shaped and honed by the centuries to articulate the predicament of a whole civilisation that had come victorious through European imposed enslavement. The stores are about animals, creatures of the forest, which, by dint of their physical limitations learned to survive the oppression of the lions and tigers of this world through cunning.

As children we never reflected on these stories. Part of our vocabulary, they were grafted on the mind from birth. The format was always the same: first, the stillness, the expectancy, the silent invocations; then, the sudden call followed by the chorus of voices — a chorus that punctuated the rendition throughout, confirming attention; and more importantly, guided the plot whichever way it wanted. The beginning and the end, we always knew. But within those two unchallenged parameters everything was possible. Relevance and meaning were ours to create and re-create. Though teeny-weeny Anansi always emerged victorious over Lion or Tiger, what mattered most to us was precisely *how* that victory was achieved.

There are many story-tellers. But the Old Voice was the one which best stirred the seeds of ancestral memory, the one which lived and echoed in the bones long after last words had fallen from the lips and settled on the brain.

> De story end
> An de wire bend

I remembered a night of stars and low moon, the last night we would hear her talk. The voice crept in on the waiting, solemn, slow. No call this time. No song. A voice slow with age and heavy — a kind of leave-taking almost:

> In de beginning wuz de word
> And de word wuz ours to change de worl as we like
> In we own image an likeness.

Her story had ended; the voice handed back to us to be passed on in turn. But those words had been planted; the legacy, left. What did she, the Old Voice, mean by that? Consciousness began to germinate. It followed me to school.

Formal education for me, the neo-colonial child, marked the beginning of a conflict of voice: the Old Voice that had gathered us, on evenings, in tight circles around small yard-fire, that had forged us a language and a link with Africa, a home we'd never really known: *that* voice, pitted against the stridulous sting of our schoolmaster's whip which constantly shamed our skins and the words that issued from our lips. Summer, autumn, winter, spring, dancing in a fairy ring; daffodils and snowdrops; the counties and the shires of England were drummed into our senses until this longed-for world of untold purity and whiteness constituted the very geography of our imaginations. Sometimes though, in sleep, the Old Voice spoke, reminding us of another school, the one not ruled by the English of Queens, but one we had lived through and surmounted in the death-heat of the cane plantations. Formal education offered 'advancement'; the Old Voice sent us *back*, searching for the source.

What do references to these folk tales have to do with language and language issues? Everything! Believe me.

> The social context for the Caribbean Creoles (the language in which these stories were told) was the Atlantic Slave Trade, involving the enslavement of Africans by Europeans for economic profit. It is also one of African resistance, readaptation and perpetuation of African culture in the teeth of an attempt to enforce European culture upon captured Africans. (Morgan Dalphinis, *Caribbean and African Languages*, Karia Press, 1985.)

Nowhere are the elements of resistance and perpetuation of African culture more evident than in the themes, motifs and *language* of the stories that the Old Voice told. And by language, I do not mean the mere concatenation of words to signify some sort of meaning. I am talking about the form, structure, gestures, music, rhythm; the silences; the way space is organised in order to define, nurture and underscore relationships in the process of communication. Early European ethnologists and ethno-linguists, basing their analyses of Afro-culture on theories of white supremacy, pointed to adults relating animal tales as proof of the 'childish simplicity of the African mind'. The credence given to this assumption by 'great' European thinkers such as Hume, who asserted 'the natural inferiority of Blacks to Whites', Thomas Jefferson, who saw this inferiority 'in both body and mind', as well as Freud who made similar claims, cannot be overlooked. Useful as Karl Marx's theories on class and class dialectics might have been to twentieth-century politics, his attitudes on race and racial aptitudes were hardly more sophisticated than Le Gobineau's, who in 1854 propounded in *Inequality of The Human Races*: 'The Negroid variety is the lowest, at the foot of the ladder. The animal character is stamped on the Negro from birth... His intellect will always move within a narrow circle.'

This is the context in which African modes of communication were perceived. The above-mentioned analysts were hardly different from the blundering Columbus who mistook the islands of the Americas for India. Communication for the Eurocentric mind operates principally at the level of the reciprocal exchange of *words* and was thus ill-equipped to deal with a civilisation that operated systems of communication so complex they often bypassed the use of words altogether. Because words could only say so much, symbols, gestures, drumming, proverbs and dance constituted a complex web of meaning that totally escaped the European mind for whom communication is heavily based on the choice of words and the way they relate to each other. It is only within recent years that socio-linguists have begun to come to terms with this complementary language system, this para-language of gestures, expressions and ritual. This system has been developed to consummate levels by our people over the centuries, often to the exclusion of words. It is, partly, within this context that I want to situate the story-telling tradition of our people, the tradition that has begun more and more to inform the work of 'young' writers like myself, the tradition of animal heroes who survive by cunning against their physically superior enemies. Gizo of the Hausa cycle becomes Anansi the spider of the Twi and Fantsti's oral culture. Zomo and Leuk (rabbit) perform the same function in the Hausa and Wolof cultures, respectively. What is often ignored is the *socio-political* role of these tales.

The function of these stories is essentially regulatory. Not only do they define the relationship between the collective and those chosen to govern their lives, they also serve as a channel of communication, a political forum, in which the collective participates and in which the excesses of a leader, a family or an individual are highlighted, challenged and democratically resolved. That Anansi/Zomo, Gizo/Leuk were always chosen as the symbolic representatives of the collective voice opposed to Lion, Tiger, Elephant, or whichever animal's characteristics best suited the offenders, points to the effective functioning of an institution which has evolved its own rules and rituals (like other models of government elsewhere) within which the affairs of the community are conducted. In this sense, audience participation — the call and response mode — is not merely a 'distinguishing feature of Afro-language structures' but a functional mode of government, the undermining of which destroyed the very fabric of social accountability and control.

Ngugi Wa' Thiong'o's, *Decolonising the Mind* addresses some of the questions raised by the imposition of alien European value systems on the language and culture of colonised African peoples. 'Language,' he states, 'is ... inseparable from ourselves as a community of human beings with a specific form and character, a specific history, a specific relationship to the world.' The most important area of domination, he adds, 'was the mental universe of how people perceived themselves and their relationship to the world.'

The strategies deployed by the colonising powers to mentally subjugate our peoples in order to seize and control their wealth, are well documented. It follows that, since culture is a product of history, and language serves both to define and articulate that history, the suppression of either history or culture limits the creative potential of language.

Like a people's history, culture cannot be destroyed; nor can it be articulated in a language that is the product of an alien history. It is for precisely this reason that suppressed languages and cultures 'co-exist' in a state of perpetual tension in which the subjugated is striving constantly to liberate itself.

I remember my first response to the term 'diglossia', dropped sonorously from the lips of a professor in full flight. The term was used to denote the perceived high/low (superior/inferior) relationship between language varieties that co-exist in the same societies, each performing different functions. The Old Voice came to mind and startled me to challenge the 'objectivity' of the term, since the very claim to objective description of language situations, covering as it did so broad a range of situations, ignored the essence of my birth-language: the fundamental element of *resistance.* Bourgeois linguistic ideologies cannot cope with the dimensions of the political inherent in colonial 'diglossic' situations where the culture/language of the oppressed are in constant tension to break loose from the ravages of an alien value system. Hubert Devonish's *Language and Liberation: Creole Language Politics in the Caribbean,* 1986, is one of the few theses to point out that 'class conflict expresses itself in diglossic situations'.

All too often I've found that as artists and arts practitioners, we unconsciously fulfil the very objectives of cultural imperialism by unquestioningly assimilating and regurgitating objective *cum* scientific terms which conveniently void our reality of its very essence. In the colonial and neo-colonial contexts, diglossia denotes nothing if its use as a 'scientific tool' does not lead us to perceive the exact role of our language in relation to the language of the coloniser. Notions of European language superiority have served as instruments of ruling class power. It is the language of government, commerce and administration to which, historically, the education system guarantees access to only the privileged few. In our world, access to European language is a precondition for access to power. It has been observed that a people's seizure of economic and political control can only be democratically sustained by the ascendancy of their own language, since it is only through their language, their world view, that they can enter into dialogue with the means of production and effect real and lasting change.

But I was talking about the stories... An obscenity, still prevalent today, is the appropriation of the world literature to signify what the Shakespeares, Chaucers, Wordsworths and Dickenses of this world have produced. Literature, even among our own critics, was non-existent until four decades ago. Young, Black, educated colonials graduated to the mother country and began to emulate Europe's literary saints. In the same way, 'culture' has come to mean that which simulates the speech, thought patterns, mannerisms, and oftentimes absurdities of Europe's upper classes. Literature has been confined to an intellectual coffin, which even in burial has to be claimed by the soil of Europe. The 1986 London Conference of Caribbean Writers at the Commonwealth Institute was in my view, based on this grossly distorted premise.

In the keynote address, the speaker presented the written language as a form sufficient unto itself, not considering the Creole-nation languages of the Caribbean as having a validity of their own, but finding excitement in the way they were 'crafted' into the structures of the English language.

The analysis was not just based on the misconception of literature. Worse, it represented a denial of a literary tradition among our people that dates back several millenia before the first scratchings on the caves of Europe. The Nansi stories of the Old Voice, like the narrations of the griots, of the Wolof and Madinka peoples, like the Marok'a of the Hausa and the oracle of the Igbo, are part of a vast body of knowledge whose functions are: education, documentation, social and political regulation, entertainment, communal celebration and mourning. One can easily respond by pointing to the written traditions of Africans of the Nile valley (hieroglyphics) or the North African-sourced written literature (ajum) among the Hausa and Yoruba. But I'm not interested in indicating the pleasure in similarities — I leave that to apologists — but rather the virtues in difference and diversity.

I owe it to the Old Voice to challenge another myth: that a society merits the distinction of being 'civilised' only if it possesses a written tradition. Apart from the fact that great civilisations have emerged, flourished and created without recourse to codifying their language in writing, the women and men of the diaspora, bearers of great traditions in orature, have carried tomes in their heads for centuries with neither the inclination nor the need to write them down. This is not to dismiss the value of scriptual traditions. It is merely a matter of clearing the records and acknowledging that the transition from an oral to the scriptual literary mode has more often than not meant the abandonment of one important faculty: the faculty of extensive recall, the ability to remember, to relate the origin, histories and evolutions of whole societies; to transmit the ideas, lessons and collective wisdom gathered and passed on over centuries by word of mouth.

In *The Struggle for Black Arts in Britain*, 1986, Kwesi Owusu speculated on how Eurocentric perceptions of the world might have led to the invention of the 'single eyed' camera. A similar logic could suggest that the effective supplanting of the oral tradition in Western culture, and the consequent fossilization of the recall faculty, might have led to the creation of memory aids such as magnetic recorders, calculators and computers.

Thinking back on the Nansi story, gatherings in the yard, warmed by a binding fire, under the pale light of a low moon, I cannot count the number of times I marvelled at the extraordinary mind for long and distant detail possessed by the old, the passed and passing generations. Perhaps we have been losing.

But there is another level where the language remains intact. History abounds with examples of the failed attempts of colonial and neo-colonial governments to stifle the birth-language. Caribbean Creole, for example, grew out of the confrontation between African modes of communication and imposed colonial languages. What resulted was a new language profoundly rooted in the African language patterns at the levels of grammar, syntax, semantics and, to a lesser extent, vocabulary. Creole linguists take pleasure nowadays in identifying the extensive Niger-Congo language family. The calypsonian replaced the griot as social commentator and documentor. The Nansi stories preserved the spaces and social structures developed at home, obtaining added relevance in the context of European slavery in the Americas. They assumed an enhanced role, functioning as a weapon of psychological resistance. The European slave master became the ravaging Lion and the oppressed, the ever-evasive Anansi, describing thus a predicament while coaching the young in strategies of physical and cultural survival. Anansi Cudjoe of Carriacou was known to have instigated rebellions using this medium.

In Britain today, young Black Africans are responding to racial and social marginalisation by mobilising around a single language. Despite the diverse national origins of its speakers, the Jamaican Creole variant has become the unifying force through which cultural assertion and racial identity are articulated for the majority. Political and cultural assertions are not dissociable. At the height of resistance, poet Linton Kwesi Johnson chants in rhythm and rhyme and the chorus that rises from the frontline unites the tides of resistance — Notting Hill, Broadwater Farm, Brixton and on, and on, and on... From the circle of eyes around the fire, beneath a tropic moon, the timeless and undying Voice has multiplied and amplified a thousand times through wire-leads and micro chips to guide the young through Babylon.

NOTTING HILL CARNIVAL

WALK WITH THE MASQUERADE

IMAGE AND TEXT TAKE A

On the road with the masquerade you don't see what you normally see. Voices hurry the boats to sea, shadows dance in the wind, blue-eyed dragons and sasabonsam inhale fire and belch out smoke. On the road with the masquerade you don't feel what you normally feel. Little chimes, arrow and shack-shack take a walk with Anansi and brigades of dancing feet along the valleys of the Kilimanjaro. There, sunrise is as sure as the volcano surge from the belly of the earth. On the road with the masquerade you don't do what you normally do. Voices wrap around the bass line and wings flap free like birds in the blue Caribbean sky. On the road with the masquerade, chains dangle loose in the dusty clouds when the people surge forward. Sound systems stay on freedom grooves and the long play of history spins round the African sun.

On the road with the masquerade, you don't use words you normally use. Soon come says the hurricane in the murmurings of the gentle breeze. Grandma feels the power in the message for it speaks at the junction of bolts and thunder. When it's ready it rushes home like Nanny on the threshold of reckoning. On the

KWESI
OWUSU

99

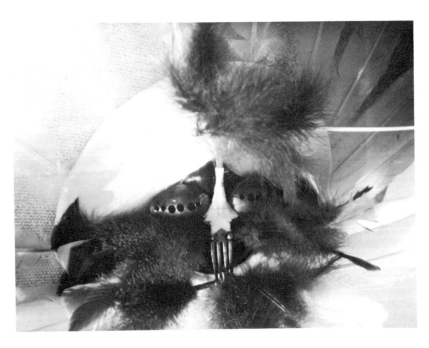

road with the masquerade, you don't hear what you normally hear. Languages long scattered by the winds of the Atlantic crossing surge forth in unison and children whisper to each other, 'It's chantwell time now, it's chantwell time now and the power Black,' and the echo takes it away, 'splendid ebony cast, worker wise and history deep'. The masquerade stands poised on the edge of the storm. A million eyes feed the hands and colours splash on the imagination of the story-tellers of our time.

The moment of the masquerade is a beauty that answers the call of a deep yearning and dream. Nature nods. There is the colour green, fresh-leaf smiling. There is gold, metal-rich and precious. There is red, sap-deep and simmering on a landscape saluting the sun. Violet dazzles from the rear of a star trek and purple tails a full moon glow. The heart is kneaded in song.

'Destroying Angels' was created with Cocoyea Mas as the theme for the 1983 Notting Hill Carnival. The masqueraders in hell-size wings turned a West London street into a celestial zone jammed by brisk brigades of dancing feet entrapped by soca and voices. When night fell, they appeared in their glitter to be filtering through a mosaic of stars and spitfire. Mangrove's 'When the Spirit Moves' (1985) and 'Me, Myself I Warrior' (1986) have themes inspired by the Burkinabe culture of West Africa. The

designs are lavishly embellished with colour. Prime colours rubricate the thin delicate lines of ink; asymmetrical patterns of black and red merge with semi-circular shapes of white tempered with yellow stripes.

In Burkina Faso, the colours evoke the tropical environment. The art is an allusion to the beauty of the natural landscape: deep brown for the soil, jaded yellow for fallen leaves blowing in the harmattan breeze and lustrous pink for sundown. The people pay homage to the rivers, the freshwater ponds and the grasslands. Costumes are made of leather and wood and finished off with tall blades of grass. The interaction with nature is the source of life and culture. The costumes function as work clothes for hunters, the camouflage which helps them blend with the landscape as they pursue game.

Hunters have intimate knowledge of the natural world and in their reproduction of sounds and synchronised imitation of movement, they evoke a fusion of work and creativity, a fusion seen also in the simultaneous act of a farmer's cutlass swing and work dance. In 1985 and 1986, Mangrove made a link with this tradition, and interpreted its significance to the Black urban reality of Britain.

One of the things which struck me on a recent visit to Burkina Faso was the accuracy of 'When the Spirit Moves' to the local tradition. The colours and designs were almost identical.

Ouagadougou is a dry, sprawling city on the edge of the Sahara, capital of the country with the lowest gross national product in the world, according to a UN statistic of the late seventies. It was a hot afternoon in front of the *maison des peuple*. As the masquerades from Koko, Warba and Tibin hit the dust into the sky, I wondered how the two traditions keep in touch in spite of the physical distance and the apparent separateness of national identities. Notting Hill is a few thousand miles from Ouagadougou, locked up in the concrete jungle of Babylon. In Ouagadougou the official language is French. Colonialism bequeathed some striking buildings of Parisian architecture which stand in the shadows of Mossi designed mosques. Every so often during the day, a steady voice rings out from the domes, calling the city to prayer. Every face turns to Mecca and foreheads humbly touch the sand.

103

From the apparent dissimilarity emerges continuity, a lifeline which connects the essence of the African experience by defying the geo-political boundaries of our modern culture. The Mas people of Notting Hill are warriors in the complex of Babylon. They engage with it in their daily lives, defying the rugged contours of its plastic landscape. In Ouagadougou when the dust goes up with the feet and the sounds emerge from the Burkinabe instruments Mangrove's creative power in Notting Hill is energised. The sound builds up into a thunderous roar and the horns bellow with the force of the winds. A masquerader moves to the centre of the circle and somersaults on two sticks. His huge frame spins in the air and folds like cloth around the intoxicated patterns of sound. The intensity of the occasion is like the climax of a carnival street jam, and if you listen carefully you will feel soca, osode, rumba and one-drop rhythm in the music from Koko and Warba.

Come closer so I can hear you beyond the oceans, the borders and the small visa print in your passport. Come closer so I can whisper to you like the water that drips from your roof in Trenchtown. Come closer so you can hear me from the Bronx, Handsworth and the little village not on the map. Come closer so I can see my face in yours and yours in mine. Come closer my sister, brother, and mother for you would not feel the thud of my heartbeat on Capital Radio nor the full range of my tonal chords on your compact disc. Come closer my uncle from Djibouti and my auntie who emigrated to Canada. This hand here and that finger there touch the notes on Coltrane's horn, and sister Holiday's voice woke grandpa after a sad, sad night. My hand holds this little gourd, vibrating with a song you used to sing. Come closer, take a step up the escalator, a tube ride on the freedom train towards home.

She may be a seamstress, a garment factory worker or just one of the many African mothers who has learnt to sew and mend garments. Few African households can do without mother's sewing tin packed to the brim with scissors, needles, balls of wool and thread. There is the kid's shirt to patch, there is baby's new cardigan to knit and new patterns in British Home Stores' catalogue to try. When she was leaving the Caribbean, grandma gave her an old sewing machine. It was manual, a Singer model, and to be honest with you, has seen better days. When she first tried to use it she had to pour a whole tin of oil into it to activate the motor. Grandma insisted she came with it, 'never know when you need it,' she said. Today it reminds her of the long evenings in the open yard, sewing and patching flour sacks and pillow cases, and, when grandma was in a good mood, a dress for herself.

Grandma had a small stall in the market and she always went with the sewing machine. When business wasn't so good, grandma would send her to friends and acquaintances to patch a few clothes for a few shillings. She would balance the portable machine gracefully on her head and click the scissors to an insistent rhythm in her head. In West Africa, we call people who earn money visiting and mending clothes, oye adie yie, a person who mends and makes things better. They usually have a hook line of a popular song on their lips and children are always at hand to respond with a chorus or a song of their own:

> I am a little child
> With no money
> My clothes are torn
> Oye adie yie please mend them and make things better.

Grandma used to say sewing a dress was like going through life. You have to go diligently: not too fast to miss out the colourful embroidery, not too slow to miss the outing. There are the trying moments and the possible disasters. Some needles are quite difficult to thread and a stubborn garment can break them. It could be your last needle. A careless swerve of the scissors can ruin a beautiful dress. Grandma is diligent in life. Her skill and intelligence simultaneously inform her creativity and attitude to life.

This consciousness is ancient. She may have been initiated into it by foreparents and the bag of ancestral knowledge stretches backwards like a shimmering silver line in the family memory. The Atlantic crossing was momentous, not least in the suppression of aspects of African culture which proved subversive to the slave system. Drumming by African slaves was, for example, periodically

105

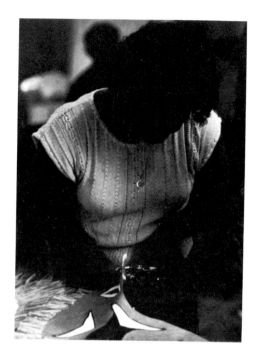

banned because slaves on different estates used it to communicate amongst themselves. African languages were also discouraged. The slave and colonial experience has resulted in a severe mutation in our contemporary consciousness. It means that we have to negotiate the expression of the silver line at every turn and within each space of our modern culture. But you see, we are a people of messages, signals, of hieroglyphics and allusive speech, and it is impossible to legislate or hammer out of existence what is second nature and lurking at the threshold of being and becoming.

Her foreparents may have come from Bonwire in pre-colonial Africa. There in Asante the community developed one of the most successful weaving cultures in the world. Kente and adinkra are its best-known products, with proverb patterns and socio-political imagery woven together with colourful thread. When the cloth is worn, it functions as a lingual tapestry depicting social mood, political association and ideological schism. In the 1960s President Kwame Nkrumah presented a gift from the people of Bonwire to the United Nations, a giant kente symbolising world peace.

Grandma connects to the tradition of Bonwire through the silver line and the instinctive/intuitive centres of remembrance. Carnival creativity is an act of historical reclamation, a departure from the alienating routine of capitalist labour. It connects the creative energy to the African experience.

In 1986, Mangrove is playing 'Me Myself, I Warrior'. 'All oppressed people of the world are warriors. We must be, to survive,' explains Arthur Peters, the designer who co-ordinates the creative process at the carnival camp. A quiet unassuming man, he moves around the room discreetly, purposefully, offering ideas and skills and hinting at creative possibilities. He is a formidable inspiration at Mangrove and an innovator in the carnival tradition both in Notting Hill and Port of Spain, Trinidad. Over the years he has contributed to the creation of mas memorable for their ingenuity and beauty.

'A visit to Disneyland' (1974) was a mark of his hand, a magical journey to Disneyland which transformed familiar characters with imaginative sculpture work and costumes. The following year he designed 'To Hell with You' for the Trinidad carnival with Peter Minshall, then his apprentice. 'Paradise Lost' (1976) made interesting use of his wire bending techniques.

Wire bending is crucial to the construction of carnival sculptures. It stabilises the infrastructure, the bare skeleton which is then elaborated and splashed with colour and ornaments. Carnival sculptures should in spite of size be strong enough to last days of gruelling duty, and at the same time, have the flexibility to facilitate easy and subtle movements. This is the test for each mas camp. On the road the sculpture should be able to dance when it is brought to life by masqueraders who stretch its durability to the limits.

Wherever you come from, you had a feel for the music.
The people dem didn't too care where you come from.
Dem people didn't have a prejudice like island thing,
you know. For the youth dem, it was just oneness. Like
when you finish work in a factory on a Friday night,
this is where you go, blues dance. All de doors close
and sounds just a drop in you head. It's like a refuge
still. It remind you of home, the feel of it. From blues
session a culture develop. I remember one on Winston
Road, played by a brother called Jucklin. One night in
1963 the door just kick down and policeman just step
in and you hear funny sound. Sound system switch off.
Dem just bust up de dance! We couldn't understand it.
De older people dem did know because it happen to
them. A couple of brethren get fling on police van and
get charge with obstructing police officers on de
Monday morning.[1]

BENEFIT IN AID
of
CARNIVAL DEFENDANTS

Acklam Hall Acklam Road W 10.
Friday 15th October 8pm to 2am

with
SPARTACUS SUKUYA
(leading london steel band)

and
CLASH

lights · sound system · fully licenced bar · food ·
donation boxes · admittance £1.
buses: 52, 7, 15, 28, 31. underground : ladbroke grove
westbourne park

 BLACK DEFENCE COMMITTEE
notting hill branch

Blues dance is walking on the edge of Babylon and claiming cultural space. Black youth articulate their experience and forge alternative aesthetics in opposition to the dominant culture. On a winter's night when the moon is frozen and chill breeze take a walk, music drop from sound system like heavy lead. Dub voices chant all the while, shaking the roof in full charge. The youth dance in combat formation, back to the wall and forward motion only. They've come from all over the Grove and beyond, for this is a vigil of testimony and incantation threaded through reggae rhythms. The trumpets take a turn and they come with force. The sounds, dub wise, just stretch big and broad. A mellow guitar groove wails through waves of drums. It's an Aswad song, 'African Children', and the youth like it. They raise their prime fingers to the deejay who lifts up Brinsley Forde's voice:

> De tribulation is so sad
> De environment is so bad
> Highrise concrete no backyard for de children to play
> African children...
> Concrete cubicles
> De rent increases every other day
> Essential repairs assessed but never done
> And when it rains de children can't go out to play...
> African children living in a concrete situation
> African children.[1]

Voices saturate the cramped basement and rise with the morning mist. The people here are below ground level and socially they occupy a strategic location for all of society is within scope. There are few real opportunities for the youth to fulfil their potential in Babylon, so they walk the edge of downpression and focus their visions beyond the dreadlines of the night. Seeds of hope grow in their hearts and the deejay chats with a fresh surge of melody. She tells them they should be ready for the eventual ritual of reckoning: 'De wicked a go drop like Twinkle Brothers dem say. See all Bagga wire catch fire an' bubble up de surface!' The echo chamber hits the words on the concrete walls and the bounced sound, a receding thud, races across the area.

Blues dance transcends mere cultural opposition. It is particularly significant for the ways in which Black youth explore and create musical forms and textures using available technologies. Many own sound systems equipment which they have partly constructed or adapted to suit their needs. Speakers are built with the appropriate wood to achieve desired sound densities. The sound chamber is made tight to maximise the sound output. A good speaker should be able to accommodate the bass line and drum calls and give them appropriate tone and resonance.

Some systems separate out the sounds and channel them into individual speakers. It gives the deejay a broader range of possibilities in the musical mix. Through decibel control and the use of effects, s/he is able to deconstruct the sound elements, vacillate tone and texture, and articulate them in a series of interactions. Over the years, the often intense competition amongst sound systems has partly hinged on experimentation which has resulted in innovations in musical styles and techniques of sound craft.

The microphone is the symbol of dialogue. The deejay engages the past and present simultaneously, livening up the session with varying delivery styles and subjects. The blues dance is a school of social and political education and everyone comes with something to give and take away. They come for a communal affirmation of their own personal experience and they celebrate with spirited choruses when the deejay calls.

Two generations of sound systems deejays have produced and popularised many styles and forms: Sir Coxsone International, Unity, Sir Lloyd, Turbo Supreme, People's War, Channel One High Power, King Tubby's Hifi, Saxon, Sister Culcha, Lorna Gee, Smiley Culcha, Ranking Ann, Pato Banton, Mad Professor, Asher Senator, Sister Audrey, Macka B, Martin Glynn and Tippa Irie. The deejay tradition echoes that of the calypsonian and hip hop rapper. Historically, deejays are rooted in the role and function of the African griot as the eyes and ears of the community.

NOTES

1 From the film *You Were Black, You Were Out*, directed by Colin Prescod, Race and Class Ltd.

KORABRA

GAVIN
JANTJES

The accompanying poetry is by Edward Kamau Brathwaite.

But no light breaks under the decks
where the sails sing
and the island resolving from water

steep steps of blue
and the anchor clumping the bottom.
tapping of water along sides of the ship

lapping away into silence;
breathe on my face
where the palm trees were,

blue drifting above them, birds
too high for shadow,
scuffed sand at my feet,

stone, roots of grass,
crushing scuttled sea shells,
claws of crabs

the soil shallow.
And I, Quaker,
praying,

my broad hat under the turmoil
of stars
and I, slaver,

slaying,
my bright whip ripping a new soil
of scars

buying
a new world of negroes, soiling
the stars.

extract from *Littoral*

108

Untitled, Gavin Jantjes.
Sand, pigment, tissue pa-
per, and acrylic on can-
vas, 180 by 200 cms,
108 1986. Photo: Focol.

Ship
house on the water
I salute you

I am a bale of straw
swish of your cask's laughter
darkest cling of the gudgeon

there are shadows about me
eyes like mine
pores sweating fears like mine
souring wine

wind carves the shape of the journey
sculpture of sails is softer than a stone
along the dolphin's trail of cloud there is no
native land

there is no grey on the sea
with wind
there is no grey in the sky
with rain

there is no sky to fall down on
no hill to run up to
and no night with its swimmers
of whiteness

it was all so sudden
it was all so very sudden
when your spirit said
I am going away
I am gone

may your journey now be straight going
may your road be a peaceful one

and on arrival
if someone should ask you how you left us
we on these islands
with their lockets of grief

say

that you left us
eyes still closed
fists still curled
bones still lapped with milk

you know the rock's teeth
you know the pathways leading up from the beaches
you know the wall with its cracks
frangi-pani blossoms
grave of the soldiers
tales of the sandbox tree

may your journey now be straight going
may your road be a peaceful one

and on arrival
tell our never-returning ancestors of old
that now they have left us
the land is unbearably dry
let there be rain.

extract from *Wake*

109

Untitled, Gavin Jantjes.
Sand, tissue paper, pig-
ment and acrylic on can-
vas, 180 by 200 cms,
109 1985. Photo: Focol.

Yes, I remember...
but what good
is recollection now
my own mock

me; my own seed,
ruined on this rock
of God, struggle
to strike me

and what need
my story
in these fields
where these cart-wheels

turn over heart
crush hard our hurt
destroy the roots of love
with pain.

Boss man makes rules:
who works, who jerks
the rope, who rips
the patient dirt.

Boss man rates gain:
I am his living vein

of sustenance:
his corn, his meal, his grain.

Boss man lacks pride:
so hides his
fear of fear and darkness
in the whip.

Boss man lacks pride:
I am his hide

of darkness. Bide
the black times, Lord, hide
my heart from the lips
that spit

from the hate
that grips
the sweat-
ing flesh

the whips
that rip
so wet, so red,
so fresh.

extract from *All God's Chillun*.

110

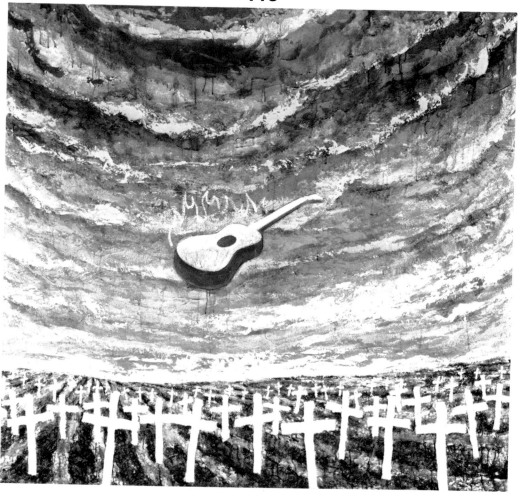

Untitled, Gavin Jantjes.
Sand, pigment, cotton
wool, sugar and acrylic
on canvas, 180 by 200
110 cms, 1986. Photo: Focol.

And so the black eye travels to the brink of vision
but not yet;
hold back the fishnet's fling of morning: unloose the sugarcane;

my spattered breast must undertake one more incision;
cut, carve, dissect
the merchant's pound of flesh, the soldier's pawn
of violence, the preacher's hymn of pain.

The black eye travels to the brink of vision:
look, the fields are wet,
the sea sits gentle on the dawn
of sand; but voices fill the green with hurricane.

And yet it is what happens
it is what happens
when they fall:

conquerors, helmets, plumes,
unloosened knots
of blood, dried river beds of iron,
rust;

it is the bird that sings,
the green that wavers, wavers, wins
the slave rebellion of the rot
of dust

that matters;
it is this that glitters
in the salt
lagoon,

that crusts the coral
with foundation stone,
that stires the resurrection
out of Tacky's bones.

extract from *Vèvè*

111

Untitled, Gavin Jantjes.
Sand, pigment and acrylic
on canvas, 180 by 200
111 cms, 1986. Photo: Focol.

We begin

with the curled embryo that will grow
to sweat
the eyes that will know

what greedy means

that will feed
on the milk of transistors
all day long.

Resurrections are stripped from the wings of trees;
Bayonets, armoured eyes, clank of the gun-butts
obscure the moon.

My tongue is heavy with new language
but I cannot give birth speech.

Pebbles surround me.
The beggaar glares; his hot eyes burn my thanks.

How many islands will be counted in this congress
of lepers, how many fathers will revoke the edicts of
their daughters?

Illegal, illegitimate,
I cannot sing.

And yet I must bring
water to the poxy bucket, its hate

scarred like the night's twinkles.
Slaughters of my innocence I must take on to
bleed the fetters

of my tribe. I must devour it all like a bank,
cell by cell, vault by vault, blinding to the void. Se

the burdens fuse to brine, the leeches
depart when there is no more marrow to kill; age

is restored and settles back to its primordial,
colourless slime; noon glistens like the dew, knees

slipping salt like oysters back to their kernel womb
Song, dirge, drag of blood, veins of beginning, nee
only this throb of a thin transparent crystal. It seen

a long way now from fat, the shaking bone, the la
But I
you what it means to eat
your god, drink his explosions of power

and from the slow sinking mud of your plunder, gr

Extract from *Eating the Dead*

112

Untitled, Gavin Jantjes.
Sand, pigment and acrylic
on canvas, 180 by 200
112 cms, 1986. Photo: Focol.

GALE FORCE

WITH GAIL THOMPSON

113

Gail Thompson. Photo:
113 Jak Kilby.

I understand you can't play the saxophone any more?

Yes, I woke up one morning and discovered I just couldn't play. That was just before the Camden Jazz Festival in 1986. My face muscles were all strained and I just could not manipulate them any more. I tried very hard and pushed myself to do the festival and prayed for the condition to improve. But it got worse. In September 1986, the muscles just gave up and now I can't blow at all. I've tried everything, acupuncture, hypnotists, I've had two of my bottom teeth out, there's nothing I haven't tried, but nothing seems to work. I think it will come back when it's good and ready.

What do you think is the problem?

I don't really know and nobody else knows, either. It's not physical. It's apparently to do with the nervous system. It started quite abruptly and got worse over a period of six months, then cut! I now have no control over my face muscles.

Must be devastating. You spend your whole life with an instrument only to find out now that you can't blow it. How are you spending your time?

I'm doing a lot of writing. I've been commissioned to write some music for the Royal Festival Hall; I'm doing a suite for the Opera House; I'm writing for the band and for the Camden Jazz Festival. I try to play the flute. I've got to blow something otherwise I'll go mad. It's so frustrating, as you can imagine, but I need to keep the muscles busy and in trim for when it comes back.

What is it about the saxophone? You can play the flute alright?

Different instruments demand different manipulation of the muscles. You use the muscles in different ways. I can't sustain a long note on the sax anymore. I've tried different saxophones, different mouthpieces, but they've done no good at all. Apparently it happened to Archie Shepp, James Moody and Fat Jones so I'm not alone in this. The problem is that not much is known about the condition in this country.

How did the others get over it?

It took Archie Shepp about four years to rebuild the muscles. There is also the subconscious. Some people tell me it's probably related to some experience or too much work. They could be right, but music is my life and that's all I know. At the time it happened I was very busy; three gigs a day, radio shows, playing with Art Blakey at Camden and doing some arranging. Stress may have a hand in it.

I have been playing the sax for 12 years and there is no way it can go away just like that.

This must be a time for some reflections on your life?

I was born in Herne Hill, at home. My parents came over from Trinidad in 1952. My father used to be a headmaster in Trinidad. His father was the head of the Royal College of Music in Trinidad. My auntie used to sing with Paul Robeson at Canegan Hall. Dad played the clarinet and mum played the piano. She tried to teach me but it didn't work. You know, it's difficult for parents to teach their own children. It just doesn't work. I took up the clarinet when I was about 14, then shopping with mum changed my life.

Shopping?

Yeah, I think it was Woolworths. I saw this Stan Getz record. You know, Stan Getz, the tenor sax player. I did not know who he was but I wanted to spend my pocket money so I bought the record. I had heard saxophone players in rock and roll bands but they never really appealed to me. Stan changed my mind. I took the clarinet back to school and brought back a saxophone. Mum of course went mad! Two of my brothers were playing the violin at the time. Her point was, how could a girl play the sax when the boys were playing the violin. I promised to take the sax back to school and collect a clarinet. I didn't; I kept it in a friend's house and practised in the park after school. Eventually I came home with it and she gradually accepted it. In fact she later bought me one.

How was school?

I have no academic qualifications. Not even CSE in music. I let my brain hold only what I want. I spent my time in school learning about life and mixing with teachers and older people. I didn't see why I had to fill my brains with British history and customs; wasn't relevant to my life at the time. I read music but I wasn't taught to play jazz or improvise. I did that myself, listening to records. I also taught myself to write and arrange. I got into the school orchestra. I enjoyed the school tours and concerts at places like the Royal Festival Hall and the Albert Hall. I went to the Soviet Union and Canada and I played baritone sax with the National Youth Jazz Orchestra. I left school when I was 19. My first job was with the long-running West End show, *Bubbling Brown Sugar*, starring Billy Daniels and Elaine Delmar. I was on the tenor sax. The musical centred around Harlem of the 1930s and 1940s, you know, the Cotton Club days with lots of jazz and tap dancing. I worked at Macari's Music shop during the day, and did a few other jobs. Let me tell you my day: I cleaned offices around Holborn at six in the morning, worked at Macari's all day and did the show till 10 o'clock. After the show, I did a night club gig at the Zanzibar in King Street till 3 in the morning.

How did you do it?

> When you're 19 you can do anything, can't you? I sometimes went to Ronnie Scott's from Zanzibar and straight to cleaning at the break of dawn.

114

Gail Thompson and Cour-
tney Pine. Photo: Jak
Kilby.

Why did you have to maintain such a hectic schedule?

I had to earn enough money so that I could have something to go home to. I learned this from the older people at school. You have to take professional work as it comes. You could be very busy one minute doing lots of gigs, but your diary could be really empty the next. I had to do other jobs to pay the rent when I was not busy. I wasn't earning enough money as a musician. I was doing gigs for £10-15 and I didn't think that was really a good life. As much as I loved music it just wasn't sensible to go on like that. After *Bubbling Brown Sugar,* I stopped playing for four years and just worked at Macari's music shop. I decided to start all over again in September 1984, when I came out with my first quartet and started a school called the Saxophone Council. The idea was to bring in some money between gigs, but a small ad in a newspaper brought in about 200 enquiries and I ended up with about ten people blowing the sax in my front room at one time. That was silly so I had to stop it. It has taken me another three years to organise a second school which started in January 87.

You've played with many bands and people, not least Art Blakey.

It was great playing with Blakey. The man is a genius and he makes you feel so comfortable. Funny how we kicked off at the first rehearsal for the Camden Festival. Blakey had invited some of us from here to play with his band, The Messengers. We were rehearsing this number and all I had to play was a simple phrase. Bobby Watson was conducting and I was so intrigued with him that I wasn't really concentrating on the notes. Then there was this big crash! Everything stopped and Blakey's voice rose. 'Hey, this ain't no good! Shit,' he yelled, 'read your goddam part'. I mumbled something like, 'but I've only got a simple....'. 'I know what you got, just read the goddam part!' I thought I was going to get the sack but he told me later that he only raised his voice because he liked me. Otherwise he would have told me to go. I learnt a lot from that because I had to take the music seriously. I had a simple phrase to play but I had to concentrate hard on it.

Music is a serious business and it's important to have that attitude. Blakey would pass on things he'd learned over many years in a few minutes. Lovely man. Jazz musicians from the States come from a long tradition. You can never do what they do in quite the same way. A British band can play a Basie number note for note but it will never sound the same, it will never have that sparkle. The immense creativity is related to the experiences they've been through. Dizzy Gillespie played his horn whilst studying agriculture because in the thirties and forties Black musicians were rarely allowed in the music colleges. When you

Gail Thompson and Courtney Pine. Photo: Jak Kilby.

115

115

hear Billie Holiday sing, you know this is some experience coming out. I also loved playing with Charlie Watts of the Rolling Stones. It was great fun at Ronnie Scott's and we also went to Berlin. We played old standards, 'Stardust', 'Jumping with Symphony Sid', 'Stomping at the Savoy', etc. It was a 35-piece band and I admire Charlie for doing it. They went to the States but I couldn't go because of my condition.

Tell us about the Black Jazz Orchestra.

It was an idea from David Donald and myself. There's always been reggae bands but until a year ago there were few avenues for young Black jazz musicians. The white jazz fraternity provided little space and the youngsters wouldn't go and sit in with the big guys. They just wanted a blow, so we decided to bring them out on their own and form a Black big band. We reckoned it was about time to move things to the forefront. We also started workshops and summer schools.

There is a new wave in jazz. What are the possibilities?

It may get better and stronger because I think there is a real movement of young Black musicians. When I worked in the music shop, many of them passed through doing all these Charlie Parker licks. They practised with records and needed a place where they could perfect them. That was the idea of the school. Courtney Pine has started Abibi Jazz so things are moving on that level. The situation for established Black jazz musicians is however slightly different. At the moment, jazz is trendy and the media is hyping it up but I think it's probably hit its peak.

You played with the Jazz Warriors?

Courtney and I formed that around the same time as the Black Jazz Orchestra for the professionals who were not getting the exposure on the circuit. Guys like Jeff Hunt, Steve Williamson and Phillip Bent. The Warriors was to tell the British jazz world that we are still here. I left it in March last year, because you can't have two leaders. Courtney is a leader and I am a leader. Unfortunately the two did not work together. We're both strong people and I wasn't really achieving what I felt I deserved. We parted amicably and that's what matters.

Let us turn finally to your compositions.

The first commissioned piece I did was performed by the Midland Jazz Orchestra at the Royal Albert Hall. It was called 'Maybe It's Me' and was for my mother. I could not play because of my condition so I conducted the orchestra. Courtney played in it and it was great to have a Black conductor and Black musicians at the front at the Albert Hall. I called it 'Maybe It's Me' because I'm always wrong in my mother's eyes. She loved it. She came to the show and said 'beautiful'.

Does she still think you're wrong?

Oh yeah. I don't know why but I'm always wrong. I also write for my band, Gail Force. One of my favourites is called 'Forget the Jazz, Let's Play This'. It's a Latin number and it was my way of saying jazz is a wide concept. 'Cutting Back the Hedge' starts with vocal intro which goes into a fast jazz swing. I wrote that one Saturday morning when mum was cutting back the hedge. I couldn't think of what to call it so I called it that. I called a piece commissioned for the Camden Festival 'Eunice', my mother's middle name.

Your mother is a constant theme in your work.

Mum plays a big part in my life. I owe everything I do to her and I dedicate my work to her.

THE FLEXED FOOT

SHOBANA JEYASINGH

As a *bharatha natyam* dancer, 'multiculturalism' is a word that I have got used to hearing, and no doubt like others of my colleagues, I often find myself the unprepared cog in the working out of this grand scheme. Facing thirty teenagers in a comprehensive school in Scunthorpe for a one-off session in Indian classical dance is only the tip of the iceberg in the constant fight to gain credibility for a different movement aesthetic in a predominantly insular culture.

There are still some who think that all that is needed is to have the product 'Indian dance' in schools and arts centres to produce a multicultural curriculum and programme. But as Indian dance is seen more and more in schools and arts centres, the goal of integration recedes further. Ironic, perhaps, but hardly surprising: when the new bride finally gets a look in to the household, both are on the threshold of a new challenge. She realizes how different the rules are and they do not comprehend that they too have to share in the work. The new bride, of course, is vastly outnumbered, and has only a meagre monetary dowry to her name, but she believes she has something of worth to offer that is uniquely hers.

There is little patience for the musician who waits to get on stage to tune his instrument, for the dancer who picks up a fallen ankle bell in mid-performance, for the presenter who announces a five-minute interval which turns into twenty. 'Unprofessional' is the word for this, and professionalism is the touchstone for the process which brings performer and audience together. In Britain that process is increasingly commercial, and packaging and marketing slickness is the medium through which the piece of art is brought to the public's attention and evaluated. In the performance, the audience and artist are separated from each other by the efficiency of 'professional' stage management. The audience pays to enter the superhuman world where bells ring, lights dim and the carefully lit scenery moves as if by magic. The smoothness of production is what distinguishes the professional from the amateur, the up-market theatre from the community venue.

Without passing judgement on the prevalent method, one needs to state that there are other processes by which the dancer meets his or her audience. In these, the ticketed performance may not be the norm, the musician tunes on stage because the audience likes it, and sticking to the printed programme is less a proof of

116

116 Shobana Jeyasingh in performance.

professionalism than of creatively responding to the audience of the evening. The audience in this situation is like a family before whom there is no need for pretence or formality to create that emotional engagement which is termed *rasa*, the aesthetic experience which is considered the aim of all art.

Another challenge is the way Indian dance techniques appear totally opposed to western ones. When a ballet dancer extends her leg and points her foot, she does so in the happy knowledge that to the majority of people the long slim line she creates is the acme of elegance. To flex the foot is a comic inversion of the western norm. One of the primary stances of *bharatha natyam* is the exact opposite of what is understood by the word 'elegance'. The body in a *demi plié* position goes earthwards with the outstretched leg ending in a firmly flexed foot. When the foot touches the ground, it is with the precision and effect of a clap of thunder. No doubt in many centres of 'alternative' dance there are challenges to the dominance of ballet. However *bharatha natyam* with its two thousand years of history wears the title of alternative awkwardly and with irony.

The technique and costuming of Indian dance is highly decorative and decoration is a difficult word to exorcise of its post-Reformation connotation of 'superficial'. Perhaps the Britons who saw no bombast in the highly decorated language of Shakespeare and Marlowe before plain speaking became the desirable dress for sincerity, would have better understood that seriousness of purpose is in no way undermined by ornament. Ornament is a product of an uncynical society where the creative process is joyous rather than angst-ridden, and where there is absolute confidence in the ability of the form to convey the content. Stylization, which is what Indian dance theatre is about, is the decoration of the ordinary and the day-to-day. On a simple level, one sees this in the vivid and ornate costume and at a deeper level, in the interpretation of character in mime and movement.

To appreciate a *thillana*, one of the modes of dance composition, is to accept the possibility that one can watch a soloist virtually static in terms of space and yet still be taken on a choreographic journey of thrilling complexity. Through footwork, a fabulously patterned structure is erected on the abstract and unseen 'stage' of Time, with rhythmic patterns as the building bricks. The appeal is mathematical as much as audial and visual. However, in a context where rhythm is intellectually suspect and choreographic interest sought in Space rather than Time, the *thillana* is bound to be underestimated. At best, it is seen as an unsubtle high energy finale, its real potential sadly unseen and unheard.

If I have dwelt on the differences, it is not through pessimism.

My aim has been to highlight the fact that where the now better-funded Indian dancer, armed with official blessings and printed programme, meets her new British audience, there lies a vast area of potential compromise. Whether the dancer will change the audience or vice versa, only time will tell.

THE IMAGE OF MARCUS GARVEY

IN REGGAE ORATURE

CECIL GUTZMORE

> Jah say, I call upon the singers and the players of instruments not
> politicians, liars and brain washers.
> Peter Tosh, 1987

MARCUS GARVEY, REGGAE, RASTAFARI
AND THE BRITISH CONNECTION

Marcus Garvey, along with the Emperor Haile Selassie 1 of
Ethiopia, is the chief icon in the visual and musical popular arts of
the Caribbean African community in Britain. It is thus correct, in a
text dealing with the cultures of Britain's African and Asian Black
communities, to speak about what one of the principal celebrants
of Garvey in reggae, Winston (Burning Spear) Rodney, invited us
to talk about as Garvey's *image.*

Reggae is the pre-eminent popular art of Caribbean Africans
in Britain and it is in this art, more strongly than anywhere else,
that Garvey's iconic, semi-sacral status is in evidence. Reggae is
one of the younger, more vibrant and strongly-rooted members of
that ever-growing family of peoples' musics which the
communities of Africa's western diaspora are constantly bringing
to birth. Reggae thus belongs, as does the record of Garvey's life
and struggle, within that broader heritage of pan-African cultural
achievement and the living practice of diasporan and continental
Africans in Britain today. With all this, the British connection is
profound.

Britain's involvement with the profitable brutalities of the
Atlantic chattel slave trade linked it to West Africa and the
Americas, including the islands of the Caribbean. One of these
islands, Jamaica, was the birthplace of Marcus Mosiah Garvey, the
Rastafari movement and reggae music. The island became an
English possession as part of Cromwell's western design in 1655,
and its colonial status persisted to 1962. (Prior to this, Spanish
power practised genocide on the island's first inhabitants, the
Arawak/Taino peoples.) British rule, slavery, colonialism and neo-
colonialism made the conditions which were to give rise to
Garvey, Rastafari and reggae. In recent decades, Britain has played
a large part in what might be termed the 'internationalisation' of
all three.

Sitting at the centre of its worldwide empire, Britain was a
magnet for many an able, adventurous, not to say potentially

117 Marcus Garvey.

17

rebellious colonial 'subject'. It was this Britain which played host to the restless young Marcus Garvey between 1912 and 1914 on his first visit to Europe. This trip enabled Garvey to make direct contact with such fellow Africans of the continent as Duce Mohamed Ali, Egyptian nationalist and editor of the West African funded *African Times and Orient Review*, and Solomon Plaatje, a founder member of the African National Congress of Azania (South Africa). From such men, Garvey soaked up concrete information on the brutalities behind the ostensibly treaty-based legality of European colonial rule in Africa (Sir E. Herslet, 1967). Garvey also travelled in Europe and took the opportunity to extend his formal education by attending lectures at London University's Birkbeck College. He visited Britain intermittently before permanently settling there in 1935. It was in London that his Universal Negro Improvement Association, originally created in Jamaica in 1914, had its international headquarters after 1935; in London that he brought out his last major publication, *The Black Man*, in 1933-39; in London that he died in 1940.

Within a decade of Garvey's death, and in the aftermath of World War II, people from his native region, the Caribbean —among whom his fellow Jamaican Africans were well represented — began a mass migration to the United Kingdom. They and their progeny failed to make real the dream of early return to the islands. They settled. The communities they formed provided the social base which supported and supplied, directly and indirectly, the capital which financed the take-off of reggae music in Britain and internationally.

The Caribbean people needed to negotiate life in a Britain whose economy and society functioned, in relation to them, as strongly racist. This racist cultural atmosphere partly determined the creative transfer to Britain of old and new Caribbean-African cultural forms like carnival, the reggae-pounding sound system and the reggae-centred blues party. The business which became Island Records, founded by the celebrated white Jamaican Chris Blackwell (Whitesick) and his now almost forgotten partner, Caribbean African, Tony Washington, encouraged the breakthrough outside Jamaica of the carefully self-nurtured musical and poetic skills of The Wailers, Bob Marley, Peter Tosh and Bunny Livingston. The capital accumulated by Whitesick through Island Records (and the ability to mobilise and manipulate African-Caribbean cultural and financial resources which flowed to Europeans such as Whitesick and Henzle) led to the making and successful promotion of the film *The Harder They Come*, a superb vehicle for the abundant talent of another Jamaican African poet-musician-singer, reggae artist Jimmy Cliff. In the final working out of these forces, reggae became the primary mode of popular musical-cultural expression of the Caribbean African community in Britain. At the same time, Rastafari, slowly established in Britain by Jamaican African migrants, forged for itself a central place in the cultural practice of that part of Britain's African community so often referred to by that problematic term, 'Black youth' (Fisher and Joshua, 1982; Gilroy, 1982; Gutzmore, 1983-4). In all these ways, there is a basis for speaking of a connection between British society on the one hand, and Marcus Garvey, reggae and Rastafari on the other.

REGGAE-RASTAFARI ORATURE AFFIRMS THE PAN-AFRICAN AND WORLD STATURE OF MARCUS GARVEY

Marcus Mosiah Garvey has been awarded posthumously the honour of First National Hero by the Jamaican neo-colonial state. It is an indication of his real status that such an honour appears to insult, to dishonour, his memory. It is difficult to conceive of Garvey — had he lived into old age — accepting this honour. Certainly his second wife, the redoubtable Amy Jacques-Garvey, was to refuse the offer of a state pension, or special stipend, in her later life. And the superficiality, not to say opportunism, of the offical commitment to the Hero is hinted at in the approach to Garvey of Jamaica's former Prime Minister, Michael Manley. In the latter's tribute to Garvey in the early pages of his book, *Jamaica: The Struggle in the Periphery* (c.1983, p.20) Manley suggests that Garvey founded the UNIA in the United States after 1935, which is well wide of the mark.

Not a few of the African citizens of Garvey's native island, influenced at least partially by Garvey's own political message, regard it as their prison. By analogy with the Jews of the Bible, they see it as the place of their Babylonian exile. They are in deadly earnest about this and expect others to take their exile from Africa equally seriously. A white journalist visiting Jamaica in the mid-1970s was counselled by Rastaman Bungo Silly:

> Dont write no joke, or nothing about Jamaica for the sportin' page. You should not say that Jamaica is full of happy folks or fookery like that. Write it out that we are in pain. Rass claat. Write it out that we are in prison and we want to go home.
>
> Davis and Simon, 1977, p.60

In any event, neither as ruthless colonial 'pigmentocracy' nor as symbol-laden neo-colonial nation-state, has Jamaica managed to imprison Garvey's spirit. He broke out from the rural confines of his place of birth on August 17, 1887 to become one of the few truly great figures of the twentieth century by virtue of the scope of his pan-African works and struggles.

Nowhere is the truth of Garvey's monumental achievement more accurately captured than in the orature of Rastaman and image-maker, Winston (Burning Spear) Rodney. Burning Spear's work contains a present-tense celebration of that 'Mister Garvey' who for him was

> The first one
> Through Black history
> Who ever control so much people.
> Hundreds!
> Thousands!
> Millions!
> It cause a eruption.
>
> Burning Spear, LP *Marcus Children,* 'Mister Garvey'

Burning Spear it is who insists that we have to talk about the image of this man. The word talk signals the fact that Burning Spear functions within the context of African orature in general and of Jamaican African orature in particular. It is not an official/'society' but a peoples/'sufferers' world of cultural practice. Here, politico-cultural products of the official world, especially language, are given a peoples' significance by way of a complex process of rejection/inversion/reversal: everything is turned downside up. Here, for example, there is not oppression but downpression. The Mona Campus of the University of the West Indies in Jamaica, formerly the University College of the West Indies (UC) becomes Ublind. The system has no possibility of an acceptable face as it becomes in a word popularised by the late Peter Tosh, the shitstem. The rejectionist, subversive linguistic practice of African Jamaica is partly what has been spoken of as 'dreadtalk' (Pollard, 1983). Note how Spear exemplifies this when he deploys the word 'image' for the word 'reality' in inviting us to see Marcus Garvey as

> One of the first Black man
> To try to uplift the masses
> The majority
> The dregs of society.
>
> Spear, LP *Far Over,* 'Image'.

Reggae-Rastafari orature speaks of Marcus Mosiah Garvey as among the greatest of men. He is spoken of as one who took a welcome politico-cultural message to the mass of the African people world-wide through his organisation, the Universal Negro Improvement Assocation, the influence and membership of which embraced millions of Africans. Garvey erupted into the history of the pan-African world in the twentieth century. He did so to the

Black Star Line share
issue.

momentary terror of the major imperialist and colonial countries.
He did so to the delight, upliftment, arousal of the pan-African
masses. In so doing, Marcus Garvey went far beyond anything
which even begins to be comprehended in an honour such as
National Hero of Jamaica.

GARVEY'S AESTHETIC THEORY AND PRACTICE AND AFRICAN ORATURE

At this point, a problem must be registered. It is that of the existence of a conflict, almost a fundamental contradiction, between Garvey's personal and organisational aesthetic and the theory and practice of the aesthetics of African orature. Most simply rendered, we can say that Garvey's aesthetic was partially Europe-derived, and the problem we must address stems from the fact that amongst Africans there is now a sharpening struggle between an African and European aesthetic standpoint, a European standpoint made to seem almost natural by centuries of colonialism and cultural imperialism.

The conflict is a function of the emergence of a politicised radical African aesthetics. This argues, with increasing boldness, that to be even minimally faithful to the reality of the practice of the arts by the African masses, it is necessary to address a concept which brings together a number of forms of performance in the arts which European aesthetics treats as distinct. That concept is orature. Radical African (pan-African) aestheticians argue that there is a distinct African aesthetic common to African peoples' musics (Bebey, 1975; Leroi Jones, 1963; Keil, 1966; Chernoff, 1979). Key texts towards the founding and development of the concept of orature include the work of Chinwezu and others (1980) and Braithwaite (1984). What is at stake is not just the determination of the nature of the African novel, African poetry, or, within the latter, the African epic. The concept of orature also forces a confrontation with the issue of the liberation of African peoples' languages. One aspect of this is concerned with the freeing of the so-called Creole languages from official neglect and subjugation (Carrington et al., 1983; Devonish, 1986). Another is concerned with resisting the attempt to treat as a creole the major language of East Africa, Swahili, as long as the old negative connotation attached to the concept of creole remain in the frame (Khalid, 1977). A third aspect wants to struggle for the maintenance of the integrity of endangered native languages of Africa, not by leaving them as repositories of this or that great 'traditional' epic or 'folklore' but by writing contemporary literature in them (Ngugi wa'Thiong'o, 1986).

The conflict between this aesthetic and some of Garvey's aesthetic conceptions is manifested in several of the African peoples' musics of the Americas of which reggae is one. The African-ness of this cultural form reveals itself at many levels. Its performers function as African griots, who not only entertain, but warn and tell truth to the nation. Its lyrics and words are mainly in the Creole/language of the Jamaican African. The African-ness of this language has been fully established by scholars. Beryl Baily (1966) used Chomskyan linguistics to show that the issue was not just a matter of the chance survival of some African words but that the syntactic structures of the Jamaican language were African, a claim since abundantly confirmed. Reggae's musical structures and performance styles are also primarily African (Kallyndyr and Dalrymple, c.1974; Clarke, 1980; White 1982, 1984; Cooper, 1987).

Reggae is the key popular, as opposed to 'high' art of the Jamaican African masses in the Caribbean. This may also be its true place within the entire Caribbean African community in Britain. It may reasonably be assumed that, were Marcus Garvey alive today, he would be comfortable both in practice and in theory with this peoples' music as he was comfortable in practice with the African popular musics of his day. In practice, but not in theory, and here lies the problem. Some of the aesthetic ideas held by Garvey are at variance with the African aesthetic of these peoples' musics.

The issues of Garvey's aesthetic theory and practice have been explored by Tony Martin in *Literary Garveyism* (1983) and by Beverly Hamilton in her article, 'Marcus Garvey: Cultural Activist' (1987). Both show that Garvey deployed both the popular and so-called 'high' arts in his work of mobilising the masses. Martin states that Garvey, in formally ascribing a propagandistic role to the arts, was an influential precursor to the cultural activists of the Black arts movements of the 1960s and 1970s, especially, but by no means exclusively, in the US. However, Martin also brings out the extent of the influence of the European aesthetic over Garvey's ideas. Martin reveals that Garvey and literary Garveyites were uncomfortable with publishing in their popular paper, *Negro World,* African American poetry which used the speech of the popular masses, so-called dialect verse. Garvey was also hostile to those novels of the so-called Harlem Renaissance which treated the lives of African Americans in the language of the masses and did not shy away from the seamy or steamy side of that life. A particular target of Garvey's condemnation was Claude McKay's novel, *Home to Harlem,* published in 1928, which he called 'a damnable libel against the Negro' before advancing the somewhat problematic credo:

> We must encourage our own Black authors who have character, who are loyal to their race, who feel proud

to be Black, and in every way let them feel that we
appreciate their efforts to advance our race through
healthy and decent literature.

Garvey, 1928, quoted in Hamilton, 1987.

Garvey had a position of some ambivalance towards such African
American musics as slave songs, spirituals, blues and jazz, all part
of the same family as reggae. Even while using them in his
popular mobilisation, he seems to have regarded them as
aesthetically second rate. He is quoted as having once expressed
the view that 'Spiritual and jazz music are credited to the
Negro... simply because we did not know any better music'. Then
there is the fact that one of the major cultural demands made by
Garvey's Peoples' Political Party in its 1929 manifesto was for a
Jamaican National Opera House. We can read this as meaning
that the 'better music' Garvey envisaged was some variant of
European classical music. What would Garvey have made of Peter
Tosh's performance at the remarkable One Love Peace Concert in
1978 at which Tosh not only sang but talked a lengthy
denunciation of the shitstem in Jamaican language replete with
variants of Jamaican swear words (Gayle, 1978)? What would
Garvey have made of Tosh's track on the LP *Wanted,* 'Oh Bumbo
Klaat', in which these words are chanted out against the shitstem
without any apology? What would Garvey have made of this
battery of (sexist, let it be admitted) verbal weapons? Garvey, the
proud and fine exponent of English elocution, would have had
some difficulty with the creole/'nation language' work of the Dub
Poets, with the style of 'Jah Ugliman':

Talkin... A nuh good English. Is not good English. It
is not good English. Dem claim say it haad fi
understan simply because dem waan yu fe be a Black
Englishman and chat like dem. Waan rob yu of yu
culcha. Well who cyaan undastan get fuk. I cannot spell
to fool Iself.

Gayle, 1978, p.4.

If we are not shocked by evidence of elements of the European
aesthetic in the approach of the foremost pan-Africanist of the
century, it is because we are aware of the pervasive influence of
European colonial culture on formally and self-educated Caribbean
Africans of Garvey's day (and, indeed, since). If so many former
colonial societies are still engaged in the struggle for cultural
decolonisation (or the decolonisation of the mind as Ngugi has it)
how much more vulnerable were those who like Garvey were born
in the colonial situation of late nineteenth century Caribbean
society. C.L.R. James, another giant of twentieth century pan-
Africanism, has given us an account of the pervasiveness of

colonial culture in the Caribbean of his youth in his semi-autobiographical text *Beyond A Boundary* (1963), while much of his other writing reveals the effects of this in its Eurocentric aesthetic. However compromised Garvey appears in theory, his practice in the field of culture was in large measure an affirmation of the African aesthetic of popular African American cultural forms. Having registered this conflict, we can examine reggae-Rastafari orature's account of Garvey. It is precisely because reggae functions as an African peoples' art and as such is functional, informative, critical, engaged, entertaining and rooted, that its exponents so often celebrate, talk about, chant up sounds to the 'image' of Marcus Mosiah Garvey.

REGGAE, RASTAFARI AND MARCUS MOSIAH GARVEY

Reggae orature puts forward a view of the importance of the relationship between Garvey and Rastafari. Reggae itself is often identified with Rastafari and Rastafari music and orature, even though this simple assertion of correspondence cannot always be assumed (O'Gorman, 1987). This identification can largely be explained by the fact that so many reggae performers, with Marley as the best example, carry Rastafari's most widely recognised symbol, dreadlocks, with many being 'dread both in the heart and in the head'. Significantly, in reggae orature, the Emperor Haile Selassie 1 of Ethiopia is even more frequently celebrated than Garvey, and Rastafari doctrine in all its variety is constantly expounded. Some African drumming and chanting techniques associated with such Rastafari practices as reasonings and bynghis have a vital place at the roots of reggae music. The griots of this music/orature talk of Garvey as precursor to Haile Selassie, whose divinity is an article of faith for most sections of Rastafari. In the celebrated historical reasoning of Rastafari by Count Ossie and the Mystic Revelations on the LP *Groundations*, the position of Haile Selassie is established as follows:

> Rastafari brethren conception
> Through the love and the study of the Bible
> The history of man on the earth.
> And since there is no limitation
> On man's faculties
> We derive the conception
> Based on the divinity
> And the character
> Of His Imperial Majesty Emperor Haile Selassie 1 of Ethiopia
> King of Kings

Lord of Lords
Conquering Lion of the Tribe of Judah.
Reggae's Rastafari practitioners often spiritualise the relationship
between Garvey and Haile Selassie, speaking of it as analogous to
that between John the Baptist and Jesus. Garvey is seen as having
been sent to 'cut and clear' the path of the divine Haile Selassie. It
is this analogy that Burning Spear makes in recounting that:
John the Baptist head was cut off
Putteth away into a saucer.
Sweet disciple of our Lord,
They stones him to death.
To death.
Spear, LP *Live*, 'Old Marcus'
In reggae, Garvey's name is regularly invoked to buttress the claim
that Haile Selassie is not dead.
My memory say.
Marcus Garvey did say
A rumour, a rumour, a rumour, Marcus say.
A rumour, a rumour, a rumour, Marcus say.
Jah nuh dead.
Jah nuh dead.
Jah nuh dead, oh!
Spear, LP *Marcus' Children*, 'Marcus Say, Jah no
Dead'
In the version of the founding of Rastafari which has had the
stamp of academic approval (despite some questioning by Hill,
1983) Marcus Garvey is presented as a founding influence (Augier,
Nettleford and Smith, 1960). Garvey certainly drew attention to
Ethiopia and ascribed significance to the crowning of Ras Tafari in
1931 in speeches and in the pages of *The Black Man*. His earlier
efforts to organise a settlement for diasporan Africans in Liberia
and build for the old 'back to Africa' dream through his Black Star
Line Steamship Corporation fed into the stream which watered
Rastafari consciousness in the early days of the movement. As
Count Ossie says on *Groundation*:
We also hold fast the conception of
redemption,
Which is repatriation to our mother home
Africa.
while another chant often heard earlier in Jamaica said:
You can take away mi lan an mi dum ting
I dont care a kick about that.
But sen me back to Ethiopia
Mek mi go mark out mi burrial spot.
For in my sickness, I've got a witness

Of Ethiopia.
                    The author from childhood memory
Some of these connections have been questioned. Haile Selassie's
divinity is an issue, and decades before the revolution and famine
of the 1970s and 1980s, Garvey disputed aspects of Haile Selassie's
rule in the pages of *The Black Man*. Adherents of Rastafari have
no difficulty with the rule or divinity of Haile Selassie. The writer
recalls a young Rastaman and reggae performer speaking in
defence of both after the Ethiopian revolution had declared the
death of the Emperor. The view he put forward was that Haile
Selassie was very much like other gods in his attitute to mortals.
Few gods seem to shy from visiting famine on people; few seem
to shy from visiting the mass deaths on populations which we
humans find so hard to take. As Shakespeare wrote in comparing
the attitude of boys to flies and gods to men, 'They kill us for
their sport'. More formally, Rastafari theology, in proclaiming the
divinity of Haile Selassie, adopts modes of proof and discourse
encountered in the theology of virtually all religions. It deploys
faith, inspiration, prophecy, revelation, experience and sacred texts
in a variety of combinations. There is simply no point in denying
the material reality of the divinity of Haile Selassie for many
Rastafari brethren and sistren.

119

119 Garvey on the eve of deportation from the US.

REGGAE RASTAFARI ORATURE AND MARCUS GARVEY

African orature generally goes beyond mere biography in speaking of 'the great ones'. Illustrative of this pattern is the way in which the reggae-Rasta griots who deal with Garvey treat his life story. What they do is chant up some powerful sounds about the hero's contribution to Black African peoples' history and culture. These chants aim to make the name of Garvey known again, to proclaim it above those seen as lesser figures who with official backing came to be more celebrated. In the land of Garvey's birth, it was long true in ruling circles, if not so true among the Jamaican African masses, that many declared National Heroes by the neo-colonial state (Nanny, Sam Sharpe, George William Gordon, Paul Bogle, Norman Washington Manley, Alexander Bustamante) received more attention than Garvey. This is what Burning Spear addresses, using typically African iterative forms in his song 'Old Marcus Garvey':

> No one remembers old Marcus Garvey.
> No one remember old Marcus Garvey.
> No one remember old Marcus Garvey.
> No one remember old Marcus Garvey.
> No one remember old Marcus Garvey.
> No one remember him. No one.
> They've been talking about Paul Bogle.
> They've been talking about George William Gordon.
> They've been talking about Norman Washington Manley.
> Including Bustamante.
> Spear, LP *Live*

By taking Garvey's contribution to the pan-African world, reggae-rasta orature addresses specific aspects of the Garvey life. The griots chant of his birth into the African race at a particular time and place; of his powers and their use in the uncompromising struggle of Africans against individual betrayers and the enemies of the African people generally; of his crucial works; and of his death, which, like that of Haile Selassie, is disputed.

THE BIRTH AND YOUTH OF THE HONOURABLE
MARCUS MOSIAH GARVEY

Garvey's birth is not presented in reggae-Rasta orature as an event specially heralded by natural forces; no star, storm or earthquake are spoken of as having accompanied his coming. That birth took place in rural Jamaica, as Burning Spear says:

> The Image.
> The Image of Marcus Mosiah Garvey,
> Let's *talk* about that.
> The Image was from the parish of St.Ann.
> The capital, St.Ann's Bay.
> That's where he is from.
> Marcus Mosiah Garvey,
> The Image!
> > Spear, LP *Farover*, 'Image'

Though the griots do not give many details of Garvey's childhood, a number of their chants highlight key virtues of the child Garvey, not least because they function as examples to fellow Africans of all ages. One such virtue is truth:

> Marcus Garvey never tell untruth.
> He always speak the truth.
> He always speak the truth.
> > Spear, LP *Marcus' Children*, 'Marcus Children Suffer'

Another virtue brought forward is Garvey's openness towards education. Even though the griots stress that Babylon's education system presents grave difficulties for Africans, amounting to deliberate robbery of our culture as they give us not our history but nursery rhymes of the 'cow jumped over the moon' variety, school is still a must:

> Mister Garvey is so cool, so cool.
> Mister Garvey is so smooth, so cool.
> That's why he goes to school.
> So smooth, so cool, so smooth.
> > Spear, LP *Marcus' Children*, 'Mister Garvey'

The necessity for a different type of school is registered. Here African children would be taught the truth about pan-African history and culture. As Dr. Alimantado cries out:

> So let we open the Marcus school
> So we can teach them the golden rule.
> > Alimantado, LP *King's Bread*, 'Marcus Garvey School'

Among the virtues to which the griots draw attention are honesty and obedience:

> He always obey his grandmother.
> He always obey his grandfather.
> He never commit no crime.
> He always do right.
> > Spear, LP *Hail H.I.M.*, 'Follow Marcus Garvey'

MARCUS GARVEY'S 'POWER' OF PROPHECY

In the African cultural world of reggae-Rasta orature, heroes and heroines are said to possess capacities termed 'powers'. Examples of this can be found in the classic epic of African orature, *Sundiata,* and in accounts of the lives of such diverse figures as Nanny, the Jamaican maroon; Haitian slave rebel leader, Makandal; Samori Toure; Asante Queen Mother and war leader Yaa Asantewa; Shona spirit mediums and rebel leaders Nehanda and Kagubi; or Kenya Land and Freedom Army general, Dedan Kimithi. Reggae-Rasta orature's account of Garvey's life fits this pattern. The key power ascribed to him is that of prophecy. Indeed, he is referred to in a song by Culture as 'earth's greatest prophet'. Garvey's power of prophecy is spoken of as of two distinct kinds: first, what may be called magico-religious; secondly, the secular and political.

GARVEY'S MAGICO-RELIGIOUS PROPHECY

In 1929, Marcus Garvey served a prison sentence for contempt of court in Jamaica's Spanish Town district prison. This was the result of a speech amplifying the fourteenth plank of the manifesto of his newly-founded Peoples Political Party in which he promised that in the event of victory he would pass 'a law to impeach and imprison judges who, with disregard for British justice and constitutional rights, dealt unfairly' (quoted in Lewis and Warner-Lewis, 1986, p.104).

Big Youth, Burning Spear and the brethren of Culture are among the reggae griots who chant up sounds about this. They tell us that on his way from serving this sentence, Marcus Garvey prophesied that no other prisoner would enter the prison through the gate by which he left. In Culture's version we hear that

> Marcus Garvey was inside Spanish Town District Prison
> And when they were about to take him out,
> He prophesied and say,
> As I pass though this gate
> No other prisoner shall enter again through.
> And so it is until now.
> The gate has been locked.
> Say what?
> Culture, LP *Two 7s Clash,* 'Two Sevens Clash'

Garvey is also said to have prophesied that Jamaica's former capital, Spanish Town (St. Jago de la Vega) and its present capital city, Kingston, would become in time a single city:

> Marcus Garvey prophecy say,
> St. Jago de la Vega and Kingston
> It is going to be.
> And I can see with mine own eyes,
> It's only a housing scheme that divides.
>> Culture, LP, *Two 7s Clash*, 'Two Sevens Clash'

In other words, the prophecy has effectively been fulfilled.
Another prophetic fate lying in store for the wicked is to 'burn',
hence

> Man like Bag-a-Wire
> Should burn in fire.
> The betrayer
> Of Marcus Garvey
>> Mighty Diamonds LP *Right Time*, 'Dem Never
>> Love Poor Marcus'

Or, as the Heptones chanted, Kingstonians *know* while 'country
boy' and everyone else will find out that

> Bag-a-Wire ketch a fire
> And Bag-a-Wire can't retire
> And Bag-a-Wire ketch a fire.
>> Big Youth, LP *Dreadlocks Dread*

This connects not just to that key background text of reggae-
Rastafari orature, the King James version of the Bible, but to the
style of a latter-day quasi-literary rant such as James Baldwin's *The
Fire Next Time* or to Bob Marley's warning chant, 'Slave Driver'
on his breakthrough LP, *Catch A Fire*. In the tradition that all
these draw upon and represent, the individual and collective
wicked merit burning. The latter it is to whom Marley says

> Slave driver
> The table is turn.
> Ketch a fire,
> You gonna get burn.
>> Marley LP *Catch a Fire*, 'Slave Driver'

In this context, the power to 'hold' the wicked under the sway of
prophecy which the reggae-Rastafari griots attribute to Marcus
Garvey, represents a spiritualised desire or an active plan for the
redemption of Africans/Ethiopians/Rastafari people from the
chains of Babylon.

GARVEY'S WORKS IN THE LIGHT OF REGGAE-RASTARAFI ORATURE

'Every man have a work fi du', Bob Marley once remarked in
response to an interviewer's query about the departure of Bunny
Wailer and Peter Tosh from The Wailers. Marcus Garvey's work
was in the struggle for African 'upliftment', redemption,

repatriation and liberation and was great enough a work to 'cause
a eruption' of millions of Africans against Babylon system. That
work remains unfinished, giving rise among some of those who
'love' and 'follow' Marcus Garvey to expressions of doubt as to
their hero's physical death. It is asked

> Is Garvey really dead?
> I wanna know for sure!

They assert:

> And they took him away,
> And they told us
> That man Garvey is dead.
> But I weep not at all,
> For I know
> That one man just caan
> Dead and bury three time
>> Culture, LP *Cumbolo,* 'Down in Jamaica'

There is in reggae-Rasta orature a call for Garvey's return to
complete his work:

> Send back Garvey down here.
> You know that we want him.
>> Culture, LP *Cumbolo,* 'Down in Jamaica'

We have heard the griot Count Ossie say in *Groundation* that
Rastafari holds fast to a specific conception of both the field in
which Garvey laboured and of the object of his labour. Within that
conception, Babylon system/shitstem is seen as holding the sons
and daughters of Africa's western diaspora in the chains of slavery,
whilst also holding some continental Africans and parts of the
African continent in the shackles of unfreedom, colonialism and
apartheid. It is against the shitstem that the battle for
redemption/liberation/repatriation is fought, and reggae-Rasta
orature is specific as to that shitstem's nature. It is spoken of as
slavery unended, going on for 'too long, too long'. The conception
of slavery is not simply the historical institution of Atlantic chattel
slavery although it includes that time when, as Marley says, the
wicked 'brutalised my very soul'. It is of this horror-time that the
griots ceaselessly speak as 'old slavery days' and recount the
terrible price paid during it by Africans. Culture's simple question
goes to this point:

> Yu tink a likkle,
> Tink a likkle,
> Tink a likkle
> Innocent blood
> Shed down here,
> Down inna Babylon city?
>> Culture, 'Innocent Blood'

On this blood and the fruits of the labour of Africans, the controllers of Babylon city grew fat during and after slavery days. Accordingly, say the griots, in so far as the redemption of the African abroad involves a return to the African motherland — the Garvey-Rastafari conception of repatriation — there can be no further payment due. In the words of the Ethiopians:

> I dont have a red, red cent to pay.
> I got my home to reach,
> And I will reach it one day.
> Cause we were taken away by force,
> Scattered all round the Caribbean pool...
> It was four hundred years ago,
> They took us from our homeland
> As we should know.
> With the slave-chains still on our hands
> They leave us here to work on their plantations.
> But Nyah man say No!
> No! Not a cent to pay!
> I have got to reach home one day.
> Ethiopians, LP *Slave Call*

But if the periods of slavery days is passed, no way is slavery dead. The chains are still there weighing down the African. Some of these chains the wicked would have Africans take as garlands and precious bracelets:

> Today they say that we are free,
> Only to be chained in poverty.
> Good God! I think it's illiteracy.
> Is only a machine that make money.
> Marley, LP *Catch A Fire*, 'Slave Driver'

What in reality Africans have is the 'sub-human bondage' of the shitstem to which the reggae-Rastafari griots ascribe certain characteristics. It is the biblical 'old dragon', the 'blood-sucker', the 'deceiver', the 'brutaliser', the subverter of African culture. Marley summarises:

> Babylon system is a vampire.
> Sucking the blood of the sufferers.
> Deceiving the children continually.
> Marley, LP *Survival*, 'Babylon System'

Against this system, the reggae-Rasta griots say Marcus Garvey directed his work, making himself a hero of Pan-Africanism through the exercise of his word and powers.

RASTA-REGGAE ORATURE, GARVEY THE SECULAR PROPHET AND SLAVERY IN THIS TIME

The end of formal, institutionalised slavery, the 'old slavery days' in the Americas, virtually coincided with the birth of Marcus Mosiah Garvey, both taking place in the 1880s. It is against the new enslavement of Africans, in this time of what deceivers call 'freedom', that his great work is directed. Reggae-Rastafari orature uses the real or poeticised word of Garvey (Garvey viewed as the great hero imbued with the special power of secular/political prophecy) to provide the means of theorising the Babylon system and inspiring Africans in the struggle for survival and/or redemption-cum-liberation. We have heard from the griots that the impact of Garvey's work was comparable to a volcanic eruption, that the key to his success lay in his being the first one to take that message to the African masses, his target that stratum described by one griot as the dregs of society. That message reached Africans 'universally', heard via a combination of traditional (bush telegraph) and modern (newspaper and steamship) means of communication.

The function of the griots, who often, on the authority of the Bible, think of themselves as divinely-called 'singers of songs and the players of instruments', is to truth-say, to chant-up truthful sounds in respect of Garvey and against the system's lies:

> Someone must know.
> Someone must know the truth.
> Someone must
> Get up, stand up and speak the truth.
> Get up, stand up and speak the truth.
> Get up, stand up and speak the truth.
>> Spear, LP *Marcus' Children*, 'Marcus Senior'

The first truth that must be told, is that under the new slavery, continual suffering is of the essence of the situation of African people. Garvey prophesied:

> Marcus Garvey *word* come to pass.
> Marcus Garvey *word* come to pass.
> Can't get no food to eat.
> Can't get no money to spend.
>> Spear LP *Live*

Or more generally

> The whole a we suffer.
> Yes, we suffer.
> Yes, we suffer.
> The whole a we suffer...
> Through this tribulation, yeah.

Through this tribulation, yeah.
Sufferation.
We suffer, we suffer.
The whole a we suffer.
Can't blame Marcus.
Can't blame Garvey.
Can't blame Marcus Garvey.
No!

> Spear LP *Marcus' Children,* 'Marcus' Children
> Suffer'

The suffering children of Garvey have to know the truth that the
wicked include

Heads of churches and politicians
Getting richer in a time of starvation.

> Joe Higgs, LP *Unity is Power,* 'Sons of Garvey'

Further, the truth is that their methods of slavery/downpression
are not just those of physical brutality:

They try to keep you down.
In poverty...
It all means that it could be.
You know that it could be
That this church and state
Psychology
Preaching love you can't never see.
When they try to keep you down
In poverty.

> Higgs, LP *Unity is Power,* 'Sons of Garvey'

The griots mobilise Garvey's name and word to counsel fellow
Africans on alternative responses to enslavement. Among these
are quietude and creative accommodation.

Marcus Mosiah Garvey say
Man who cannot get no work
Should make work/make work/make work
Be creative/be creative/ be creative.
Come let's talk...

> Spear, 'The Image'

Or somewhat more disturbingly, since what Spear advises
immediately above goes to the heart of the need, the struggle for
day-to-day survival by the sufferers:

They take us away from our homeland
They take us away from our homeland
And we are slaving down here in Babylon.
We are waiting on an opportunity
We are waiting on an opportunity
For the Black Star Liner wishes to come...

> Let man meekly wait and murmur not
> Meekly wait and murmur not
> For the Black Star Liner shall come.
> You better do right
> For the Black Star Liner shall come.
>> Fred Locks, LP *Black Star Liner,* 'Seven miles of
>> Black Star Liner'

More often, the reggae-Rasta griots put forward positive lines of response to downpression for Marcus' children to follow. The issue is not peace and meekly waiting, whether counselled by Rastaman or by one of the wicked peddling Babylon's 'church and state psychology'. Rather it is equal rights and justice:

> Everyone is crying out for peace.
> None is crying out for justice.
> Everyone is crying out for peace.
> None is crying out for justice.
> I don't want no peace.
> I want equal rights and justice.
> I've got to get it.
>> Peter Tosh, LP *Equal Rights,* 'Equal Rights'

This is the message that Marcus Garvey roared forth out of rural Jamaica, prophesying to African people:

> Earth's greatest prophet
> Was born down in St. Ann's Bay.
> He was going about
> Prophesying equal rights
> And justice to the nation
> I know.
>> Spear, 'Down in Jamaica'

He took this message everywhere:

> From parish to parish.
> From district to district,
> From village to village,
> From town to town,
> From country to country,
> From state to state,
> Through all around,
> Garvey go all around.
>> Spear, LP *Marcus' Children,* 'Marcus Senior'

Given that these efforts at mobilisation had dramatic effects among Africans at home and abroad, the question must be asked, why are we still held captive by the shitstem? Or, as the griot asks, 'whose fault?'. Obviously, as another says, we 'can't blame Garvey. No!'. Several blame our tendency to wait for extreme circumstances before taking action. Big Youth puts it:

> I seen it many, many times before
> A Mr. Marcus Garvey say
> Black people down here
> Will never *see themselves*
> Until them back against the wall.
> You never *know yourself*
> Until you back against the wall.
> Some will rise and some will fall
> But Black people will never know themself
> Until dem back against the wall.
> And that is what Mr. Marcus Garvey say.
>> Big Youth, LP *Dreadlocks Dread*

Spear varies this theme:

> Marcus Garvey did say
> People! Black People!
> You got to wait
> Until your backs against the wall
> Before you start to enquire
> Whose fault?
>> Spear, LP *Marcus' Children,* 'Marcus' Children
>> Suffer'

The griots are clear that the way to achieve equal rights, justice and redemption/liberation is through African unity in action now. Joe Higgs, for one, makes this point in an archetypally African call and response song:

> Sons of Garvey, the time is *now*
> We'll never get nowhere
> Till we live as one...
> If you heard the words
>> Sons of Garvey
> Of Marcus Mosiah Garvey
>> Sons of Garvey
> Unity is power
>> Sons of Garvey
> The power to the hour. Oh yeah!
>> Sons of Garvey, our time is now.
>> Higgs, LP *Unity is Power,* 'Sons of Garvey'

Higgs gets into the basic call and response form via the following opening lines:

> Right now I would like to sing this song
> About the greatest exponent of Black liberation
> The giant from our little island of Jamaica
> Marcus Mosiah Garvey.
> And I am gonna ask the sisters
> To help me sing that song

Help me sing that song, yeah!

Other griots address the urgency and necessary sharpness of the
struggle for Black liberation espoused by Garvey. Though their
local references are to Jamaica, the point is meant to apply
elsewhere:

Marcus Garvey prophesy say
Oh yeah!
Man a go find him back against the wall
On yeah!
It a go bitter, when the right time come...
Swallow Field a go be the battlefield
Yeah! Yeah!
Natty dread will never run away.
No my bredren.
Dis ya a prophecy.
Hold dem Marcus.
Dis ya a prophecy.
Hold dem Marcus.

Mighty Diamonds, LP *Right Time,* 'Right Time'

In other words, serious Africans will not run away from the fray.
The struggle was, is and will remain one in which the wicked
throw everything they have at Africans who stand up. To Garvey

They tried to do to him everything
Which is wrong.
They did to him everything,
Which is bad.
They tried to buy him out
Materially.

Spear, LP *Marcus' Children,* 'Marcus Senior'

But there can be no question of giving in before the objective is
achieved. Garvey is held up as an example:

He never subdue
Garvey never.
Marcus never, never...
Marcus never, never, never, never.
Never, never, never, never
Never subdue
Little did they know.

Spear, LP *Marcus' Children,* 'Marcus Senior'

This is why his message and memory live on. This is why in the
tradition of the great African hero ancestors, we can be invited by
griot Peter Tosh to

Remember Marcus.
Remember Garvey.   .
Him no ded

Dat man no ded
Dat man no ded.
De man a trod earth still
That man a trod earth still
Watching his prophecy fulfil.
Tosh, LP *Bush Doctor,* 'Moses — The Prophet'

BIBLIOGRAPHY

F. Bebey, *African Music: A People's Art,* Harrap 1975.

A. Booth, V. Goldman, *Bob Marley: Soul Rebel — Natural Mystic,* Eel Pie 1981.

E.K. Braithwaite, *History of the Voice,* New Beacon Books 1984.

A. Booth, M. Thomas, *Jamaica: Babylon on a Thin Wire,* Schocken Books 1977.

L. D. Carrington, D. Craig eds., *Studies in Caribbean Language,* University of the West Indies, Trinidad and Tobago 1983.

J. M. Chernoff, *African Rhythms and African Sensibility,* University of California Press 1979.

Chinweizu et al, *Towards the Decolonialisation of African Literature,* Fourth Dimension Publishers 1980.

C. Cooper, 'Chanting Down Babylon: Bob Marley's Songs as Literary Texts', *Jamaica Journal* vol. 19/4.

J. Copastic, 'Johnny Cool and the Isle of Sirens' in *Rock File,* C. Gillett ed., New English Library 1972.

H. Dalrymple, *Bob Marley: Music, Myth and the Rastas,* Carib-Arawak Publishing Ltd., London 1976.

R. Kallyndyr, H. Dalrymple, *Reggae: A Peoples' Music,* Carib-Arawak 1974.

S. Davis et. al., *Reggae International,* Thames and Hudson 1982.

S. Davis et. al., *Reggae Bloodline: In Search of the Music and Culture of Jamaica,* Heinemann Educational Books 1977.

H. Devonish, *Language and Liberation: Creole Language Politics in the Caribbean,* Karia Press 1986.

G. Fisher, H. Joshua, 'Social Policy and Black Youth' in *Black Youth in Crisis,* Cashmore & Troyna eds, Allen & Unwin 1982.

C. Gayle, ed., *Jah Ugliman,* vol.1 no.1, October 1978.

P. Gilroy, 'The Myth of Black Criminality', in *Socialist Register* 1982.

C. Gutzmore, 'Capital, Black Youth and Crime' in *Race and Class* vol xxv,2, 1983.

S. Hall et.al., *Policing the Crisis: Mugging, the State and Law and Order,* Macmillan Press 1978.

B. Hamilton, 'Marcus Garvey: Cultural Activist' in *Jamaica Journal,* vol 20/3.

I. F. Hancock ed., *Journal of Creole Studies,* 1977 et. seq.

Sir E. Herslet, *The Map of Africa by Treaty,* 3 vols, Frank Cass 1967.

R. Hill ed., *Marcus Garvey's The Black Man,* Kraus-Thompson 1975.

R. Hill, 'Leonard P. Howell: Millenarian Vision in Early Rastafari', *Jamaica Journal,* vol. 16, No. 1, Feb. 1983.

C. L. R. James, *Beyond a Boundary,* Hutchinson 1963.

H. Johnson et. al.,*Reggae: Deep Roots Music,* Proteus Books and Channel 4 TV 1982.

L. Jones, *Blues People,* Wm. Morrow & Co. 1963.

A. Khalid, *The Liberation of Swahili from Appropriation,* East African Literature Bureau 1977.

C. Keil, *Urban Blues,* University of Chicago Press 1966.

R. Lewis, M. Warner-Lewis, *Garvey, Africa, Europe and the Americas,* Institute of Social and Economic Studies, Kingston, Jamaica 1986.

M. Manley, *Jamaica: The Struggle in the Periphery*, Writers and Readers c.1983.

P. O'Gorman, 'On Reggae and Rastafarianism — and a Garvey Prophecy' in *Jamaica Journal* vol. 30 no.3.

Ngugi wa 'Thiong'o, *Decolonialisation of the Mind: The Politics of Language in African Literature,* James Curry, Heinemann, and Zimbabwe Publishing House.

M. Thomas, A. Booth, *Jah Revenge: Babylon Revisited,* Eel Pie 1982.

G. White, *The Development of Jamaican Popular Music: With Special Reference to the Music of Bob Marley: A Bibliography,* African Caribbean Institute of Jamaica 1982.

DISCOGRAPHY

Dr. Alimantado, *Kings Bread,* Ital Sounds 1979.

Big Youth, *Dread Locks Dread,* Klick Records 1975.

Burning Spear, *Dry and Heavy,* Island/Mango Records 1977.

Burning Spear, *Hail H.I.M.,* Tuff Gong 1980.

Burning Spear, *Farover,* EMI 1982.

Burning Spear, *Live,* Island Records 1977.

Burning Spear, *Man in the Hills,* Island Records 1976.

Burning Spear, *Marcus' Children,* Sonic Sounds 1978.

Burning Spear, *Garvey Ghost,* Island Records 1976.

Count Ossie and the Mystic Revelations of Rastafari, *Groundation,* Ashanti Records 1973.

Culture, *Africa Stands Alone,* April Records.

Culture, *International Herb,* Virgin Records 1979.

Culture, *Cumbolo,* Virgin Records 1979.

Culture, *Two Sevens Clash,* Lightening Records 1978.

Diamonds, *Planet Earth,* Virgin Records 1978.

The Ethiopians, *Slave Call,* Third World Records 1979.

Joe Higgs, *Unity is Power,* I Stop Records 1979.

Fred Locks, *Black Star Liner,* Vulcan Records 1973.

Mighty Diamonds, *Right Time,* Virgin Records 1976.

Tapper Zukie, *M.P.L.A.,* Klick Records 1976.

Peter Tosh, *Equal Rights,* Virgin Records 1977.

Twinkle Brothers, *Love,* Virgin Records 1978.

UNITY IS POWER

Right now I would like to sing this song
About the greatest exponent of Black liberation
The giant from our little island of Jamaica, yeah!
Marcus Mosiah Garvey.

And I'm gonnan ask the sisters
To help me to sing this song
Help me to sing this song, yeah!
    Sons of Garvey, the time is now
    We'll never get nowhere
    Till we live as one
That's for true. That's for sure
    Heads of churches, and politicians
All right now
    Getting richer in a time of starvation
One more time
    Starvation
Oh! Alright
    Sons of Garvey
Oooooh
    Sons of Garvey
Oh yeah!
    Sons of Garvey
Hear me call you now
    Sons of Garvey
Did you really love him?
    Sons of Garvey
Did you really love Marcus Garvey?
    Sons of Garvey
Did you really love Mosiah?
    Sons of Garvey
Did you really love him? Oh yeah!
    Sons of Garvey
Our time is now./Our Time is now.
We'll never, never, never/Get nowhere till we live as one
The time is now
    Heads of churches and politicians

All right!
                    Getting richer in a time of starvation.
Oh! What did you say?
                    Starvation!
Alright, I can feel it.
You know that it could be
                    Sons of Garvey
You know that it could be
                    Sons of Garvey
That this church and state psychology
                    Sons of Garvey
Preaching love
                    Sons of Garvey
That you could never never see
                    Sons of Garvey
While they try to keep you down
                    Sons of Garvey
In poverty. Yeah! Yeah!
                    Sons of Garvey, our time is now
                    We'll never get nowhere
                    Till we live as one
Get the power to do right
                    Heads of churches
Unity is power
                    And politicians
That is right!
                    Getting richer in a time of starvation
Put yourselves together
                    Starvation
It all means that it could be
                    Starvation
You know, you know, that it could be
That this church and state psychology
                    Sons of Garvey
All right! They preaching love
                    Sons of Garvey
You will never see. Oh no!

Sons of Garvey
While they keep you down
Sons of Garvey
In poverty
That's it sisters
Sons of Garvey, the time is now
Oh! Alright, yeah, yeah!
We'll never get nowhere till we live as one
Alright, yeah, yeah, yeah!
Heads of churches and politicians
Oh! Ooh!
Getting richer in a time of starvation
Ummmmm!
Starvation
It all means that it could be
Sons of Garvey
That this church and state
Sons of Garvey
Psychology
Sons of Garvey
If you heard the words
Sons of Garvey
Of Marcus Mosiah Garvey
Sons of Garvey
Unity is power
Sons of Garvey
The power to the hour. Oh yeah!
Sons of Garvey our time is now
Getting richer now
We'll never get nowhere till we live as one
Heads of churches and politicians
That's the direction now
Getting richer in a time of starvation
Unity is power...

Transcription by Cecil Gutzmore

NOTES ON CONTRIBUTORS

Rasheed Araeen was born in Karachi, Pakistan, and came to England in 1964. Was founder and editor with Mahmoud Jamal of *Black Phoenix*, the 1970s radical Black arts magazine, and is author of *Making Myself Visible*, Kala Press, 1984. A visual artist and political activist, his work has appeared in exhibitions in England, Europe and Asia.

David A Bailey was born in 1961. He is a writer and cultural practitioner working in the field of the new technologies, particularly photography.

Sonia Boyce is a painter who was born in London in 1962 and studied at London Stourbridge College of Art. She has exhibited widely in Britain.

Ceddo Film and Video Workshop is franchised by the ACTT and works under the Workshop Declaration. Apart from producing films and videos, the group offers training programmes and encourages new film makers and writers. The group is involved in film/video documentation of Black cultural and political events.

Merle Collins grew up in Grenada. A collection of her poetry, *Because the Dawn*

Breaks, was published by Karia Press. She is editor with Rhonda Cobham of *Seekers and Watchers, Creative Writing by Black Women in Britain* (Women's Press 1987). Her first novel *Angel* was published in 1987 by The Women's Press. She is a member of The African Dawn, an orature collective based in London.

Carolyn Cooper is a lecturer at the University of the West Indies, Jamaica and a literary critic. She is a regular participant in the Black, Radical and Third World Book Fair in Britain and has lectured in British universities.

David Dabydeen is a lecturer in Caribbean studies at Warwick University and an activist. He is the author of *Slave Song*, (Dangeroo Press, 1984) which was awarded the 1984 Commonwealth Prize for Poetry and *Hogarth's Blacks* (Dangeroo Press, 1985).

J. D. Douglas was educated in Curaçao, St. Lucia and Wales. He attended the University of Essex and the University of Wales, graduating in economics. He is well known on the poetry circuit and is the author of *Caribbean Man's Blues* (Akira Press 1985). To date, six of his plays have been staged. He has written the successful musical

Black Heroes in the Hall of Fame.

Armet Francis was born in Jamaica and came to Britain aged eight. He began working as a professional photographer in the late sixties, covering fashion, advertising and reportage. His work has been published in many journals and he has exhibited internationally He is the author of *The Black Triangle* (Seed Publications 1985). 'Every face is a landscape... I see you not through mine eyes but through your reflections of me.'

Cecil Gutzmore was born in the Jamaican north coast parish of Portland. He arrived in Britain aged sixteen to join his migrant family. Worked on factory floor and in the civil service before studying at the universities of Leicester and London. Lectured before turning to community work in London's Notting Hill from which base he engaged in Black community activism. He has published articles on philosophy, politics and history in the *Guardian, Race and Class, Marxism Today* and *The Black Liberator*, of which he was a member of the editorial collective.

Kofi Hagan was born in Ghana. He came to Britain in 1975 and studied at the London College of Printing, East Ham College of Printing and Glasgow College of Printing. Has worked as a graphic designer, lecturer in visual communications, freelance journalist and for the Campaign for Press Freedom. In 1984 he won the Mohammed Maiga journalism award for Africa.

Shaheen Haque was born in East London and works as an architect for a London local authority. She is interested in developing non-Eurocentric architectural practices.

Ruhi Hamid was born in Tanzania in 1956. She studied graphic design at Middlesex Polytechnic and the Royal College of Art and has worked in Holland and Zimbabwe. Currently working at the BBC in news graphics and freelancing as a designer and part-time tutor in art colleges: 'My work is primarily concerned with designing for need. At the same time, making political comments aimed at raising consciousness and contributing towards the creation of a new design language.'

Yusuf Hassan was born in Kenya and educated there and at the University of London. He is an editor with the monthly *Africa Events*. He is chair of Ukenya, the Movement for Unity and Democracy in Kenya.

Gavin Jantjes was born in Cape Town, South Africa and studied in Germany. He now lives and works in Britain. His work has appeared in exhibitions in Britain and abroad, including Ljubljana Biennale, Yugoslavia, 1979; Culture and Resistance Festival, Gaborone, Botswana, 1982; and *Into the Open,* Mappin Gallery, Sheffield, 1984. He has written for *Artrage* and other arts magazines.

Tunde Jegede is fifteen and one of the few people performing on the kora in Britain. He was introduced to the music by the Senegalese musician Bouly Cissohoko. His first appearance in London, at the age of nine, was with the African Dawn in 1981. He has featured on albums by the African Dawn and Gaspar Lawal and on Ewan McColl/Peggy Seeger's cassette 'White Wind/Black Tide'. He is the author with Galina Chester (his mother and a painter) of *The Silenced Voice: Hidden Music of the Kora* (Diabate Kora Arts 1986).

Shobana Jeyasingh was born in Madras, South India. She is a solo bharatha natyam dancer who has worked extensively in Britain. She has sat on dance advisory panels of the Arts Council and Greater London Arts. She has an MA in Renaissance Studies from the University of Sussex.

Tam Joseph was born in Dominica and came to England in 1965. He studied at the Central School of Art and the Slade which he left after two months, frustrated by Eurocentric teaching and inadequate curriculum content. Worked as a painter and tracer on the Beatles film *Yellow Submarine* and travelled through Europe and overland to India. On his return he studied at the London College of Printing and worked for *Africa* magazine. He now works as a freelance artist.

Pitika Ntuli was born in Azania where he was actively involved in creative and trade union movements. He came to Britain in 1978 and has worked as a painter, performance poet, sculptor and activist. He is a founder member of PITSO, the Association of Azanian artists and writers, and Monti-Wa-Marumo, an Azanian Orature collective. He has worked closely with the African Dawn collective and Dade Krama. His sculpture includes a twelve foot, free standing stone carving at Swaziland airport and a fifteen-foot stone mural. He has exhibited internationally.

Jan McKenley was born in Brixton in 1955, and is a lecturer at a college in Hackney where she has lived for fifteen years. She has a daughter, Ama, who is four.

Jide Odusina: 'I was born in 1959 into a conservative, deeply nationalist Yoruba family with aristocratic connections, who were living in London. I grew up in Notting Hill and North Paddington running with the boys. From my early teens I was involved with the organised struggle for Black Liberation guided by comrades at Grassroots. I am married to Winsome and we have a wonderful son, who is a constant reminder of why I am engaged in struggle. I have worked as editor of *Gemini* community arts magazine and for *Relay*, the community radio magazine. Currently I work as publicity and information worker for the Organisation for Black Arts Advancement and Learning Activities(OBAALA).

Ben Okri is a Nigerian writer living in London. He has published two novels, *Flowers and Shadows* and *The Landscapes Within*. His latest work is a volume of short stories, *Incidents at the Shrine* (William Heinemann 1986).

Kwesi Owusu is a member of the African Dawn, an orature collective based in London. He is the author of *The Struggle for Black Arts in Britain* (Comedia 1986) and *Behind the Masquerade: The Story of Notting Hill Carnival* with Jacob Ross (Arts Media Group 1988).

Pratibha Parmar was born in Kenya and migrated to England at the age of eleven. She lives in London. She has worked as a lecturer, youth worker, publisher, film researcher and is currently a freelance writer and film-maker.

Keith Piper was born in 1960 and grew up in Birmingham. He studied at Trent Polytechnic and Slade School of Art. He has been a member of the Black Art Group since 1981.

Donald Rodney was born in 1961 and grew up in Birmingham. He studied art at Trent Polytechnic and Slade School of Art. He has been a member of the Black Art Group since 1983.

Jacob Ross was born in Grenada and is editor of *Black Arts in London*. He is the author of *Songs for Simone*, a collection of short stories (Karia Press, 1986) and *Behind the Masquerade: The Story of Notting Hill Carnival* with Kwesi Owusu (Arts Media Group 1988).

Suzanne Scafe was born in Jamaica in 1954. Having taught English in secondary schools in London and Jamaica, she now teaches at and co-ordinates a Black supplementary school in Brixton. She has worked with the Committee of Women for Progress in Jamaica, and has been a member of the Brixton Black Women's Group for several years. She lives in South London.

Adeola Solanke is a Nigerian journalist and writer based in London. She has written for arts magazines, radio, newspapers and television. She is a founder member of Zora Press, publishers of *Jagged Edges* by Yamide Hazeley.

Nadir Tharani is an architect and graphic designer who has participated in several exhibitions. He was the founder editor of *9H* architectural magazine and has worked as a cartoonist and reviewer.

Ngugi wa' Thiong'o was born in Kenya in 1938. His many novels include *Petals of Blood* and *Devil on the Cross* and essays include 'Barrel of a Pen', 'Decolonising the Mind', and 'Writing Against Neo-colonialism'. He has written children's stories, *Njanba Nene, Njanba Nene Pitol,* in the Gĩkuyu and made a film, *Blood, Grapes and Black Diamonds.* This exposes the economic self-interest behind the forces in the West that oppose sanctions against the racist white minority régime in South Africa, and calls for all democratic forces to unite behind the Liberation Movement in South Africa.

Gail Thompson was born in Herne Hill, South London. Her parents are from Trinidad. She began her musical training on clarinet, moving to flute and tenor sax. She has played in several bands including Art Blakey, Charlie Watts and Black Jazz Orchestra and led her own, the Gail Thompson Approach and Gail Force. She has appeared on TV and radio, written music for festivals and concerts in England and Europe and started a music school in South London.

Jatinder Verma is a founder member and director of Tara Arts Group, now a major international arts organisation. He has written several plays since 1976 and recently turned to producing and directing adaptations of Indian folk texts.

Amrit Wilson is a journalist and political activist. She is the author of *Finding a Voice, Asian Women in Britain* and *But My Cows Aren't Going to England,* a study of divided families, with Sushma Lal (Manchester Law Centre, 1986).

PERMISSIONS AND ACKNOWLEDGEMENTS

We are grateful to the following publishers and publications for allowing us to reprint the articles listed below.

Rasheed Araeen, 'Come On, Cheer Up', from *Making Myself Visible*, Kala Press, 1984.

David Dabydeen, 'Blacks in Eighteenth Century Art and Society', from *Hogarth's Blacks*, Dangeroo Press, 1985.

Kofi Hagan, 'Crossfire', *West Africa*, December 8, 1986.

Yusuf Hassan, 'Drumpolitik' and 'What is Ours?', *Africa Events*, May 1987.

Tunde Jegede and Galina Chester, 'Walking Away With the Music', from *The Silenced Voice: Hidden Music of the Kora*, Diabate Kora Arts, 1986.

Kwesi Owusu, 'Notting Hill Carnival: Image and Text Take a Walk with the Masquerade' from *Behind the Masquerade: The Story of the Notting Hill Carnival*, Arts Media Group, 1988.

Extracts from *The Arrivants* by Edward Kamau Brathwaite, 1973, by permission of Oxford University Press.

ART BOOKS

FROM CAMDEN PRESS

THE CORRESPONDENCE OF BERTHE MORISOT
edited by Kathleen Adler and Tamar Garb

CANVASSING: RECOLLECTIONS BY SIX VICTORIAN
WOMEN ARTISTS
edited by Pamela Gerrish Nunn

THE NEW ART HISTORY
edited by A. L. Rees and F. Borzello

VISIBLY FEMALE: FEMINISM AND ART TODAY
edited by Hilary Robinson

PUTTING MYSELF IN THE PICTURE:
A POLITICAL, PERSONAL AND PHOTOGRAPHIC
AUTOBIOGRAPHY
by Jo Spence